ISBN 978-2-84707-154-2
«Formula 1 Yearbook 2008-09» is also published
in French language under the title «L'Année Formule 1 2008-09» (ISBN 978-2-84707-147-4)

© December 2008, Chronosports S.A.

Le Vergnolet Parc, CH-1070 Puidoux, Switzerland. Phne : (+41 21) 694 24 44. Fax : (+41 21) 694 24 46.

E-mail: info@chronosports.com   Internet: www.chronosports.com

Printed in France by Imprimerie Clerc s.a.s., Rue de la Brasserie, F-18206 St-Amand Montrond.
Bound by Reliures Brun, F-45331 Malesherbes Cedex
Clerc s.a.s. & Reliures Brun are both Qualibris companies.

Special thanks to Robert Rui, Jean-Philippe Lavergne, Nicolas Brunet and all the Clerc team.

FORMULA 1 YEARBOOK

2008-09

Photos
Darren Heath
Steve Domenjoz
Agence WRI2

Editor
Luc Domenjoz

Page layout
Loraine Lequint & Cyril Davillerd

Results and statistics
Loraine Lequint & Cyril Davillerd

Drawings
Pierre Ménard

Gaps and lap charts
Michele Merlino

Translated by
Eric Silbermann & Stuart Sykes

CHRONOSPORTS
EDITEUR

CONTENT

SEASON ANALYSIS

The duel between Lewis Hamilton and Felipe Massa was never ending. All season long, both men ran into problems of one sort or another, struggling to take the wins that seemed to be handed them on a plate. A strange season.

> Sao Paulo, midday, a last handshake before the final confrontation.

The unbelievable inventory of missed opportunities for Lewis and Felipe

It's a safe bet that, in years to come, the 2008 Formula 1 season will still be the subject of heated discussion and motor sport pub quizzes, or reminiscences by a roaring fire on New Year's Eve.

Of course, the part that will stick in the memory will be the mind blowing conclusion to this world championship. Fans had already been spoilt in 2007, with a three way shoot-out between Lewis Hamilton, Fernando Alonso and Kimi Raikkonen. For the Finn, it seemed like mission impossible, but he still did it at the end of a race which saw the world title change hands no less than five times. This time, it was a straightforward duel between Lewis Hamilton and Felipe Massa. But while the race might have been more straightforward than the 2007 version, the tension increased with every passing lap, as the chequered flag beckoned.

Lewis Hamilton should have been easily capable of securing the fifth place he needed, whatever the circuit, even if his engine only had six cylinders, but yet again, he was almost the victim of the same misfortune that cost him the title the previous year. As the finish line hove into view, he was finding it ever more difficult to hang onto fourth place, then fifth place, which he then gave up to Sebastian Vettel, with two laps remaining.

Could we believe our eyes? Lewis Hamilton was going to finish sixth and let Felipe Massa snatch the crown away from him. At Interlagos, in the pits, in the media centre, in the McLaren garage, everyone was holding their breath, giddy from watching this incredible scenario being played out before their eyes. At McLaren, Hamilton's family, his mechanics, friends of the team, all of them were mesmerised, refusing to believe it, watching with their mouths open, eyes glued to the TV monitors.

The last 400 metres of the season will remain forever in the memories of those who witnessed them. Felipe Massa wins the race. In the Ferrari camp there are shouts of joy and the champagne comes out. But on the screens, it's confusion all round. It's black outside as the rain beats down on Interlagos. In the press room, the journalists are on their feet, no one says a word, the tension is palpable, with all eyes on the monitors. From his on-board camera, one sees Hamilton fighting to catch Sebastian Vettel with some desperate moves. The two drivers come up behind backmarkers. Someone shouts "Glock!" Confusion. No one understands what's happening. In the Ferrari camp, Gino Rosato, a team member, known for his great intelligence, screams with joy at the camera, but he is damned. Lewis Hamilton then crosses the line and the timing screen has him down as fifth and the McLaren garage erupts in delight. At Ferrari, Massa's father is hugging someone, with tears of joy streaming down his face. Then, someone behind him shouts, "no, no!" It's the whole human condition in one moment - paroxysms of pleasure and pain.

What is striking in the moments that follow is the dignity shown by Felipe Massa. Of course, he cries for this championship that flew away when he had it in his grasp for a few seconds. He grits his teeth on the podium, holding back from sobbing in pain. But a few moments later, during the post-podium press conference, he stresses how much Hamilton deserves this title and what a worthy champion he is. Felipe Massa proves to be more of a man than if he had taken the title. Of course, this is just about motor racing, a simple amusement. But the incredible intensity of those last few minutes had never been seen before in the 59 year history of Formula 1 and nothing like it had ever been seen in any other sport. Everything in this Brazilian drama, from the weather, to the nationality of the loser, had been turned into a true drama. A football world cup final won with the last kick of the game, would never have matched it for intensity. Only Formula 1, with its teams of around a thousand people, its colossal budgets and its global audience could ever reach such a dramatic conclusion. But if it all played out between Hamilton and Massa in that famous final dash for the line, they only have themselves to blame. Because, with hindsight, looking at their 2008 season overall, both men threw away several opportunities for scoring points, which would have seen one of them wrap up the title well before the final 400 metres of the season.

Hamilton's first world title came, in large part, thanks to mistakes from Ferrari and Massa

---

More so for Massa. As can be deduced from the fact that Ferrari took the Constructors' title, the Scuderia's car was generally superior to the McLaren MP4-23. On fast circuits, that make up the bulk of the venues, the F2008 was hard to beat and Hamilton only managed it twice, at Hockenheim and in China. His three other wins, came either on street circuits (Melbourne and Monaco) or in the rain (Silverstone).

The Ferrari did indeed seem a tricky handful in the wet and if its drivers are to be believed, that stemmed from the difficulty of getting the grooved tyres up to temperature, as the chassis was very stiff. In the damp, one has to soften the suspension as much as possible so that the tyres

->>>

<
Lewis Hamilton at
Silverstone. In front of his
home crowd, in a wet
race, the Englishman took
one of his most
convincing wins of the
season.

hug the track surface better.

In 2008, it rained relatively often over the Grand Prix weekends. That was the case in Monaco, France, England, Germany, Belgium, Italy, Japan and Brazil. The Scuderia was thus at a disadvantage more often than it should have been, which affected its results, most obviously at Silverstone and Monza, even if in England, it aggravated its own problems by relying on the absurd forecast from Meteo France, its weather forecast partner, which predicted sunshine that eventually took a week to arrive!

Massa's season was therefore badly hobbled by his team. In Australia, the little Brazilian saw his engine let go just after the halfway point.

A week later in Malaysia, he made his only real mistake of the year, going off the track all on his

own, like a grown-up.

After two Grands Prix, Massa had yet to trouble the scorer and these two blank Sundays would cost him the title six months later. The Brazilian then saw victories taken from him through team error in Hungary and Singapore. In Budapest, he was strolling along in the lead, with the win in his pocket when his V8 suddenly exploded in a huge cloud of smoke. He was leading in Singapore, when a mechanic gave him the green light to leave the pits, while the refuelling line was still attached to the car.

Two wins and another twenty points had just gone out the window. Doing the maths, all these mistakes cost Massa between 30 and 36 points, given what he should have picked up also in Australia, Malaysia and Silverstone.

Therefore, Hamilton's first world title came, in large part, thanks to mistakes from Ferrari and Massa. Also driving an F2008, Kimi Raikkonen should have been in contention for the title again. However, the reigning world champion finished third, a long way behind the first two.

Immediately after being crowned in 2007, the brand new world champion claimed he would be even stronger in 2008, as he now had a better understanding of how things worked at Scuderia Ferrari.

However, this year, Raikkonen appeared uninterested, not really on the case and seemed de-motivated. He too had a number of mechanical problems - starting at the opening round in Australia, when his engine let him down. He also had his fair share of bad luck,

->>>

<
Felipe Massa head on. A
mistake in Malaysia,
technical problems, a
mistake from his team in
Singapore...probably over
30 points went to waste
in these missed
opportunities, which sent
the world title scuttling
over to Lewis Hamilton.

>
"What? Another win…" Fernando Alonso seems stunned with this second consecutive win, as he steps out of the cockpit in Mount-Fuji.

something that has dogged his career, but had generally stayed away in 2007. In Montreal, he was doing well until Hamilton crashed into him from behind. At Silverstone, he followed the disastrous instructions from his team and stayed out on dry tyres too long in the wet. The problem is that, even looking Kimi in the eye, it's hard to know what he is really thinking.

With the two Ferrari drivers accumulating troubles and effectively putting themselves out of contention, Hamilton had a clear path ahead of him. At the wheel of the extremely reliable McLaren MP4-23, that never let him down all season long, that was very quick, albeit one notch below the level of the Ferrari at most circuits, the young Englishman naturally made the most of Ferrari's woes.

He also had some difficult days, but there were definitely fewer of them for him than for Massa. Like his Brazilian rival, Hamilton could also have wrapped up the title well before the final straight of the season. In Bahrain for example, he forgot to select the correct launch sequence on his steering wheel. This finger trouble was followed by a collision with Fernando Alonso and ended in a meagre 13th place at the flag. Then there was the infamous Canadian incident, where he didn't see the red light, which in this instance was blue, at the pit lane exit and rammed Raikkonen's stationery car, missing out on another points scoring opportunity. The collision resulted in a ten place grid penalty at the next round in Magny-Cours where, starting 13th, he was then given a drive-through penalty for having cut a chicane. He ended up tenth and, for the second consecutive race, failed to score any points.

Hamilton might also regret his over anxious start in the Japanese Grand Prix, which saw him take to the escape road at the first corner, which then meant he was hit by Felipe Massa a bit further down the road.

Apart from these lapses, the Englishman was brilliant. His mastery of a sliding car is phenomenal, as demonstrated in the rain at Silverstone and Monza. In the dry, he is very aggressive and relies heavily on his car control. He is one of the few drivers who can hold a long slide, masterfully controlling any oversteer. Even if he was greatly helped by the roll of the dice, Hamilton richly deserved this first title which is no doubt not the last. At the age of 23, he still has plenty of time to pick up more crowns and with more experience should come fewer mistakes. As long as the McLaren continues to match his talent, between them, they should prove to be a formidable force in the coming years.

The 2008 season also witnessed a remarkable return to form for the Renault team. By signing up with Renault again, Fernando Alonso knew he would not enjoy the level of success that could have been his, if he had stayed with McLaren. Who knows, he might even have become the 2008 World Champion. But the Spaniard probably did not expect to find the French team in such a state of disarray. Right from the off, he complained the car was terrible. "*It has to be admitted, the chassis wasn't perfect,*" agrees Denis Chevrier, the head of the engine side at Renault. "*Fernando complained of a lack of traction at every debrief.*

>
Fernando Alonso ahead of Nelsinho Piquet. The Brazilian's season got off to a difficult start, before he managed to score points in Japan and China, saving his 2009 seat in the nick of time.

He could not get the power down as it was sliding. That meant he was over-driving and sliding around even more. In Canada, he went over the limit and went off."

The team and its driver seemed to have reached an impasse that might lead to divorce. Or at least, that was the case until July, when Alonso decided to deal with the situation. *"Fernando then set himself the goal of helping Renault to finish fourth in the championship, behind Ferrari, McLaren and BMW. He got down to work and thanks to his analyses, we managed to fight back."*

The Renault engineers are all in awe of the Spaniard's abilities, rating Alonso as the best of the current drivers. *"We have to admit that, at the moment, no one is at his level,"* continues Chevrier. *"Lewis is very quick, but he makes a lot of mistakes. Felipe is a bit inconsistent and seems one notch down. As for Kimi, he has not been on the case this year. Fernando is really the best. He is always flat out on every lap and never goes off."*

In Formula 1, the majority of drivers can be very quick over one lap. The difference then comes down to mental attitude. *"Here too, Fernando is impressive,"* concludes Chevrier. *"In qualifying, Nelsinho Piquet (the team's second driver, Ed.) is very nervous. Fernando can just sit in his car and calmly wait for several minutes before going out. He never feels any pressure."*

These strengths translated into a surprise win in Singapore, followed by the one in Mount Fuji. In Japan, the surprise was the pace which the Spaniard and his Renault could maintain; almost a second a lap faster than Lewis Hamilton. This late charge was confirmed in Brazil, when Alonso made it to the second step on the final podium of the season.

Other teams also provided some surprises. Within the Red Bull family, the little Toro Rosso team and its staff of 120, managed to do better than its big sister, with the same chassis and less money. But it benefited from the no-nonsense management style of workaholic Franz Tost and the indisputable talent of Sebastian Vettel who made the most of the opportunity presented him to become the youngest ever Grand Prix winner at Monza.

A pleasant surprise also from the Toyota team, which is back on the right road after a catastrophic 2007 season. Just as its president had promised, the Japanese car maker got a

podium finish, in Magny-Cours and will now be aiming for wins in 2009.

2008 also witnessed a rapid evolution in the championship itself, with the appearance of two new emblematic venues, in Valencia and Singapore and with the announcement that two seemingly eternal fixtures on the calendar, Canada and France, were no more.

With the series in a state of perpetual motion, those events will one day be replaced by others in Abu Dhabi, India and Korea. Failing to achieve perpetual motion was the Super Aguri team which did not manage to finish the season, running out of funds after the Spanish Grand Prix. It was hardly a surprise, as the Japanese team only just made it to the Australian Grand Prix. Honda, which was its sole form of support, could no longer reasonably be expected to finance two teams, just to satisfy Takuma Sato's Japanese fans, by providing him with a seat.

In conclusion, the 2008 season has been very rewarding from all points of view. In the background, the global economic crisis, which surfaced at the end of the summer, seems to have had the effect of a detonator. Up to that point, everyone seemed to be burying their heads in the

sand, with the FIA in the middle. But the stock market collapse and talk of a recession caused panic among the team bosses, because a crisis signals a reduction in budgets. Whenever this happens, the first casualty for car companies and other sponsors, is always the marketing budget and that's where F1 derives its income.

As this edition of the "Formula 1 Yearbook" goes to press, it is too early to measure the full extent of the crisis and its consequences for F1, the championship and the teams. However, it seems likely that 2008 will have been the last year of conspicuous consumption. It is a fair bet that this past season will, in a few years time, be seen as a turning point for the aesthetes of motor sport, when they gather by the fireside to reminisce.

∧
Nico Rosberg: a lucky podium in Melbourne, another very lucky one in Singapore and that was it. A tough season for Williams.

<
Robert Kubica took his first Grand Prix win in Montreal. He then even topped the points table, without ever believing he could be champion. He knew what he was talking about: come the end of the season, the BMWs slumped into anonymity. For his part, Jarno Trulli made the most of a good season for Toyota, to finish ninth in the championship.

Sebastien Bourdais turned his dream into reality: to race in F1. He didn't realise that dreams can sometimes turn into nightmares…
< ∨

2008 CHAMPIONSHIPS

Drivers

1. L. Hamilton ◊	McLaren Mercedes	5♦	98
2. F. Massa	Ferrari	6♦	97
3. K. Räikkönen	Ferrari	2♦	75
4. R. Kubica	BMW	1♦	75
5. F. Alonso	Renault	2♦	61
6. N. Heidfeld	BMW		60
7. H. Kovalainen	McLaren Mercedes	1♦	53
8. S. Vettel	STR Ferrari	1♦	35
9. J. Trulli	Toyota		31
10. T. Glock	Toyota		25
11. M. Webber	Red Bull Renault		21
12. N. Piquet	Renault		19
13. N. Rosberg	Williams Toyota		17
14. R. Barrichello	Honda		11
15. K. Nakajima	Williams Toyota		9
16. D. Coulthard	Red Bull Renault		8
17. S. Bourdais	STR Ferrari		4
18. J. Button	Honda		3
19. G. Fisichella	Force India		0
20. A. Sutil	Force India		0
21. T. Sato	Super Aguri Honda		0
22. A. Davidson	Super Aguri Honda		0

Constructors

1. Scuderia Ferrari Marlboro ◊	8♦	172
2. Vodafone McLaren Mercedes	5♦	151
3. BMW Sauber F1 Team	2♦	135
4. ING Renault F1 Team	2♦	80
5. Panasonic Toyota Racing		56
6. Scuderia Torro Rosso	1♦	39
7. Red Bull Racing		29
8. AT&T Williams		26
9. Honda Racing F1 Team		14
10. Force India F1 Team		0
11. Super Aguri F1 Team		0

>
2008 Monaco Grand Prix, Saturday evening: a relaxed Lewis Hamilton is on top of his game. The next day he would go on to win the most prestigious race of the season.

Lewis Hamilton, programmed to be champion

By finishing fifth in the Brazilian Grand Prix, Lewis Hamilton became the 2008 Formula 1 World Champion. Just over a year ago, such an exploit would have been totally unthinkable, as he had yet to take part in a Grand Prix. Lewis Hamilton's rise has been so meteoric that it seems unreal. At the start of 2007, with no other obvious candidates available, he was taken on by McLaren-Mercedes to back up Fernando Alonso. Going into his first ever Grand Prix, the youngster himself affirmed that he would be very happy if he managed "to finish on the podium at least once this season." He did much better than that: Lewis Hamilton, then aged 22, soon put his team-mate in the shade and was far too good to play a supporting role.

This year, understanding what he had just witnessed and wishing to avoid a repeat of the turbulent times of 2007, his boss Ron Dennis pretty much handed him over the keys to the McLaren team, making Lewis the undoubted leader of the famous English team.

In the space of just one season, Lewis Hamilton went from being a complete unknown to a global star. Within the Formula 1 establishment, his rise had the same effect as a thunderbolt. Until his arrival, it had been thought that experience was one of the most important factors in becoming world champion, but the Englishman has turned that theory on its head. Ron Dennis had promised him he could test the Formula 1 car "if he wins the GP2 championship" in 2006. The test duly took place at Silverstone and one year later, Hamilton only just missed out on a first world title, getting his hands on it one year later, robbing Fernando Alonso of the record for being the youngest ever champion in the sport's history.

Of course, Hamilton was at the wheel of a McLaren-Mercedes, one of the two best cars in the field, an opportunity which does not usually come the way of rookie drivers. And yes, he arrived in Formula 1 in the best possible way, having been mollycoddled and protected by the McLaren organisation since 1998, since when he has become something of the darling of the team and a spiritual son to team boss Ron Dennis. When little Lewis was just ten, he went up to Dennis and asked if he could drive one of his cars and Dennis immediately warmed to the lad. "He's

the best prepared novice in the history of F1," reckoned three times world champion, Jackie Stewart, even before Hamilton had taken part in his first Grand Prix.

Up to that point, the young Englishman had won every championship in which he had taken part, from karting to GP2, via Formula Renault and Formula 3. Each step of the way, he made his mark as an exceptional driver, maybe not always the quickest over a single lap, but the most accomplished when all the parameters of race driving were taken into account: tyre use, braking skill, managing the race and making daring passing moves.

He is also very interested in the technical side of the sport, wanting to understand every detail about the aerodynamics and suspension. Hamilton is a late braker. He attacks deep into the corners and combines the style of Ayrton Senna with the analytical approach of Alain Prost and he undoubtedly has Michael Schumacher's aptitude for building a team around him.

It's hard to find fault with him, which explains why he is not so popular with the other drivers, who would love to be travelling down the same path. Hamilton makes very few mistakes, has had the occasional lucky break and won't be bullied on track, which means that sometimes he drives in a style that comes close to the limit of what is acceptable.

It is not just all the records he has broken over the past two years that makes the Englishman stand out from the crowd. He is also the first champion who has been more or less put together piece by piece by a team. Up until now, drivers who have won the world championship, have tended to be to a greater or lesser degree, tough individualists, strong headed and full of self belief in their superiority over their rivals. They had put their careers together, building their character, as they struggled up the slopes of the lower formulae before making it to F1.

Lewis Hamilton does not fit that description, having been taken under the McLaren wing at the age of ten and today, he is the epitome of perfection as a result of all that schooling.

In Formula 1, drivers are part of a much larger whole. No other sport relies on such a complex team

structure made up of hundreds of people. When Felipe Massa goes up against Lewis Hamilton on track at Interlagos, he can rely on the support of the 850 employees of the Maranello Scuderia, who are fighting the 600 staff from the Woking factory in England, allied to the 400 engine specialists, who build the Mercedes V8.

There is a strong sense of team spirit within these organisations. Team members spend more time together than they do with their families, all of them identically dressed in team kit, even when travelling to races. For most of them, their only family is to be found at work.

Usually, the drivers are not part of this family. With their preferential treatment, their million dollar salaries and their private jets, they are more often than not seen as mercenaries, who offer their services to the highest bidder, have no soul and are quite capable of switching from one team to another without giving the matter a second thought.

This might be the main difference between Hamilton and those who have gone before him on the Formula 1 world championship role of honour. Far from being an individualist offering his services to McLaren, Hamilton is as much part of the family as any one of his mechanics.

He lives and breathes McLaren, he knows ever member of the team and feels really comfortable in their company. For the past ten years, this has been his home and he spends days at the factory, patting everyone on the back, from the canteen lady to the technical director.

Maybe it is this new approach that has allowed him to win the world title so soon. At the age of 23, Hamilton is still very young and only McLaren could have offered him the protection which has allowed him to concentrate solely on his driving, which has seen him pull off the extraordinary feats we have seen since 2007.

As he matures, it is possible that, one day, Lewis Hamilton will cut the umbilical cord that ties him to the Woking team. In the meantime, his contract has been extended to the end of 2012. That should give him enough time to pick up some more world titles. He is easily capable of it....

Lewis Hamilton at the wheel of the 2008 McLaren: a winning combination, even if the title only came his way in the final metres.

V

> (opposite)
A 16 year old Lewis Hamilton competes in the karting world championship, in Kerpen.

(right)
In the rain in Kerpen, the karting world championship final. McLaren's support is already visible in the colours on his kart.

> (opposite)
At the F3 "Bahrain Superprix," on 10 December 2004.

(on right)
17 April 2005: at Hockenheim, at the wheel of his Formula 3 Dallara-Mercedes.

> (opposite)
Monza: congratulated by his father, Anthony, Lewis Hamilton is declared the winner of the 2006 GP2 championship, after Giorgio Pantano's fastest race lap is disallowed.

(right)
2006, in his GP2 days, with frizzy hair…

<
(left)
Lewis Hamilton jumps for joy on his ART Grand Prix car, having won the GP2 title.

(opposite)
15 January 2007: Lewis Hamilton has just secured his seat in the second McLaren. At the team launch, he is seen with Gary Paffett (test driver, on left) Fernando Alonso and Pedro de la Rosa (reserve driver.)

<
(left)
Lewis Hamilton has always been very close to his family. Here with his younger brother, Nicholas.

(opposite)
McLaren demands a lot of its drivers, who have to attend many sponsor events. Here's one, the day before first practice for the Australian Grand Prix, on the beach in Melbourne.

<
(left)
Another swanky evening event, this time for Mercedes, before the German Grand Prix weekend.

(opposite)
Sao Paulo, getting out of his car, displaying the joy and emotion of becoming the youngest world champion in history.

THE ACTORS

Drivers of course, but also team bosses, engineers, technicians, mechanics, press and marketing officers: thousands of people work in the Formula 1 paddock. Team reviews.

Ferrari

The reigning world champion had a bad season. Several weeks after the final race, the Finn pretty much admitted he lost interest once things didn't go his way. Räikkönen is certainly no Schumacher in terms of the amount of work he is prepared to put in from outside the cockpit and this showed, once it was clear that his car's understeering characteristics didn't suit him. Rather than work hard to fix the problem, he seemed to accept it and the Scuderia soon switched its attention to Massa. In Malaysia, France, where he was robbed of victory through a cracked exhaust, and Belgium, he showed why, on his day, he is supremely quick and talented, but his poor qualifying meant he spent too many races stuck behind slower cars. In the later part of races, when the tyres would start behaving to his liking, he would often set the race fastest lap, but by then it was too late to pose a threat. Räikkönen is an enigma, but an enigma who will need to change his attitude, work hard in winter testing, get fit, because even that was a weak point this year, if he wants to ever see the number one on his car again, or indeed be considered a number one driver. But maybe, he just doesn't care enough to bother.

1 | Kimi RÄIKKÖNEN

DRIVER PROFILE

- Name — *RÄIKKÖNEN*
- Firstname — *Kimi Matias*
- Nationality — *Finnish*
- Date of birth — *October 17, 1979*
- Place of birth — *Espoo (FIN)*
- Lives in — *Pfäffikon (CH), Espoo (FIN)*
- Marital status — *married to Jenni*
- Kids — *-*
- Hobbies — *snowboard, skateboard, jogging*
- Favorite music — *U2, Darude, Bomfunk Mc, Eminem*
- Favorite meal — *mushrooms pasta, chicken*
- Favorite drinks — *pineapple juice, water and milk*
- Height — *175 cm*
- Weight — *71 kg*
- Web — *www.kimiraikkonen.com*

STATISTICS

• Grands Prix	140	• Podiums	57
• Starts	139	• GP in the lead	51
• Wins	17	• Laps in the lead	1027
• Pole positions	16	• Km in the lead	5137
• Fastest laps	35	• Points scored	531

CAREER

2008	F1 *Ferrari, 75 pts, 3rd*	
2007	F1 *Ferrari, 110 pts,* **World Champion**	
2006	F1 *McLaren-Mercedes, 65 pts, 5th*	
2005	F1 *McLaren-Mercedes, 112 pts, 2nd*	
2004	F1 *McLaren-Mercedes, 45 pts, 7th*	
2003	F1 *McLaren-Mercedes, 91 pts, 2nd*	
2002	F1 *McLaren-Mercedes, 24 pts, 6th*	
2001	F1 *Sauber-Petronas, 9 pts, 10th*	
2000	F. *Renault (GB) Champion; (EUR)* • F1 *tests Sauber*	
1999	F. *Renault 3rd; "Winter Series" Winner*	
	Karting (FIN) FA, 2nd; (World) F. Super A, 10th	
1998	*Karting (FIN) FA, Champion; (Nordic) Champion;*	
	Super A (EUR) 2nd; Monaco Cup Super A, 3rd; (World) F. Super A	
1997	*Karting (FIN) Class Intercontinental A, Champion;*	
	(Nordic) Class Intercontinental A, 4th • *KWC*	
1996	*Karting (European Series, World, Nordic & FIN); FA, 4th*	
1995	*Karting FA*	
1994-93	*Karting (National) Class Raket, Finnish Cup*	
1988-92	*Karting (National) Class A, B, C, Mini, Raket Jr.*	

2 | Felipe MASSA

DRIVER PROFILE

- Name — *MASSA*
- Firstname — *Felipe*
- Nationality — *Brazilian*
- Date of birth — *April 25, 1981*
- Place of birth — *São Paulo (BR)*
- Lives in — *Monaco (MC)*
- Marital status — *married to Rafaela*
- Kids — *-*
- Hobbies — *nautical skiing, football, cinema, music*
- Favorite music — *all, black music, hits*
- Favorite meal — *pasta, brazilian food, churrascaria*
- Favorite drinks — *champagne of the podiums*
- Height — *166 cm*
- Weight — *59 kg*
- Web — *www.felipemassa.com*

STATISTICS

• Grands Prix	106	• Podiums	27
• Starts	105	• GP in the lead	25
• Wins	11	• Laps in the lead	819
• Pole positions	15	• Km in the lead	3951
• Fastest laps	11	• Points scored	298

CAREER

2008	F1 *Ferrari, 97 pts, 2nd*	
2007	F1 *Ferrari, 94 pts, 4th*	
2006	F1 *Ferrari, 80 pts, 3rd*	
2005	F1 *Sauber-Petronas, 11 pts, 13th*	
2004	F1 *Sauber-Petronas, 12 pts, 12th*	
2003	F1 *Ferrari, test driver*	
2002	F1 *Sauber-Petronas, 4 pts, 13th*	
2001	*Euro F3000 Champion* •	
	F1 *Sauber tests* • *FIA ETC* • *24H Sicilia 2nd*	
2000	F. *Renault (I) Champion* • F. *Renault Eurocup Champion*	
1999	F. *Chevrolet (BR) Champion*	
1998	F. *Chevrolet (BR) 5th*	
1990-97	*Karting national and international level*	

Second in the world championship by one little point, decided in the most exciting F1 finale of all time. The dignity that the Brazilian showed at home, winning in Interlagos from pole, was the final affirmation that he is now a world class driver, who has definitely shaken off his wild boy reputation. Massa was written off by the media, after a poor start to the season, but eventually, the team had to shift its focus from their Finnish world champion to the Brazilian understudy. Much has been made of Massa listening to advice from Michael Schumacher and the main thing he learnt was to listen and take advice from the team. This he did to fantastic effect, thanks to a very close and trusting relationship with his race engineer, Rob Smedley, famous for shouting at his driver over the radio that he was "driving like a girl!" Felipe was helped by the fact that the tendency to understeer of the F2008 suited him much better than it did Kimi and he used this to devastating effect, completely dominating some race meetings, with pole, lights to flag wins and race fastest laps. Next year, he will bring all that confidence with him and this time, the team won't start the year thinking Räikkönen is their number one.

Stefano Domenicali

Aldo Costa

Chris Dyer

Luca Baldisseri

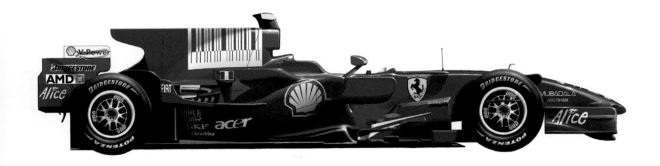

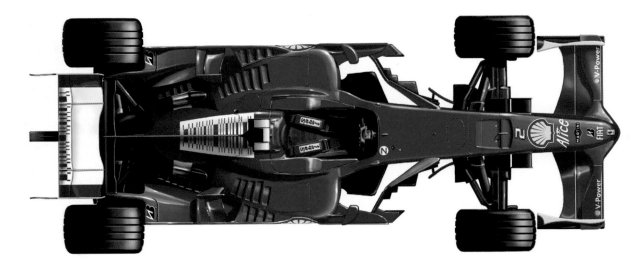

FERRARI F2008
FELIPE MASSA
BRAZILIAN GRAND PRIX

SPECIFICATIONS

• Chassis	Ferrari F2008
• Type	Carbon-fibre and honeycomb, composite structure
• Suspensions (Front & Rear)	Aluminium alloy uprights, upper and lower carbon wishbones and pushrods, torsion bar springs and anti roll bars
• Dampers	Sachs
• Transmission	Semi-automatic sequential electronically controlled gearbox / quick shift 7 speeds + reverse
• Clutch	not revealed
• Electronic systems	McLaren Electronic Systems-Microsoft SECU
• Spark plugs / battery	NGK / not revealed
• Engine	Ferrari Type 056 V8 (90°) <95 kg
• Capacity	2,398cc
• Horsepower	more than 700 bhp
• Max rpm	19,000 rpm
• Number of valves	32 valves pneumatic distribution
• Fuel / lubricants	Shell V-Power ULG 64 / Shell SL-1098
• Brakes (discs)	Brembo ventilated carbon-fibre
• Brakes (calipers)	Brembo
• Tyres	Bridgestone Potenza
• Wheels dimensions	13"
• Wheels	BBS
• Wheel base	not revealed
• Overall length	not revealed
• Overall width	not revealed
• Overall height	not revealed
• Front track	not revealed
• Rear track	not revealed
• Weight	605 kg, driver + camera + ballast

TEAM PROFILE

• Address	Ferrari SpA Via A. Ascari 55-57 41053 Maranello (MO) Italy
• Telephone	+ 39 (0)536 949 450
• Fax	+ 39 (0)536 949 049
• Web	www.ferrariworld.com
• Founded in	1929
• First Grand Prix	Monaco 1950
• Official Name	Scuderia Ferrari Marlboro
• President	Luca Cordero di Montezemolo
• General Director	Stefano Domenicali
• Technical Director	Aldo Costa
• Sporting Director	Luca Baldisserri
• Engine and Electronic	Gilles Simon
• Director of operations	Mario Almondo
• Chief Designer	Nikolas Tombazis
• Racing Engineer Car n°1	Chris Dyer
• Racing Engineer Car n°2	Rob Smedley
• Race Engine Manager	Mattia Binotto
• Test Team and Test Operations Manager	Luigi Mazzola
• Consultant	Michael Schumacher
• Number of employees	900
• Sponsor en titre	Philip Morris (Marlboro)

• Sponsors *Fiat, Shell, Telecom Italia (Alice), Bridgestone, AMD, Martini, Acer, Mubadala Abu Dhabi, Etihad Airways*
• Official Suppliers *Magneti Marelli, Mahle, OMR, SKF, Europcar, Iveco, NGK, Infineon, Finmeccanica, Puma, Sanbittèr, Tata Consultancy Services, Brembo* • Suppliers *BBS, Selex Communications, Sabelt, TRW, Microsoft*

STATISTICS

• Grands Prix	776	• Constructors' World titles 16
• Wins	209	(1961, 64, 75, 76, 77, 79, 82, 83, 99,
• Pole positions	203	2000, 01, 02, 03, 04, 07 & 08)
• Fastest laps	218	• Drivers' World titles 15
• Podiums	622	(1952 & 1953: Alberto Ascari,
• One-two	79	1956: Juan Manuel Fangio,
• GP in the lead	370	1958: Mike Hawthorn, 1961: Phil Hill,
• Laps in the lead	13030	1964: John Surtees, 1975 & 1977: Niki
• Km in the lead	67846	Lauda, 1979: Jody Scheckter,
• Points scored	3876,5	2000, 2001, 2002, 2003 & 2004:
	(4023,5)	Michael Schumacher & 2007: Kimi
		Räikkönen)

POSITION IN CHAMPIONSHIP

1958	2nd, 40(57) pts	1971	3rd, 33 pts	1984	2nd, 57,5 pts	1997	2nd, 102 pts
1959	2nd, 32(38) pts	1972	4th, 33 pts	1985	2nd, 82 pts	1998	2nd, 133 pts
1960	3rd, 26(27) pts	1973	6th, 12 pts	1986	4th, 37 pts	1999	1st, 128 pts
1961	1st, 40 (52) pts	1974	2nd, 65 pts	1987	4th, 53 pts	2000	1st, 170 pts
1962	5th, 18 pts	1975	1st, 72,5 pts	1988	2nd, 65 pts	2001	1st, 179 pts
1963	4th, 26 pts	1976	1st, 83 pts	1989	3rd, 59 pts	2002	1st, 221 pts
1964	1st, 45 (49) pts	1977	1st, 95 (97) pts	1990	2nd, 110 pts	2003	1st, 158 pts
1965	4th, 26(27) pts	1978	2nd, 58 pts	1991	3rd, 55,5 pts	2004	1st, 262 pts
1966	2nd, 31(32) pts	1979	1st, 113 pts	1992	4th, 21 pts	2005	3rd, 100 pts
1967	4th, 20 pts	1980	10th, 8 pts	1993	4th, 28 pts	2006	2nd, 201 pts
1968	4th, 32 pts	1981	5th, 34 pts	1994	3rd, 71 pts	2007	1st, 204 pts
1969	5th, 7 pts	1982	1st, 74 pts	1995	3rd, 73 pts	2008	1st, 172 pts
1970	2nd, 52(55) pts	1983	1st, 89 pts	1996	2nd, 70 pts		

2008 TEST DRIVERS

• Luca BADOER (I)
• Marc GENÉ (E)

SUCCESSION OF DRIVERS 2008

• Kimi RÄIKKÖNEN (FIN)	the 18 Grands Prix
• Felipe MASSA (BR)	the 18 Grands Prix

Officially, Ferrari are world champions again and indeed they are, as they finished first in the Constructors' classification, but despite the age old protestations from every car maker that's been in this situation in F1, namely that the team prize is important, the Italian team lost, because a McLaren driver won the far more mediatised Drivers' crown. In fact, Ferrari would have taken the Drivers' title too, but for Massa's heartbreaking engine failure just three laps from a comfortable win in Hungary and that silly, silly, fuel line incident in the Singapore pit lane. And for that matter, if they had not let Räikkönen beat Massa in Spain. Generally, the F2008 was a quicker race car than its rivals, but suffered a little in qualifying, ironically, because it was almost too easy on its tyres. With overtaking as near impossible as ever this year, starting anywhere other than the front row meant a difficult Sunday afternoon. This was also an important year for the Prancing Horse, as it was the first under the stewardship of Stefano Domenicali, who took over from the father of the team's renaissance, Jean Todt. The young man's style is less dictatorial, but he is just as strong as the fearsome Frenchman. Domenicali showed his mettle, riding the storm of the Hungary, Valencia engine failures, and the pit stop fiascos with Räikkönen ignoring their own traffic light system and Massa being let go with the fuel line still attached.

BMW Sauber

3 | Nick HEIDFELD

DRIVER PROFILE

- Name — *HEIDFELD*
- Firstname — *Nick*
- Nationality — *German*
- Date of birth — *May 10, 1977*
- Place of birth — *Moenchengladbach Rheydt (D)*
- Lives in — *Staefa (CH)*
- Marital status — *engaged to Patricia*
- Kids — *a daughter (Juni) and a son (Joda)*
- Hobbies — *tennis, golf, motorcycle, music, cinema*
- Favorite music — *hits, Outkast*
- Favorite meal — *pasta, appetizers*
- Favorite drinks — *orange juice with sparkling water*
- Height — *165 cm*
- Weight — *59 kg*
- Web — *www.motorsport-magazin.com/nickheidfeld*

STATISTICS

• Grands Prix	153	• Podiums	11
• Starts	150	• GP in the lead	8
• Best result	7 x 2^{e}	• Laps in the lead	25
• Pole positions	1	• Km in the lead	118
• Fastest laps	2	• Points scored	200

CAREER

2008	F1 *BMW, 60 pts, 6th*	
2007	F1 *BMW, 61 pts, 5th*	
2006	F1 *BMW, 23 pts, 9th*	
2005	F1 *Williams-BMW, 28 pts, 11th*	
2004	F1 *Jordan-Ford, 3 pts, 18th*	
2003	F1 *Sauber-Petronas, 6 pts, 14th*	
2002	F1 *Sauber-Petronas, 7 pts, 10th*	
2001	F1 *Sauber-Petronas, 12 pts, 8th*	
2000	F1 *Prost-Peugeot, 0 pt, 20th*	
1999	F3000 *Champion* • F1 *McLaren tests*	
1998	F3000 *2nd* • F1 *McLaren tests*	
1997	F3 *(D) Champion; GP Monaco Winner* • F1 *McLaren tests*	
1996	F3 *(D) 3rd; GP Macau, 6th; Masters Zandvoort, 3rd*	
1995	F. Ford 1800 Inter *Champion* • F. Ford *(D) 2nd*	
1994	F. Ford 1600 *(D) Champion*	
1993	F. A Laval *(F)*	
1992	Karting *(D) Junior, 5th*	
1991	Karting ADAC Jr. Kart Trophy, *3rd; World and European Championship*	
1986-90	Karting *(D)*	

4 | Robert KUBICA

DRIVER PROFILE

- Name — *KUBICA*
- Firstname — *Robert*
- Nationality — *Polish*
- Date of birth — *December 7, 1984*
- Place of birth — *Cracovia (PL)*
- Lives in — *Cracovia (PL)*
- Marital status — *single*
- Kids — *-*
- Hobbies — *karting, bowling, video games*
- Favorite music — *pop/rock*
- Favorite meal — *italian food*
- Favorite drinks — *orange juice*
- Height — *184 cm*
- Weight — *73 kg*
- Web — *www.kubica.pl*

STATISTICS

• Grands Prix	40	• Podiums	8
• Starts	40	• GP in the lead	8
• Wins	1	• Laps in the lead	74
• Pole positions	1	• Km in the lead	337
• Fastest laps	0	• Points scored	120

CAREER

2008	F1 *BMW, 75 pts, 4th*	
2007	F1 *BMW, 39 pts, 6th*	
2006	F1 *BMW, 6 pts, 16th*	
2005	World Series by Renault *Champion* • F3 *GP Macau, 2nd*	
2004	F3 Euro Series *7th; F3 GP Macau, 2nd*	
2003	F3 Euro Series *12th; F3 Masters Sardaigne Winner*	
2002	F. Renault 2000 *(I), 2nd*	
2001	F. Renault 2000 *(I)*	
2000	Karting *(EUR) Formule A, 4th; (Monde) Formule A, 4th*	
1999	Karting *(I & D) Champion Junior ; Monaco Trophy Winner*	
1998	Karting *(I) Champion Junior; (EUR) Junior, 2nd; Monaco Trophy Winner*	
1995-97	Karting *(PL) Champion Junior*	

Mario Theissen

Willy Rampf

Beat Zehnder

Mike Krack

While Kubica gave his team their first ever win, Nick Heidfeld had to settle for that worst of all places for any sportsman – second. He finished runner up four times this year, Australia, Canada, Britain and Belgium. When he wasn't finishing second, the German spent his time cultivating one of the biggest beards ever since in F1, which made him look like the captain of a ship. This was a particularly apposite analogy for much of his season, as Heidfeld was all at sea when it came to getting the best out of his car. The F1.08 perfectly suited Kubica's aggressive late braking, aggressive style, but Nick's Prost-like love of smooth and gentle into and out of the corner, meant he never really got the tyres to work for him, which especially affected his qualifying performance. However, he finally changed his style later in the year, by which time, development on the car had stalled, so it was hard to tell what he might have done. However, he closed the performance gap to Kubica, guaranteed his 2009 seat...and trimmed his beard a bit.

Finally in Bahrain, the English language media were able to use a headline they'd been waiting ages to dust off: "Pole on Pole" graced many a newspaper and web site, after Robert Kubica was fastest in qualifying at the third race of the season, having missed out on pole in Melbourne, when he ran wide at one corner. He went on to do better than that, taking his and the team's first ever F1 victory in Montreal and he also briefly led the Drivers' Championship. The car perfectly suited his late braking driving style and in the early part of the season, the talented Pole presented a real threat to the McLaren-Ferrari quartet. Kubica's name suddenly appeared on a lot of team's shopping lists and his dissatisfaction with the lack of late season development from BMW meant he seemed ready to consider other offers. However, this was all bluff and Robert stays with the Hinwil crew for 2009. It's customary to put the world champion as number one in any driver top ten of the year list, but in my book, Kubica could well have been the most accomplished driver of 2008.

BMW SAUBER F1.08
ROBERT KUBICA
MALAYSIAN GRAND PRIX

SPECIFICATIONS

• Chassis	BMW Sauber F1.08
• Type	Carbon-fibre monocoque and honeycomb composite structure
• Suspensions (Front & Rear)	Upper and lower wishbones, inboard springs and dampers, actuated by pushrods
• Dampers	Sachs
• Transmission	BMW 7-speed quick shift gearbox + reverse, longitudinally mounted, carbon-fibre clutch
• Clutch	AP Racing
• Electronic systems	McLaren Electronic Systems-Microsoft SECU
• Spark plugs / battery	NGK / not revelated
• Engine	BMW P86/8 V8 (90°), 95 kg
• Capacity	2,400cc
• Horsepower	more than 700 bhp
• Max rpm	19,000 rpm
• Number of valves	4 valves per cylinder pneumatic distribution
• Fuel / lubricants	Petronas / Petronas
• Brakes (discs)	Brembo ventilated carbon-fibre
• Brakes (calipers)	Brembo
• Tyres	Bridgestone Potenza
• Wheels dimensions	13"
• Wheels	O.Z. Racing
• Wheel base	3,130 mm
• Overall length	4,600 mm
• Overall width	1,800 mm
• Overall height	1,000 mm
• Front track	1,470 mm
• Rear track	1,410 mm
• Weight	605 kg, driver + camera + ballast

TEAM PROFILE

• Address	BMW Motorsport - Sauber Wildbachstrasse 9 CH - 8340 Hinwil Switzerland
• Telephone	+41 (0)19 37 90 00
• Fax	+41 (0)19 37 90 01
• Web	www.bmw-sauber-f1.com
• Founded in	1970 (Sauber); 2006 (BMW)
• First Grand Prix	Bahrain 2006
• Official Name	BMW Sauber F1 Team
• BMW Motorsport Director	Prof. Dr.-Ing. Mario Theissen
• Technical Director	Willy Rampf
• Technical Director (transmission)	Markus Duessman
• Head of Track Engineering	Mike Krack
• Head of Aerodynamics	Willem Toet
• Chief designer	Christoph Zimmermann
• Team Manager	Beat Zehnder
• Consultant	Peter Sauber
• Chief Mechanic	Urs Kuratle
• Race Engineer (Heidfeld)	Giampaolo Dall'Ara
• Race Engineer (Kubica)	Antonio Cuquerella
• Test Team Engineer	Ossi Oikarinen
• Number of employees	650
• Premium Partner	Petronas
• Official Corporate Partner	Intel
• Official Partners	Credit Suisse, T-Systems, Dell, Puma
• Technical Partner	Bridgestone
• Official Suppliers	Ansys Fluent, Cadence, Certina, Dalco, Dräxlmaier, DuPont, NGK, Walter Meier, Würth, ZF Sachs
• Promotional Suppliers	Brütsch/Rüegger, Mitsubishi Electric, Oerlikon Balzers, OZ, Sika

STATISTICS

• Grands Prix	53	• Best classification in
• Wins	1	constructors' championship
• Pole positions	1	2nd (2007)
• Fastest laps	2	• Best classification in
• Podiums	15	drivers' championship
• One-two	1	4th (2008: Robert Kubica)
• GP in the lead	13	
• Laps in the lead	98	
• Km in the lead	450	
• Points scored	272	

POSITION IN CHAMPIONSHIP

2006	5th,	36 pts
2007	2nd,	101 pts
2008	3rd,	135 pts

2008 TEST DRIVERS

- Christian KLIEN (A)
- Marko ASMER (EST)

SUCCESSION OF DRIVERS 2008

• Nick HEIDFELD (D)	the 18 Grands Prix
• Robert KUBICA (PL)	the 18 Grands Prix

A promising start followed by a disappointing finish, pretty much sums up the year for the Hinwil based BMW-Sauber team. Its performance was a perfect example of how, in Formula 1, you can't afford to ease off developing your car right the way through to the final race, at least, not if you want to challenge the two giants of the sport that are McLaren and Ferrari. BMW finished third again and this year, the points gap to the top two was much reduced. It also finally saw one of its drivers stand on the top step of the podium and to reinforce the fact it was definitely on the up and up, Canada GP winner Robert Kubica was joined in second place by his team-mate Nick Heidfeld. But if Montreal was the high point, it was also the start of the slide down the order, or at least a period of treading water rather than swimming forward. The team had evidently sacrificed pushing forward with the 2008 car, switching its focus to the 2009 version, as the rest of the season saw it often out-paced by Renault, with Toyota and Toro Rosso occasionally causing it more problems. But we can expect Mario Theissen and his crew to have learnt from this lesson and come back stronger in 2009.

Renault

5 | Fernando ALONSO

DRIVER PROFILE

- Name — *ALONSO DÍAZ*
- Firstname — *Fernando*
- Nationality — *Spanish*
- Date of birth — *July 29, 1981*
- Place of birth — *Oviedo (E)*
- Lives in — *Mont-sur-Rolle (CH) & Oxford (GB)*
- Marital status — *married to Raquel del Rosario*
- Kids — *-*
- Hobbies — *sports on tv, movies, computers*
- Favorite music — *Spanish groups*
- Favorite meal — *pasta*
- Favorite drinks — *mineral water*
- Height — *171 cm*
- Weight — *68 kg*
- Web — *www.fernandoalonso.com*

STATISTICS

• Grands Prix	123	• Podiums	52
• Starts	122	• GP in the lead	51
• Wins	21	• Laps in the lead	1221
• Pole positions	17	• Km in the lead	5845
• Fastest laps	11	• Points scored	551

CAREER

2008	F1 *Renault*, 61 pts, *5th*
2007	F1 *McLaren-Mercedes*, 109 pts, *3rd*
2006	F1 *Renault*, 134 pts, **World Champion**
2005	F1 *Renault*, 133 pts, **World Champion**
2004	F1 *Renault*, 59 pts, *4th*
2003	F1 *Renault*, 55 pts, *6th*
2002	F1 *Renault, test driver*
2001	F1 *Minardi-European*, 0 pt, *23rd*
2000	F3000 *4th* • F1 *Minardi test driver*
1999	F. Nissan Euro Series *Champion*
1998	Karting *(E) Champion Inter-A*
1997	Karting *(E & I) Champion Inter-A*
1996	Karting *(E & World) Champion Jr.*
1993-95	Karting *(E) Champion Jr.*
1984-92	Karting *(E) Asturian Champion kids category*

6 | Nelsinho PIQUET

DRIVER PROFILE

- Name — *PIQUET*
- Firstname — *Nelson Angelo*
- Nationality — *Brazilian*
- Date of birth — *July 25, 1985*
- Place of birth — *Heidelberg (D)*
- Lives in — *London (GB)*
- Marital status — *single*
- Kids — *-*
- Hobbies — *water sports, video games, football*
- Favorite music — *electro*
- Favorite meal — *sushis*
- Favorite drinks — *fruits juice*
- Height — *177 cm*
- Weight — *70 kg*
- Web — *www.npiquet.com*

STATISTICS

• Grands Prix	18	• Podiums	1
• Starts	18	• GP in the lead	2
• Best result	1 x 2e	• Laps in the lead	14
• Best qualif.	1 x 7e	• Km in the lead	64
• Fastest laps	0	• Points scored	30

CAREER

2008	F1 *Renault*, 19 pts, *12th*
2007	F1 *Renault, third driver*
2006	GP2 Series *2nd* • A1GP *2nd* • 24H du Mans (GT1) *4th* • Mil Milhas (GTP1) *(BR) Winner*
2005	GP2 Series *8th* • F1 *BAR tests*
2004	F3 *(GB) Champion* • F3 European Cup *4th*; GP Macau, *2nd*; F3 Masters, *8th* • F1 *Williams tests*
2003	F3 *(GB) 3rd*; Korea Super Prix, *3rd*; GP Macau, *8th*; F3 Masters, *2nd* • F1 *Williams tests*
2002	F3 *(South Am.) Champion* • F. Renault 2.0 *(BR) 15th*
2001	F3 *(South Am.) 5th* • F. Renault 2.0 *(BR) 15th*
2000	Karting *(BR) 3 x Champion*
1997-99	Karting *(BR) 3 x Champion Brasilia Federal District; 1x Champion Copa Brazil…*
1993-96	Karting

Flavio Briatore

Bob Bell

The double world champion was damaged goods when he returned to Renault, after a bruising year with McLaren and this was clear to see in some inconsistent performances from the Spaniard, who, after a positive fourth place in Melbourne at the start of the year, seemed to lose interest for a while in the middle of the year. He even made some uncharacteristic mistakes, tangling with other drivers or just crashing on his own, most of these incidents born from frustration with the package. It's understandable, given the machinery he was given to work with. However, once the car showed signs of improvement, so did the Spaniard. Fernando raised his game and reminded us why he is considered the most complete driver package on the grid. With the Renault car still no match for the top three teams, Alonso produced some stirring drives and on-boards shots of him behind the wheel, were a delight to watch for real racing fans: here was a master at work. Sure, the Singapore win was very lucky indeed, but Mount Fuji a week later was totally deserved.

It can be tough having a famous name: just ask the Andretti clan or Jacques Villeneuve. It might help open doors, but if you're not careful, just as you've walked through it, the door swings the other way and hits you in the back. Paddock gossip had it that Nelsinho only got the driver because of Piquet Senior's close relationship with Renault boss Flavio Briatore and certainly, the early part of the season, marred by accidents and no worthwhile results, seemed to indicate that the Italian's ability to talent spot had been clouded by nostalgia for the Piquet name. But in time, the youngster calmed down, took some deep breaths and began to make it into Q3 – even if the best grid position he ever managed was seventh - and score some significant points, including his best result, a second place in the German Grand Prix. By the end of the year, the Brazilian had gone from having a "For Sale" sign hanging round his neck to Renault confirming they wanted to hang onto him.

Pat Symonds

Denis Chevrier

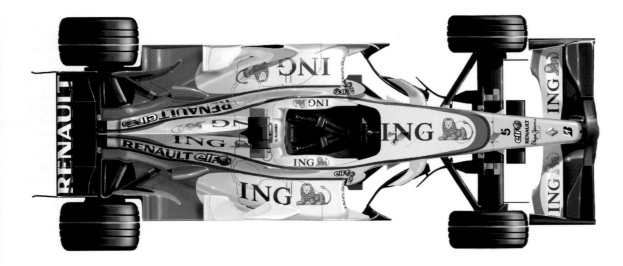

RENAULT R28
FERNANDO ALONSO
SINGAPORE GRAND PRIX

SPECIFICATIONS

- **Chassis** — *Renault R28*
- **Type** — *Moulded carbon fibre and aluminium honeycomb composite monocoque*
- **Front Suspension** — *Carbon fibre top and bottom wishbones, inboard rocker/pushrod system, torsion bar and damper units*
- **Rear Suspension** — *Carbon fibre top and bottom wishbones, vertically-mounted, torsion bars and horizontally-mounted damper on the top of the gearbox casing*
- **Dampers** — *Renault F1*
- **Transmission** — *seven-speed semi-automatic titanium gearbox with one reverse gear longitudinally mounted. "Quickshift" system.*
- **Clutch** — *not revelated*
- **Electronic systems** — *McLaren Electronic Systems-Microsoft SECU*
- **Spark plugs / battery** — *Champion / Renault F1 Team*
- **Radiateurs** — *Secan / Marston*
- **Engine** — *Renault RS27 V8 (90°) of 95 kg*
- **Capacity** — *2,400cc*
- **Horsepower** — *more than 700 bhp*
- **Max rpm** — *19 000 rpm*
- **Number of valves** — *32 valves pneumatic distribution*
- **Fuel / lubricants** — *Elf / Elf*
- **Brakes (discs)** — *Hitco ventilated carbon-fibre*
- **Brakes (calipers)** — *AP Racing*
- **Tyres** — *Bridgestone Potenza*
- **Wheels dimensions** — *13"*
- **Wheels** — *O.Z. Racing*
- **Wheel base** — *3,100 mm*
- **Overall length** — *4,800 mm*
- **Overall width** — *1,800 mm*
- **Overall height** — *950 mm*
- **Front track** — *1,450 mm*
- **Rear track** — *1,400 mm*
- **Weight** — *605 kg, driver + camera + ballast*

TEAM PROFILE

- **Address** — *Renault F1 UK, Whiteways Technical Centre, Enstone, Chipping Norton, Oxon OX7 4EE, Great Britain* — *Renault F1 France, 1-15, avenue du Pdt Kennedy, 91177 Viry-Châtillon, France*
- **Telephone** — *+44 (0) 1608 678 000* — *+33 (0)1 69 12 58 00*
- **Fax** — *+44 (0) 1608 678 609* — *+33 (0)1 69 12 58 17*
- **Web** — *www.ing-renaultf1.com*
- **Founded in** — *1973*
- **First Grand Prix** — *Great Britain 1977*
- **Official Name** — *ING Renault F1 Team*
- **President Renault F1 Team** — *Bernard Rey*
- **Managing Director** — *Flavio Briatore*
- **Technical Director (chassis)** — *Bob Bell*
- **Executive Director of Engineering** — *Pat Symonds*
- **Deputy Managing Director, Technical (engine)** — *Rob White*
- **Deputy Managing Director, Support Operations** — *André Lainé*
- **Head of Engine Trackside Operations** — *Denis Chevrier*
- **Chief Race Engineer** — *Alan Permane*
- **Chief Designer** — *Tim Densham*
- **Assistant Chief Designer** — *Martin Tolliday*
- **Engine Project Manager** — *Malcolm Stewart*
- **Sporting Manager** — *Steve Nielsen*
- **Chief Mechanic** — *Gavin Hudson*
- **Engineering Coordinator** — *Paul Seaby*
- **Race Engineers (Alonso)** — *D. Greenwood, R. Taffin, S. Rennie*
- **Race Engineers (Piquet)** — *P. Charles, R. Penteado, A. Komatsu*
- **Head of Communications** — *Jean-François Caubet*
- **Communications Manager** — *Patrizia Spinelli*
- **Number of employees** — *470 (GB) / 280 (F)*
- **Title Sponsor** *ING* • **Partners** *Elf, Bridgestone, Mutua Madrilena, Pepe Jeans, Universia, Chronotech, Sanho Human Service* • **Official Suppliers** *Altran, Avus, Champion, GF AgieCharmilles, DMG, Elysium, Magneti-Marelli, Network Appliance, Processia Solutions, Puma, Steria, Symantec, SDL Tridion, Vistagy* • **Technology Collaborator** *Phantom Works*
- **CFD Partner** *APC, APPRO, CD Adapco, ABM, Bose, Trilux*
- **HPC/RDD Partners** *Fitlinxx, Johnson, Leisurelines, Marin, Puma, Quicksilver*

STATISTICS

- **Grands Prix** — 245
- **Wins** — 35
- **Pole positions** — 50
- **Fastest laps** — 27
- **Podiums** — 94
- **One-two** — 2
- **GP in the lead** — 86
- **Laps in the lead** — 2500
- **Km in the lead** — 12084
- **Points scored** — 1056
- **Constructors' World titles** — 2 (2005 & 2006)
- **Drivers' World titles** — 2 (2005 & 2006: Fernando Alonso)

POSITION IN CHAMPIONSHIP

1977 *n.c.*	1981 *3rd, 54 pts*	1985 *7th, 16 pts*	2005 *1st, 191 pts*
1978 *12th, 3 pts*	1982 *3rd, 62 pts*	2002 *4th, 23 pts*	2006 *1st, 206 pts*
1979 *6th, 26 pts*	1983 *2nd, 79 pts*	2003 *4th, 88 pts*	2007 *3rd, 51 pts*
1980 *4th, 38 pts*	1984 *5th, 34 pts*	2004 *3rd, 105 pts*	2008 *4th, 80 pts*

2008 TEST DRIVERS

- Lucas DI GRASSI (BR)
- Romain GROSJEAN (F)
- Ben HANLEY (GB)
- Sakon YAMAMOTO (J)

SUCCESSION OF DRIVERS 2008

- Fernando ALONSO (E) — *the 18 Grands Prix*
- Nelsinho PIQUET (BR) — *the 18 Grands Prix*

Renault had a terrible time in 2007, with Fernando Alonso switching to McLaren and the Enstone-built car struggling to adapt to the fact it couldn't run Michelin tyres anymore, as Bridgestone had the monopoly on tyre supply. The Anglo-French team seemed to lack direction and it looked as though 2008 was going to see a repeat of that downward trend, even if Renault's lucky talisman, Alonso, had returned to his spiritual home. We don't know what the double world champion's first words were when he tried the '08 car for the first time, but they were probably not polite: the Renault engine was reckoned to be anywhere between 30 and 40 horsepower down on the best in the field and lacked torque too. The chassis suffered with poor traction and was slow off the line. But, a gradual, almost invisible transformation took place, as various departments came up with small improvements, some aero, some engine and even a major power hike courtesy of a new Elf fuel towards the end of the year. Certainly, Alonso's win in Singapore owed a lot to luck and the timing of the safety car, but a fortnight later in Japan, when McLaren and Ferrari tied themselves in knots, the Renault was quick enough to be in the right place to take its second consecutive win.

Williams Toyota

When the car allowed, mainly on the slower tracks with not too many high speed corners, the man who looks like an advertisement for hair care products, proved that he was worth it. Like most talented drivers, Nico wasn't bothered by oversteer and could make up for some of the car's shortcomings at tracks where aero efficiency is not the key to a fast lap. He came third in the curtain raiser in Melbourne, admittedly helped by one of the safety car periods and he was incredibly lucky to finish second in Singapore, even though he was given a drive-through penalty for refuelling when the pit lane was closed. He also looked to be heading for the podium in Canada, but got stuck behind the road traffic accident when Hamilton rammed Räikkönen in pit lane. In simple terms, he did the best he could with the equipment he was given.

7 | Nico ROSBERG

DRIVER PROFILE

- Name — ROSBERG
- Firstname — Nico
- Nationality — German
- Date of birth — June 27, 1985
- Place of birth — Wiesbaden (D)
- Lives in — Monaco (MC)
- Marital status — single
- Kids — -
- Hobbies — football, snowboarding, jet-ski
- Favorite music — 3 Doors Down
- Favorite meal — vegetable pasta, chocolate cake
- Favorite drinks — Apfel Schorler
- Height — 178 cm
- Weight — 69 kg
- Web — www.nicorosberg.com

STATISTICS

• Grands Prix	53	• Podiums	2
• Starts	53	• GP in the lead	1
• Best result	1 x 2nd	• Laps in the lead	11
• Best qualif.	1 x 3rd	• Km in the lead	56
• Fastest laps	1	• Points scored	41

CAREER

2008 F1 Williams-Toyota, 17 pts, 13th
2007 F1 Williams-Toyota, 20 pts, 9th
2006 F1 Williams-Cosworth, 4 pts, 17th
2005 GP2 Series Champion • F1 Williams tests
2004 F3 Euro Series 4th • F1 Williams tests
2003 F3 Euro Series 8th • F1 Williams tests
2002 F. BMW ADAC (D) Champion • F1 Williams tests
2001 Karting (World) Super A
2000 Karting (EUR) FA, 2nd
1999 Karting (I) ICA Jr., 2nd; (EUR) ICA Jr., 4th
1998 Karting (North USA) Champion ICA Jr.
1997 Mini-Kart (F) Champion
1996 Mini-Kart (F) Champion Regional "Côte d'Azur"

8 | Kazuki NAKAJIMA

DRIVER PROFILE

- Name — NAKAJIMA
- Firstname — Kazuki
- Nationality — japanese
- Date of birth — January 11, 1985
- Place of birth — Aichi (J)
- Lives in — Oxford (GB) & Okazaki (J)
- Marital status — single
- Kids — -
- Hobbies — soccer, music
- Favorite music — japanese music
- Favorite meal — japanese and italian food
- Favorite drinks — Sprite
- Height — 175 cm
- Weight — 62 kg
- Web — www.kazuki-nakajima.com

STATISTICS

• Grands Prix	19	• Podiums	0
• Starts	19	• GP in the lead	0
• Best result	1 x 6th	• Laps in the lead	0
• Best qualif.	1 x 10th	• Km in the lead	0
• Fastest laps	0	• Points scored	9

CAREER

2008 F1 Williams-Toyota, 9 pts, 15th
2007 F1 Williams-Toyota, 0 pt, 22nd • GP2 Series 5th
2006 F3 Euro Series 7th
2005 F3 (J) 2nd; GP Macau, 5th • Super GT GT300 Class 11th
2004 F3 (J) 5th
2003 F. Toyota Champion
1996-2000 Karting

Son of the first Japanese driver to make some sort of impression in F1, Honda-backed Satoru Nakajima, Toyota-backed Kazuki at least showed a willingness to adapt to his surroundings and a more international and cosmopolitan attitude than many of the drivers from the Land of the Rising Son, who followed in his father's pioneering footsteps. But would he be sitting in the Williams if he did not have a Toyota engine nestling behind his head and is he any good? The answer to the first part of the question is probably not, whereas the answer to the second part is harder to find, given that his Williams was not the sort of car to let a driver show his talent. Nakajima proved to be a clever driver who knew how to keep out of trouble and would generally see the chequered flag. And in races where other hotheads had thrown away their chances, he even picked up points from the lower end of the scale. Only if the '09 car is significantly better, will we find out if he can be a real Grand Prix driver, rather than part of a Nippon engine deal.

Sir Frank Williams

Adam Parr

Sam Michael

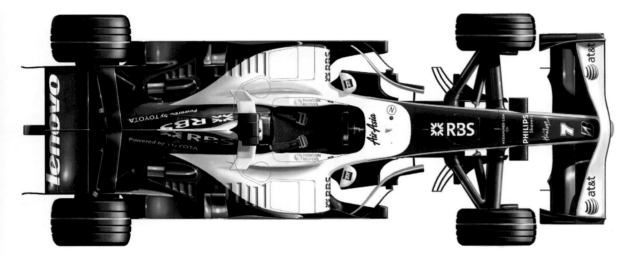

WILLIAMS FW30-TOYOTA
NICO ROSBERG
TURKISH GRAND PRIX

SPECIFICATIONS

- Chassis — Williams FW30
- Type — Monocoque construction fabricated from carbon aramid epoxy and honeycomb composite structure
- Front Suspension — Carbon fibre double wishbone arrangement, with composite toelink and pushrod activated torsion springs
- Rear Suspension — Double wishbone and pushrod activated torsion springs and rockers
- Dampers — Williams F1
- Transmission — Williams F1 7-speed seamless sequential semi-automatic shift + reverse gear in an aluminium maincase, gear selection electro-hydraulically actuated
- Clutch — not revelated
- Electronic systems — McLaren Electronic Systems-Microsoft SECU
- Spark plugs / battery — ND / not revelated
- Engine — Toyota RVX-08 V8 (90°) of 95 kg
- Capacity — 2,398cc
- Horsepower — around 740 bhp
- Max rpm — 19 000 rpm
- Number of valves — 32 valves pneumatic distribution
- Fuel / lubricants — Petrobras / Petrobras
- Brakes (discs) — Carbon Industrie carbon discs and pads
- Brakes (calipers) — AP Racing
- Tyres — Bridgestone Potenza
- Wheels dimensions — 13", 350 mm (AV) / 375 mm (AR)
- Wheels — RAYS forged magnesium
- Wheel base — 3,100 mm
- Overall length — 4,500 mm
- Overall width — 950 mm
- Overall height — 1,800 mm
- Front track — not revelated
- Rear track — not revelated
- Weight — 605 kg, driver + camera + ballast

TEAM PROFILE

- Address — Williams F1 Team, Grove, Wantage, Oxfordshire, OX12 0DQ - Great Britain
- Telephone — +44 (0)1235 777 700
- Fax — +44 (0)1235 777 739
- Web — www.williamsf1.com
- Founded in — 1969
- First Grand Prix — Argentina 1975
- Official Name — AT&T Williams
- Team Principal — Sir Frank Williams
- CEO, Williams F1 Team — Adam Parr
- Director of Engineering — Patrick Head
- Technical Director — Sam Michael
- Chief Designer — Ed Wood
- Chief Aerodynamicist — Jon Tomlinson
- Chief Operations Engineer — Rod Nelson
- Team Manager — Tim Newton
- Team Manager (tests) — Mike Condliffe
- Operating Manager — Alex Burns
- Marketing Manager — Scott Garrett
- Engineering Senior — John Russell
- Chief Mechanic — Carl Gaden
- Race Engineer (Rosberg) — Tony Ross
- Race Engineer (Nakajima) — Xevi Pujolar
- Press Officers — Liam Clogger, Claire Williams, Silvia Hoffer
- Number of employees — 450
- Partners — Hamleys, RBS, AT&T, Philips, Lenovo, Petrobras, Accenture, Air Asia, All Saints, McGregor, Mydiamonds, ORIS, Thomson Reuters, Allianz, Battery, DeWALT, MAN, PPG, Randstad, Reys, Sparco

STATISTICS

- Grands Prix — 529
- Wins — 113
- Pole positions — 125
- Fastest laps — 129
- Podiums — 296
- One-two — 33
- GP in the lead — 217
- Laps in the lead — 7477
- Km in the lead — 34692
- Points scored — 2565,5

- Constructors' World titles — 9 (1980, 1981, 1986, 1987, 1992, 1993, 1994, 1995, 1996 & 1997)
- Drivers World titles — 7 (1980: Alan Jones, 1982: Keke Rosberg, 1987: Nelson Piquet, 1992: Nigel Mansell, 1993: Alain Prost, 1996: Damon Hill & 1997: Jacques Villeneuve)

POSITION IN CHAMPIONSHIP

1975 9th, 6 pts	1984 6th, 25,5 pts	1993 1st, 168 pts	2002 2nd, 92 pts
1976 n.c., 0 pt	1985 3rd, 71 pts	1994 1st, 118 pts	2003 2nd, 144 pts
1977 n.c., 0 pt	1986 1st, 141 pts	1995 2nd, 112 pts	2004 4th, 88 pts
1978 9th, 11 pts	1987 1st, 137 pts	1996 1st, 175 pts	2005 5th, 66 pts
1979 2nd, 75 pts	1988 7th, 20 pts	1997 1st, 123 pts	2006 8th, 11 pts
1980 1st, 120 pts	1989 2nd, 77 pts	1998 3rd, 38 pts	2007 4th, 33 pts
1981 1st, 95 pts	1990 4th, 57 pts	1999 5th, 35 pts	2008 8th, 26 pts
1982 4th, 58 pts	1991 2nd, 125 pts	2000 3rd, 36 pts	
1983 4th, 36 pts	1992 1st, 164 pts	2001 3rd, 80 pts	

2008 TEST DRIVER

- Nico HÜLKENBERG (D)

SUCCESSION OF DRIVERS 2008

- Nico ROSBERG (D) — the 18 Grands Prix
- Kazuki NAKAJIMA (J) — the 18 Grands Prix

Williams was in trouble both on the track and off it: in racing terms the FW30 was not quick or consistent enough to allow its drivers to know what to expect from one circuit to the next, while away from the circuit, Sir Frank Williams' once proud team, a nine times winner of the Constructors' championship, was struggling financially. The money problems got even worse, when the world markets began to collapse because not only did obvious casualties among its sponsor portfolio, such as the Royal Bank of Scotland suffer, but it turned out that unfortunately, other partners were actually owned by similarly struggling financial institutions. This year's car was a development of the 2007 Toyota-powered version and, while it immediately proved to be quicker in winter testing, it was not enough and it did not even have the pace to match the cars fielded by its engine supplier, Toyota. One major problem, especially in the second half of the season, was that development on FW30 virtually came to a complete halt as the team decided to cut its losses and concentrate on the 2009 car. We must now wait and see if Williams has sufficient resource to keep moving forward in the hope of making a significant step next year. The entire future of one of the most famous names in Formula 1 could depend on it.

Red Bull Renault

9 | David COULTHARD

DRIVER PROFILE

- Name   COULTHARD
- Firstname   David
- Nationality   British (Scotish)
- Date of birth   March 27, 1971
- Place of birth   Twynholm (Scotland, GB)
- Lives in   Monaco (MC)
- Marital status   engaged to Karine Minier
- Kids   -
- Hobbies   Golf, swimming, cyclism, cinema
- Favorite music   Maroon 5, Scissor Sisters
- Favorite meal   pasta, thaï food
- Favorite drinks   tea and mineral water
- Height   183 cm
- Weight   72,5 kg
- Web   www.davidcoulthard.co.uk

STATISTICS

• Grands Prix	247	• Podiums	62
• Starts	246	• GP in the lead	62
• Wins	13	• Laps in the lead	897
• Pole positions	12	• Km in the lead	4211
• Fastest laps	18	• Points scored	535

CAREER

2008 F1 Red Bull-Renault, 8 pts, 16th
2007 F1 Red Bull-Renault, 14 pts, 10th
2006 F1 RBR-Ferrari, 14 pts, 13th
2005 F1 RBR-Cosworth, 24 pts, 12th
2004 F1 McLaren-Mercedes, 24 pts, 10th
2003 F1 McLaren-Mercedes, 51 pts, 7th
2002 F1 McLaren-Mercedes, 41 pts, 5th
2001 F1 McLaren-Mercedes, 65 pts, 2nd
2000 F1 McLaren-Mercedes, 73 pts, 3rd
1999 F1 McLaren-Mercedes, 45 pts, 4th
1998 F1 McLaren-Mercedes, 56 pts, 3rd
1997 F1 McLaren-Mercedes, 36 pts, 3rd
1996 F1 McLaren-Mercedes, 18 pts, 7th
1995 F1 Williams-Renault, 49 pts, 3rd
1994 F1 Williams-Renault, 14 pts, 8th • F3000 9th
1993 F3000 3rd • F1 Williams tests • 24H du Mans Winner GT
1992 F3000 9th • F1 Benetton tests
1991 F3 (GB) 2nd; GP Macau & Marlboro Masters Zandvoort Winner
1990 F. Vauxhall-Lotus (GB) 4th • GM Lotus Euroseries 5th
1989 F. Ford 1600 (GB) Champion; F. Ford Festival 3rd
1986-88 Karting (Scotland) Open Kart, 3x Champion;
         (GB) Super Kart 1, 2x Champion
1983-85 Karting (Ecosse) Junior, 3x Champion

10 | Mark WEBBER

DRIVER PROFILE

- Name   WEBBER
- Firstname   Mark Alan
- Nationality   Australian
- Date of birth   27th August 1976
- Place of birth   Queanbeyan, (NSW-AUS)
- Lives in   Buckinghamshire (GB)
- Marital status   engaged to Ann
- Kids   -
- Hobbies   VTT, guided planes, PS2
- Favorite music   INXS, U2, "Red Hot", Pink, Oasis…
- Favorite meal   pasta, pizza, chocolate, ice cream & desserts
- Favorite drinks   apple juice, limonade & sparkling water
- Height   184 cm
- Weight   74 kg
- Web   www.markwebber.com

STATISTICS

• Grands Prix	123	• Podiums	2
• Starts	122	• GP in the lead	4
• Best result	2 x 3rd	• Laps in the lead	10
• Best qualif.	4 x 2nd	• Km in the lead	45
• Fastest laps	0	• Points scored	100

CAREER

2008 F1 Red Bull-Renault, 21 pts, 11th
2007 F1 Red Bull-Renault, 10 pts, 12th
2006 F1 Williams-Cosworth, 7 pts, 14th
2005 F1 Williams-BMW, 36 pts, 10th
2004 F1 Jaguar, 7 pts, 13th
2003 F1 Jaguar, 17 pts, 10th
2002 F1 Minardi-Asiatech, 2 pts, 16th
2001 F3000 2nd • F1 Benetton tests
2000 F3000 3rd • F1 Arrows & Benetton tests
1999 24H du Mans • F1 Arrows tests
1998 FIA-GT 2nd
1997 F3 (GB) 4th; Marlboro Masters Zandvoort, 3rd; GP Macau, 4th
1996 F3 (GB) 2nd • F. Ford Festival Winner; F. Ford Cup (EUR), 3rd
1995 F. Ford (AUS) 4th; F. Ford Festival, 3rd
1994 F. Ford (AUS) 14th
1993 Karting "King of Karting Clubman" Winner;
      Coupe Canberra Winner
1992 Karting (AUS) NSW & ACT Champion
1991 Karting (AUS) Junior

"Did you hear DC is retiring after Brazil?" "Oh, I thought he retired after Canada!" This rather unkind joke was doing the rounds in the paddock, but it's fair to say, the Scotsman's fifteenth and final season did not provide a fitting finale to what has been a long and illustrious career in the sport, which includes 13 Grand Prix victories. He only made it through to Q3 a total of five times and in the races, he had an uncanny knack of crashing into other drivers, who had assumed the politest gentleman racer had kindly left the door open for them at a corner, only for the Red Bull to charge into them. His best race came in Montreal, where he made his final appearance on an F1 podium, having finished third in a race where he showed that, even in a young man's sport, experience can still count for something. It was a shame that a great career ended on a down note, going out at the very first corner of his final race in Brazil, because very few people have a bad word to say about "DC." He will still be at the races in '09, as a consultant to his current team and quite possibly as an expert commentator on British TV.

The only Aussie driver on the grid, Webber had a good season in terms of qualifying, nearly always getting the better of team-mate Coulthard and regularly making it through to Q3 on Saturday afternoons. But his best race result was a fourth place in the Monaco Rain Lottery and as other teams made more progress, life got tougher in the second half of the year. While he therefore maintained his reputation as a strong qualifier, he still has to prove he has the ability to master the complex art of grand prix racing over a distance of 300 kilometres. Next year, he shares the Red Bull garage with Sebastian Vettel, who carries the "star of the future" badge on his overalls. Webber will have to raise his game considerably to match the young German, or it could be time to move on. Away from the track, the outspoken Australian deserves recognition for all his work in the cause of safety through the GPDA and he gets a special mention this year, for being one of a very select band of drivers brave enough to speak their mind over the "Mosley" affair.

Dietrich Mateschitz

Christian Horner

Adrian Newey

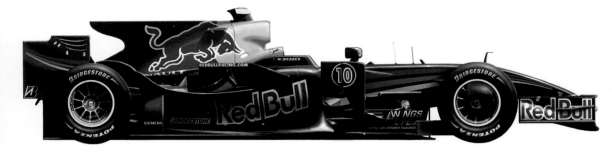

RED BULL RB4-RENAULT
MARK WEBBER
SPANISH GRAND PRIX

SPECIFICATIONS

• Chassis	Red Bull RB4
• Type	Carbon-fibre monocoque and honeycomb composite structure
• Suspensions (Front & Rear)	Aluminium alloy uprights, upper and lower carbon wishbones and pushrods, torsion bar springs and anti roll bars
• Dampers	Multimatic
• Transmission	seven-speed + reverse gearbox, longitudinally mounted with "seamless" hydraulic system for power shift and clutch operation
• Clutch	AP Racing
• Electronic systems	McLaren Electronic Systems-Microsoft SECU
• Spark plugs / battery	Champion / Renault F1 Team
• Engine	Renault RS27 V8 (90°) of 95 kg
• Capacity	2,400cc
• Horsepower	more than 700 bhp
• Max rpm	19,000 rpm
• Number of valves	32 valves pneumatic distribution
• Fuel / lubricants	Elf / Elf
• Brakes (discs)	Hitco ventilated carbon-fibre
• Brakes (calipers)	Brembo
• Tyres	Bridgestone Potenza
• Wheels dimensions	12.7"-13 (AV) / 13.4"-13 (AR)
• Wheels	O.Z. Racing
• Wheel base	not revelated
• Overall length	not revelated
• Overall width	not revelated
• Overall height	not revelated
• Front track	not revelated
• Rear track	not revelated
• Weight	605 kg, driver + camera + ballast

TEAM PROFILE

• Address	Red Bull Racing
	Bradbourne Drive, Tilbrook,
	Milton Keynes, MK7 8BJ
	Great Britain
• Telephone	+44 (0)1908 279 700
• Fax	+44 (0)1908 279 711
• Web	www.redbullracing.com
• Founded in	2005
• First Grand Prix	Australia 2005
• Official Name	Red Bull Racing
• President Red Bull	Dietrich Mateschitz
• Consultant Red Bull	Helmut Marko
• Team Principal Red Bull Racing	Christian Horner
• Chief Technical officer, RBT	Adrian Newey
• Technical Director, RBT	Geoff Willis
• Team Manager (race), RBR	Jonathan Wheatley
• Head of R&D, Red Bull Technology	Andrew Green
• Head of Race and Test Engineering	Paul Monaghan
• Chief Aerodynamicist, RBT	Peter Prodromou
• Chief Designer, Red Bull Technology	Rob Marshall
• Race Engineer (Coulthard)	Guillaume Rocquelin
• Race Engineer (Webber)	Kieran Pilbeam
• Chief Mechanic	Kenny Handkammer
• Head of Communications	Eric Silbermann
• Press Officers	Katie Tweedle, Britta Roeske
• Number of employees	300
• Partners	Hangar-7, Renault, Quehenberger, Bridgestone, Metro, Mac Tools, Magneti Marelli, Siemens, Platform, MSC Software, Leica Geosystems

STATISTICS

• Grands Prix	71	• Best classification in
• Best result	3 x 3°	constructors' championship
• Best qualification	1 x 2°	5° (2007)
• Fastest laps	0	
• Podiums	3	• Best classification in
• One-two	0	drivers' championship
• GP in the lead	5	10° (2007: David Coulthard)
• Laps in the lead	9	
• Km in the lead	43	
• Points scored	103	

POSITION IN CHAMPIONSHIP

2005	7°, 34 pts	2007	5°, 24 pts
2006	7°, 16 pts	2008	7°, 29 pts

2008 TEST DRIVER

• Sébastien BUEMI (CH)

SUCCESSION OF DRIVERS 2008

• David COULTHARD (GB)	the 18 Grands Prix
• Mark WEBBER (AUS)	the 18 Grands Prix

In 2007, Red Bull Racing had definitely lacked the fizz that is the trademark of the drink's company that gives the team its name. Therefore, much was expected of 2008, thanks to the continuity of keeping the same driver line-up, the same Renault engine, of having finished overhauling the workforce and having had a winter with Geoff Willis tidying up the whole technical operation. 2008 got off to a bad start with suspension breakages so spectacular they attracted the attention of the FIA. However, progress soon followed, especially on the reliability front, which had been the weakest point the previous year. In fact, until Webber's retirement in Singapore, where it was claimed that a freak power surge from an underground railway, had caused the problem, the team didn't suffer a single car related failure all season. The points kept coming in the early part of the year, so the team looked to be heading for a solid fourth place in the championship. But apart from Coulthard's visit to the podium with a third place in Canada and Webber's front row start in Silverstone, the points then dried up, to give the team its worst finish ever. It blamed a lack of power from its Renault engine for much of its woes, but had to give up on this excuse after Alonso won two grands prix for the French team! More realistically, the Newey designed car lacked traction and was no good in slow sections.

Toyota

11 | Jarno TRULLI

DRIVER PROFILE

- Name — *TRULLI*
- Firstname — *Jarno*
- Nationality — *Italian*
- Date of birth — *July 13, 1974*
- Place of birth — *Pescara (I)*
- Lives in — *St Moritz (CH) & Pescara (I)*
- Marital status — *married to Barbara*
- Kids — *two sons (Enzo et Marco)*
- Hobbies — *music, cinema, karting, computers*
- Favorite music — *pop, rock, jazz, blues*
- Favorite meal — *pizza*
- Favorite drinks — *Coca-Cola, Fanta*
- Height — *173 cm*
- Weight — *60 kg*
- Web — *www.jarnotrulli.com*

STATISTICS

Grands Prix	202	Podiums	8
Starts	199	GP in the lead	14
Wins	1	Laps in the lead	160
Pole positions	3	Km in the lead	666
Fastest laps	0	Points scored	214

CAREER

2008 F1 *Toyota, 31 pts, 9th*
2007 F1 *Toyota, 8 pts, 13th*
2006 F1 *Toyota, 15 pts, 12th*
2005 F1 *Toyota, 43 pts, 7th*
2004 F1 *Renault & Toyota, 46 pts, 6th*
2003 F1 *Renault, 33 pts, 8th*
2002 F1 *Renault, 9 pts, 8th*
2001 F1 *Jordan-Honda, 12 pts, 9th*
2000 F1 *Jordan-Mugen Honda, 6 pts, 10th*
1999 F1 *Prost-Peugeot, 7 pts, 11th*
1998 F1 *Prost-Peugeot, 1 pt, 15th*
1997 F1 *Minardi-Hart & Prost-Mugen Honda, 3 pts, 15th*
1996 F3 *(D) Champion*
1995 F3 *(D) 4th* • Karting *(I) Champion 100 FSA;
      "Ayrton Senna" World Cup Winner 100 FSA*
1994 Karting *(World) Champion 125 FC;
      (EUR & North USA) Champion 100 FSA;
      "Ayrton Senna" World Cup Winner 100 FSA*
1993 Karting *(World) 100 SA, 2nd...*
1992 Karting *(World) 125 FC, 2nd*
1991 Karting *(World) Champion 100 FK*
1988-90 Karting *(I) Champion 100 National Class*
1987 Karting *Gold medal "Youth Games" Junior class 100*
1983-86 Mini-Kart

12 | Timo GLOCK

DRIVER PROFILE

- Name — *GLOCK*
- Firstname — *Timo*
- Nationality — *German*
- Date of birth — *March 18, 1982*
- Place of birth — *Lidenfels (D)*
- Lives in — *Cologne (D)*
- Marital status — *single*
- Kids — *-*
- Hobbies — *karting, fitness*
- Favorite music — *Red Hot Chili Peppers, Guns N'Roses*
- Favorite meal — *pasta, sushis*
- Favorite drinks — *none*
- Height — *169 cm*
- Weight — *64 kg*
- Web — *www.timoglock.com*

STATISTICS

Grands Prix	22	Podiums	1
Starts	22	GP in the lead	1
Best result	1 x 2nd	Laps in the lead	3
Best qualif.	1 x 5th	Km in the lead	13
Fastest laps	0	Points scored	27

CAREER

2008 F1 *Toyota, 25 pts, 10th*
2007 GP2 Series *Champion*
2006 GP2 Series *4th*
2005 Champ Car *8th*
2004 F1 *Jordan-Ford, 2 pts, 19th*
2003 F3 Euro Series *5th*
2002 F3 *(D) 3rd*
2001 F. BMW ADAC *(D) Champion*
2000 F. BMW ADAC Jr. *(D) Champion*
1998 Karting

Ninth in the Drivers' World Championship might not sound like anything special, but Jarno Trulli really worked hard for his 31 points. It's all too easy to watch the race for first place and ignore what's going on further back. But the Italian driver produced some great drives, the most obvious being his visit to the podium after a very tough drive to finish third in France. It was a poignant moment, given that the architect of much of Toyota's success in all forms of motor sport, Ove Anderson had died earlier that week. In Spa, he looked set for a remarkable drive, charging from eleventh on the grid – one of his less successful qualifying postions – to be right up there with the lead Ferraris by the time they got to the first corner. Jarno also put up some great qualifying performances and all this on top of the fact that he made a great contribution to the development of the car throughout the year.

Vettel's the rising star, Heidfeld has a huge beard, Sutil's the tall one at the back, Rosberg is the pretty one. But there were five German drivers on the grid this year and Timo Glock is the anonymous one. In his second season, Glock proved that he is a driver who can make rapid progress, learning every time he sits in the cockpit. Highlight of his season came when he gave Toyota its best finish of the year, coming home second in Budapest. Sure, he moved up a place thanks to Massa's untimely engine exploding retirement, but the Toyota man had already done half the job on Saturday, qualifying an excellent fifth. Coming second showed what he could do on a circuit where Toyota's less than wonderful aero package weighed less heavily than usual on the car's overall performance. Anonymous? Not anymore, not after the final corner of the final race in Brazil. Glock will forever be remembered as the man who couldn't hold off Hamilton, thus allowing the Englishman to grab the championship crown. He's probably not very popular in Italy!

Tadashi Yamashina

John Howett

Pascal Vasselon

Frank Dernie

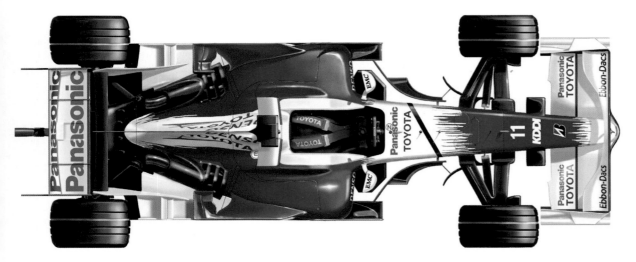

TOYOTA TF108
JARNO TRULLI
FRENCH GRAND PRIX

SPECIFICATIONS

- Chassis — Toyota TF108
- Type — Moulded carbon fibre and honeycomb construction
- Suspensions (Front & Rear) — Carbon fibre double wishbone arrangement, with carbon fibre trackrod and pushrod
- Dampers — Penske
- Transmission — Toyota/Williams F1 sequential, longitudinally mounted, semi-automatic /seamless 7-speed + reverse
- Clutch — not revealed
- Electronic systems — Toyota / Magneti Marelli + MES SECU-Microsoft
- Spark plugs / battery — DENSO / not revealed
- Engine — Toyota RVX-08 V8 (90°) of 95 kg
- Capacity — 2.398cc
- Horsepower — around 740 bhp
- Max rpm — 19,000 rpm
- Number of valves — 4 valves per cylinder pneumatic distribution
- Fuel / lubricants — Esso / Esso
- Brakes (discs) — Hitco ventilated carbon-fibre
- Brakes (calipers) — Brembo
- Tyres — Bridgestone Potenza
- Wheels dimensions — 13"
- Wheels — BBS Magnesium
- Wheel base — 3,090 mm
- Overall length — 4,636 mm
- Overall width — 1,800 mm
- Overall height — 950 mm
- Front track — not revealed
- Rear track — not revealed
- Weight — 605 kg, driver + camera + ballast

TEAM PROFILE

- Address — Toyota Motorsport GmbH, Toyota-Allee 7, 50858 Köln-Marsdorf, Deutschland
- Telephone — +49 (0) 223 418 23 444
- Fax — +49 (0) 223 418 23 37
- Web — www.toyota-f1.com
- Founded in — 1999
- First Grand Prix — Australia 2002
- Official Name — Panasonic Toyota Racing
- Chairman and Team Principal TMG — Tadashi Yamashina
- President TMG — John Howett
- Executive Vice-President TMG — Yoshiaki Kinoshita
- Executive Vice-Président TMC — Kazuo Okamoto
- Managing Officer TMC — Masayuki Nakai, Hisayuki Inoue
- Director Technical Co-ordination — Noritoshi Arai
- Senior General Manager Chassis — Pascal Vasselon
- Senior General Manager Engine — Luca Marmorini
- Team Manager — Richard Cregan
- Project Managers — John Litjens, Mark Tatham
- Chief aerodynamicist — Mark Gillan
- Chief Engineer Race and Test — Dieter Gass
- Consultant — Frank Dernie
- Race Engineer (Trulli) — Giancula Pisanello
- Race Engineer (Glock) — Francesco Nenci
- Chief Mechanic — Gerard Lecoq
- Number of employees — 600
- Title Partner — Panasonic
- Partners — DENSO, Bridgestone, Dassault Systèmes, Ebbon-Dacs, EMC, KDDI, Alpinestars, KTC, Magneti Marelli Motorsport, MAN, Takata, Time Inc., Würth

STATISTICS

- Grands Prix — 122
- Best result — 3 x 2nd
- Pole positions — 2
- Fastest laps — 1
- Podiums — 8
- One-two — 0
- GP in the lead — 9
- Laps in the lead — 53
- Km in the lead — 271
- Points scored — 219

- Best classification in constructors' championship — 4th (2005)
- Best classification in drivers' championship — 6th (2005: Ralf Schumacher)

POSITION IN CHAMPIONSHIP

2002 10th, 2 pts
2003 8th, 16 pts
2004 8th, 9 pts
2005 4th, 88 pts
2006 6th, 35 pts
2007 6th, 13 pts
2008 5th, 56 pts

2008 TEST DRIVER

- Kamui KOBAYASHI (J)

SUCCESSION OF DRIVERS 2008

- Jarno TRULLI (I) — the 18 Grands Prix
- Timo GLOCK (D) — the 18 Grands Prix

With reputedly the biggest budget on the grid, but no race wins to show for it, something had to change at the Japanese team and this year it did, as the 2008 car was created from a clean sheet of paper. The technical team was tightened up as technical director, Pascal Vasselon was joined by Mark Gillan as head of aerodynamics while the eternal Frank Dernie, his hand eternally clasped around a mug of nice English team, came on board as a consultant. The trick worked and the TF108 was a much less nervous and temperamental beast than the 2007 car, partly thanks to a Ferrari-like long wheelbase. This made the car kind to its tyres and its engine also had plenty of driveability, making the whole thing much more user friendly. Another aspect of the car's performance that had dramatically improved was its speed off the start line: previously a weak point, this year, Trulli and Glock often seemed to be strapped into rocket launchers when the red lights went out. Toyota used to have an advertising slogan that read: "the car in front is a Toyota." If progress continues, it might well come true on a race track soon.

Toro Rosso Ferrari

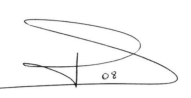

14 | Sébastien BOURDAIS

DRIVER PROFILE

- Name — *BOURDAIS*
- Firstname — *Sébastien*
- Nationality — *French*
- Date of birth — *February 28, 1979*
- Place of birth — *Le Mans (F)*
- Lives in — *Morges (CH)*
- Marital status — *married to Claire*
- Kids — *a daughter (Emma)*
- Hobbies — *informatic, music, cinema, reading*
- Favorite music — *pop, classic rock, Queen…*
- Favorite meal — *pasta*
- Favorite drinks — *Red Bull*
- Height — *179 cm*
- Weight — *72 kg*
- Web — *www.sebastien-bourdais.com*

STATISTICS

• Grands Prix	18	• Podiums	0
• Starts	18	• GP in the lead	1
• Best result	2 x 7th	• Laps in the lead	3
• Best qualif.	1 x 4th	• Km in the lead	14
• Fastest laps	0	• Points scored	4

CAREER

2008 F1 *STR-Ferrari, 4 pts, 17th*
2007 Champ Car World Series *Champion •*
   24H du Mans *(LMP1) 2nd*
2006 Champ Car World Series *Champion*
2005 Champ Car World Series *Champion*
2004 Champ Car World Series *Champion • 24H du Mans (LMP1)*
2003 Champ Car World Series *4th • F1 Tests Arrows*
2002 F3000 *Champion • FIA Sportscar (SR1) 4th •*
   24H du Mans *(LMP 900) 10th*
2001 F3000 *4th • FIA Sportscar (SR1) •*
   24H du Mans *(LMP 900) 4th*
2000 F3000 *9th • 24H du Mans (LMP 900) 4th*
1999 F3 *(F) Champion; Masters of F3, 10th • 24H du Mans (GTS)*
1998 F3 *(F) 6th; Masters of F3, 20th*
1997 F. Renault *(F) 2nd*
1996 F. Renault *(F) 7th*
1995 F. Renault Campus *(F) 9th*
1991-94 Karting *(F) Ligue de Bretagne, 2 x Champion;*
   Ligue Cadets, Champion; Cadets, 4th

15 | Sebastian VETTEL

DRIVER PROFILE

- Name — *VETTEL*
- Firstname — *Sebastian*
- Nationality — *German*
- Date of birth — *July 3, 1987*
- Place of birth — *Heppenheim (D)*
- Lives in — *Heppenheim (D)*
- Marital status — *single*
- Kids — *-*
- Hobbies — *VTT, swimming, snowboarding, fitness*
- Favorite music — *rock, house…*
- Favorite meal — *pasta*
- Favorite drinks — *Red Bull*
- Height — *174 cm*
- Weight — *64 kg*
- Web — *www.sebastianvettel.de*

STATISTICS

• Grands Prix	26	• Podiums	1
• Starts	26	• GP in the lead	2
• Wins	1	• Laps in the lead	52
• Pole positions	1	• Km in the lead	298
• Fastest laps	0	• Points scored	41

CAREER

2008 F1 *STR-Ferrari, 35 pts, 8th*
2007 F1 *BMW & STR-Ferrari, 6 pts, 14th •*
   World Series by Renault 3rd
2006 F3 Euro Series *2nd; F3 Masters 6th • World Series by*
   Renault 15th • F1 BMW. Sauber test driver
2005 F3 Euro Series *5th; F3 (E) 15th; F3 Masters 11th*
2004 F. BMW ADAC *(D) Champion*
2003 F. BMW ADAC *(D) 2nd*
2002 Karting *(EUR) ICA, 6th; (D) 10th*
2001 Karting *(EUR) Champion ICA Jr.; (D) Champion Jr.;*
   Monaco Junior Cup & Paris-Bercy Winner
2000 Karting *(D) Junior, 5th;*
1995 Karting

The other half of the Seb & Seb duo was actually more of a rookie than Vettel, having never raced in F1 before Melbourne. Nevertheless, as a four time Champ Car champion, he obviously knew a bit about racing. Indeed, in the usual chaos of the opening round in Australia, he nearly managed a fairy tale debut, as he was heading for fourth place, when he suffered a technical problem in the last few laps. He eventually finished seventh, his best result, which he later repeated in Spa. Sebastien Bourdais definitely preferred the STR2B with which the team started the year and the Frenchman struggled at first with the new car. But, in the second half of the year, he made it through to Q3 every time, except Singapore and even qualified on row 2 in fourth spot in Monza. But Sebastien is not the easiest guy to work with from a team point of view and Franz Tost and Gerhard Berger were harsh critics whenever he made a mistake. At the time of writing, it is unclear whether or not he is being given a second chance in 2009, or if he will head back to happier hunting grounds across the Atlantic.

A star is born! Sebastian Vettel hated being tagged as "the next Schumacher" by the German media, but you can see what they meant. For a lad who only turned 21 towards the end of the year, he showed a level of maturity way beyond his tender years and he coupled this with a level of intelligence and skill behind the wheel that has put him on every team's shopping list. After a bad start to the season, where he only managed 39 laps from the first four races, he learnt not to get involved in first lap tangles and later on, he avoided these by regularly qualifying in the top ten. His technical feedback also improved considerably over the course of the season and his skill in the wet was breathtaking. It all seems to come very easily to him and some members of his team would need to check if he was actually on track rather than in the garage, as he was so cool over the car-to-pit radio that sometimes it was hard to tell. For 2009, he has been "promoted" to Red Bull Racing, a move which privately he was none too keen on. But if his career stalls, it won't be for long, as he is surely destined for a top two team in the not too distance future.

Gerhard Berger

Franz Tost

Giorgio Ascanelli

TORO ROSSO STR3-FERRARI
SEBASTIAN VETTEL
ITALIAN GRAND PRIX

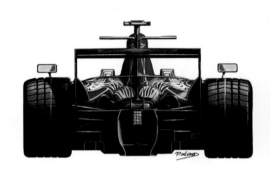

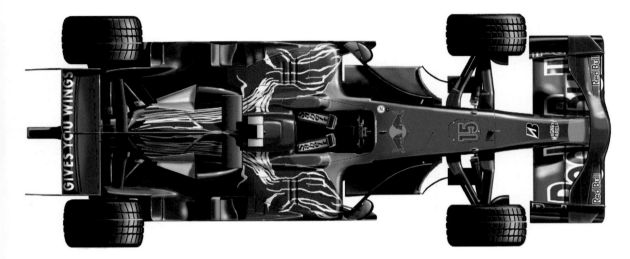

SPECIFICATIONS

• Chassis	Toro Rosso STR2B (AUS > TUR) Toro Rosso STR3 (MC > BR)
• Type	Carbon-fibre monocoque and honeycomb composite structure
• Suspensions (Front & Rear)	Aluminium alloy uprights, upper and lower carbon wishbones and pushrods, torsion bar springs and anti roll bars
• Dampers	Multimatic
• Transmission	seven-speed + reverse gearbox, longitudinally mounted with "seamless" hydraulic system for power shift and clutch operation
• Clutch	AP Racing
• Electronic systems	Magneti Marelli + MES SECU-Microsoft
• Spark plugs / battery	not revealed
• Engine	Ferrari Type 056 V8 (90°) of 95 kg
• Capacity	2,398cc
• Horsepower	more than 700 bhp
• Max rpm	19,000 rpm
• Number of valves	32 valves pneumatic distribution
• Fuel / lubricants	Castrol / Castrol
• Brakes (discs)	Brembo, Hitco, Carbone Industrie
• Brakes (calipers)	Brembo
• Tyres	Bridgestone Potenza
• Wheels dimensions	12.7"-13 (AV) / 13.4"-13 (AR)
• Wheels	O.Z. Racing
• Wheel base	not revelated
• Overall length	not revelated
• Overall width	not revelated
• Overall height	not revelated
• Front track	not revelated
• Rear track	not revelated
• Weight	605 kg, driver + camera + ballast

TEAM PROFILE

• Address	Scuderia Toro Rosso Via Spallanzani, 21 48018 Faenza (RA) Italy
• Telephone	+39 (0)546 696 111
• Fax	+39 (0)546 620 998
• Web	www.scuderiatororosso.com
• Founded in	2006
• First Grand Prix	Bahrain 2006
• Official Name	Scuderia Toro Rosso
• Co-Owner	Dietrich Mateschitz
• Co-Owner	Gerhard Berger
• Team principal	Franz Tost
• Technical Director	Giorgio Ascanelli
• General Director	Gianfranco Fantuzzi
• Team Manager	Massimo Rivola
• Chief Engineer	Laurent Mekies
• Technical Coordinator	Sandro Parrini
• Race Engineer (Bourdais)	Claudio Balestri
• Race Engineer (Vettel)	Riccardo Adami
• Chief Mechanic	Paolo Piancastelli
• Head of Communications	Eric Silbermann
• Press Officers	Fabiana Valenti
• Number of employees	170
• Partners	Hangar-7, VolksWagen, USAG, Bridgestone, Puma, Magneti Marelli, Advanti

STATISTICS

• Grands Prix	53
• Wins	1
• Pole positions	1
• Fastest laps	0
• Podiums	1
• One-two	0
• GP in the lead	3
• Laps in the lead	55
• Km in the lead	311
• Points scored	9

• Best classification in constructors' championship — 6° (2008)
• Best classification in drivers' championship — 8° (2008: Sebastian Vettel)

POSITION IN CHAMPIONSHIP

2006 9°, 1 pt
2007 7°, 8 pts
2008 6°, 39 pts

2008 TEST DRIVER

• None

SUCCESSION OF DRIVERS 2008

• Sébastien BOURDAIS (I)	the 18 Grands Prix
• Sebastian VETTEL (D)	the 18 Grands Prix

When Red Bull owner Dietrich Mateschitz bought the Minardi team and turned it into Scuderia Toro Rosso, he was asked how he would feel if his new little team beat the more established Red Bull Racing. "It would be great, as that's part of racing." Well, this year, that's exactly what happened, as the little Italian outfit finished one place ahead of its big brother, giving Mr. Mateschitz his first ever F1 win, courtesy of Sebastian Vettel's remarkable pole position to chequered flag victory in Monza. For a team with just over 150 staff in total, it totally embarrassed organisations three times its size. How? Well, the very promising Vettel was one factor, allied to a well integrated engine from Ferrari and the technical wisdom and expertise of Giorgio Ascanelli. These elements were masterfully controlled by meticulous team principal Franz Tost, with team co-owner Gerhard Berger adding his great experience and charisma to the equation. The Ferrari engine provided around 30 horsepower more than Red Bull's Renault, but that's not the whole story as the Italian V8 was thirstier and required a more compromised aero package to achieve the necessary level of cooling. The team also coped very well with only switching to this year's car as from the Monaco Grand Prix and Ascanelli wisely chose not to adopt all the modifications to the chassis proposed by Red Bull Technology, only picking those that he understood and could work with. In 2009, the Faenza squad will have to make do without Vettel, but the team itself has proved capable of taking on the big boys.

Honda

16 | Jenson BUTTON

DRIVER PROFILE

- Name — *BUTTON*
- Firstname — *Jenson*
- Nationality — *British*
- Date of birth — *January 19, 1980*
- Place of birth — *Frome, Somerset (GB)*
- Lives in — *Monaco (MC)*
- Marital status — *engaged to Florence*
- Kids — *-*
- Hobbies — *web surfing, video games, shopping*
- Favorite music — *Jamiroquaï, Kool And The Gang, the 70'*
- Favorite meal — *curry, fish and pasta*
- Favorite drinks — *water and orange juice*
- Height — *183 cm*
- Weight — *68,5 kg*
- Web — *www.jensonbutton.com*

STATISTICS

• Grands Prix	157	• Podiums	15
• Starts	153	• GP in the lead	13
• Wins	1	• Laps in the lead	104
• Pole positions	3	• Km in the lead	522
• Fastest laps	0	• Points scored	232

CAREER

2008	F1	*Honda, 3 pts, 18th*
2007	F1	*Honda, 6 pts, 15th*
2006	F1	*Honda, 56 pts, 6th*
2005	F1	*B·A·R-Honda, 37 pts, 9th*
2004	F1	*B·A·R-Honda, 85 pts, 3rd*
2003	F1	*B·A·R-Honda, 17 pts, 9th*
2002	F1	*Renault, 14 pts, 7th*
2001	F1	*Benetton-Renault, 2 pts, 17th*
2000	F1	*Williams-BMW, 12 pts, 8th*
1999	F3	*(GB) 3rd ; GP Macau, 2nd*
1998		*F. Ford (GB) Champion; F. Ford (EUR) 2nd; F. Ford Festival Winner*
1997		*Karting (EUR) Super A, Champion; Winter Cup, 2nd; A. Senna Memorial Cup Winner-Suzuka*
1996		*Karting (EUR) FA, 5th; (AMER.) 3rd; World Cup, 3rd*
1995		*Karting (I) Senior ICA, Champion; (World) FA, 3rd*
1994		*Karting (GB) Jr. TKM, 4th; (EUR+ITA) Intercontinental A Jr.*
1990-93		*Karting (GB) Open, 3x Champion; Jr. TKM, Champion; (GB) Junior, 2x Champion*
1989		*Karting (GB) Super Prix Winner*

17 | Rubens BARRICHELLO

DRIVER PROFILE

- Name — *BARRICHELLO*
- Firstname — *Rubens Gonçalves*
- Nationality — *Brasilian*
- Date of birth — *May 23, 1972*
- Place of birth — *São Paulo (BR)*
- Lives in — *Monaco (MC)*
- Marital status — *married to Silvana*
- Kids — *two sons (Eduardo and Fernando)*
- Hobbies — *golf, karting, bowling*
- Favorite music — *pop, rock, Biagio Antonacci*
- Favorite meal — *pasta*
- Favorite drinks — *Red Bull*
- Height — *172 cm*
- Weight — *70 kg*
- Web — *www.barrichello.com.br*

STATISTICS

• Grands Prix	271	• Podiums	62
• Starts	268	• GP in the lead	45
• Wins	9	• Laps in the lead	729
• Pole positions	13	• Km in the lead	3517
• Fastest laps	15	• Points scored	530

CAREER

2008	F1	*Honda, 11 pts, 14th*
2007	F1	*Honda, 0 pt, 20th*
2006	F1	*Honda, 30 pts, 7th*
2005	F1	*Ferrari, 38 pts, 8th*
2004	F1	*Ferrari, 114 pts, 2nd*
2003	F1	*Ferrari, 65 pts, 4th*
2002	F1	*Ferrari, 77 pts, 2nd*
2001	F1	*Ferrari, 56 pts, 3rd*
2000	F1	*Ferrari, 62 pts, 4th*
1999	F1	*Stewart-Ford, 21 pts, 7th*
1998	F1	*Stewart-Ford, 4 pts, 14th*
1997	F1	*Stewart-Ford, 6 pts, 14th*
1996	F1	*Jordan-Peugeot, 14 pts, 8th*
1995	F1	*Jordan-Peugeot, 11 pts, 11th*
1994	F1	*Jordan-Hart, 19 pts, 6th*
1993	F1	*Jordan-Hart, 2 pts, 17th*
1992	F3000	*3rd*
1991	F3	*(GB) Champion*
1990		*GM Lotus series Champion • F. Vauxhall Lotus 11th*
1989		*F. Ford 1600 (BR) 4th*
1981-88		*Karting (BR) 5x Champion*

Those of you with long memories might recall the fuss that surrounded Jenson Button's arrival on the F1 scene back in 2000 when the 20 year old youngster joined Williams. It was similar to the media frenzy accorded to fellow countryman Lewis Hamilton last year: spot the difference? One of them is now a world champion with a great future ahead of him, while the other has one rather lucky Grand Prix victory to his name. If there is any bad driver management advice on offer, Button will usually go for it and it seems his only consolation is that he will retire a very wealthy man, thanks to some lucrative contracts with the wrong teams at the wrong time. Jenson struggled with the lack of front end grip provided by the Honda and also made a few too many mistakes and only made it through to Q3 once all year. He is very definitely a wasted talent, as some great drives in past years have shown, but all he can do now is sit and wait and see if Ross Brawn can work his magic in Brackley - and Tochigi for that matter - over the winter.

What a pity it will be if Rubens Barrichello is not on the F1 grid in 2009. The little Brazilian with the baby face and the silly podium dance, set a new record this year when he overtook Riccardo Patrese at the head of the list for most Grand Prix starts. The enthusiasm and dedication is still there. While he might lack team-mate Button's outright pace, Barrichello had the better season, thanks to a more analytical approach, learned at Ferrari, which meant he provided better feedback to the engineers. He learned to live with the faults – and god knows there were enough of them – of his Honda and his smooth driving style occasionally tamed the recalcitrant beast. At Silverstone, one of his favourite tracks, thanks to his apprenticeship years spent in England, he made an inspired call, persuading the team to put him on extreme rain tyres before the conditions demanded them and splashed his way through the puddles to his and Honda's only podium of the year, finishing third in the British Grand Prix.

Ross Brawn

Nick Fry

Jacky Eeckelaert

Jock Clear

HONDA RA108
RUBENS BARRICHELLO
MONACO GRAND PRIX

SPECIFICATIONS

- Chassis — *Honda RA108*
- Type — *Moulded carbon fibre and honeycomb composite structure*
- Suspensions (Front & Rear) — *Wishbone and pushrod-activated torsion springs and rockers, mechanical anti-roll bar*
- Dampers — *Showa*
- Transmission — *Honda F1 sequential, semi-automatic, hydraulic activation 7-speed + reverse, Honda internals*
- Clutch — *Alcon*
- Electronic systems — *Honda PGM-IG / Honda PGM-FI + McLaren Electronic Systems-Microsoft SECU*
- Spark plugs / battery — *NGK / 3Ah lead acid*
- Engine — *Honda RA808E V8 (90°) of 95 kg*
- Capacity — *2,400cc*
- Horsepower — *more than 700 bhp*
- Max rpm — *19,000 rpm*
- Number of valves — *4 valves per cylinder; pneumatic valve system*
- Fuel / lubricants — *ENEOS / ENEOS*
- Brakes (discs) — *Alcon ventilated carbon-fibre*
- Brakes (calipers) — *not revealed*
- Tyres — *Bridgestone Potenza*
- Wheels dimensions — *13"*
- Wheels — *BBS forged magnesium*
- Wheel base — *not revelaled*
- Overall length — *4,700 mm*
- Overall width — *1,800 mm*
- Overall height — *950 mm*
- Front track — *not revelaled*
- Rear track — *not revelaled*
- Weight — *605 kg, driver + camera + ballast*

TEAM PROFILE

- Address — *Honda Racing F1 Team F1 Team Operations Centre, Brackley, Northants NN13 7BD Great Britain*
- Telephone — *+44 (0)1280 84 40 00*
- Fax — *+44 (0)1280 84 40 01*
- Web — *www.hondaracingf1.com*
- FOUNDED IN — *1964*
- First Grand Prix — *Allemagne 1964*
- Official Name — *Honda Racing F1 Team*
- Chairman, Honda Racing F1 Team — *Yasuhiro Wada* General Manager, Honda Motor Motorsports Division
- Team Principal, Honda Racing F1 Team — *Ross Brawn*
- CEO, Honda Racing F1 Team — *Nick Fry*
- President, Honda Racing Development, Ltd. — *Hiroshi Abe*
- Deputy MD (Technical) — *Shuhei Nakamoto*
- Deputy Technical Director — *Jörg Zander*
- Director of Advanced Research — *Jacky Eeckelaert*
- Sporting Director — *Ron Meadows*
- Head of Aerodynamics — *Loïc Bigois*
- Head of Race & Test Engineering — *Steve Clark*
- Chief Engineer, Vehicle Engineering — *Craig Wilson*
- Senior Race Engineer (Button) — *Andrew Shovlin*
- Senior Race Engineer (Barrichello) — *Jock Clear*
- Chief Mechanic — *Alistair Gibson*
- Head of Medias — *Tracy Novak, Nicola Armstrong*
- Number of employees — *360 (GB) / 370 (J)*
- Team Partners *Bridgestone, ENEOS, Fila, NGK, NTN, Ray-Ban, Seiko,*
- Technical Partners *Alcon, Avaya, Haas Automation, Showa, PerkinElmer, TÜV SÜD Automotive*
- Team Suppliers *+GF+ AgieCharmilles, Alpinestars, Barco, CIBER UK, CYTEC, DAF Trucks, Endless Advance Ltd, Hitachi High-Technologies, IBM, Instron, Kyowa Electronic Instruments, Laverstoke Park, Lincoln Electric, MTS Systems, NCE, Oliver Sweeney, Quadrant, Sandvik Coromant, Snap-on Tools, STL Communications Ltd, Takata, Tripp Luggage, Vialtus Solutions* • Charity Partner *Helen & Douglas House*

STATISTICS

- Grands Prix — 88
- Wins — 3
- Pole positions — 2
- Fastest laps — 2
- Podiums — 9
- One-two — 0
- GP in the lead — 10
- Laps in the lead — 111
- Km in the lead — 623
- Points scored — 154

- Best classification in constructors' championship — *4th (1967 et 2006)*
- Best classification in drivers' championship — *4th (1967: John Surtees)*

POSITION IN CHAMPIONSHIP

1964	9th, 0 pt	2006	4th, 86 pts
1965	6th, 11 pts	2007	8th, 6 pts
1966	8th, 3 pts	2008	9th, 14 pts
1967	4th, 20 pts		
1968	6th, 14 pts		

2008 TEST DRIVERS

- Alex WURZ (A)
- Mike CONWAY (GB)
- Luca FILIPPI (I)
- Will STEVENS (GB)

SUCCESSION OF DRIVERS 2008

- Jenson BUTTON (GB) — *the 18 Grands Prix*
- Rubens BARRICHELLO (BR) — *the 18 Grands Prix*

What a disaster! This was the year Honda decided to show the world its "green" credentials, but surely it was not part of the plan to save the world's fuel by driving very slowly and doing fewer laps than the other cars? Everything, apart from the drivers, was wrong about the Japanese team this year, right down to its ridiculous lime-green trousers. When the RA108 was first rolled out of the gates, it was actually much worse than the 2007 car, but just before Melbourne, a last-minute aero update produced a dramatic improvement. However, it was not enough. Ross Brawn had been tempted out of post-Ferrari retirement to head up the technical side, but by the time he joined, he could only stick the metaphorical band-aid on the worst of the problems. And there was nothing he could do about the fact that the engine – something Honda usually prides itself on doing well – was possibly the worst on the grid and couldn't pull the skin off a rice pudding. Just about everything else that could be modified was, but the team couldn't escape the fact that the car was a dog and eventually, development tailed off as the focus shifted to the '09 car.

Super Aguri Honda

18 | Takuma SATO

DRIVER PROFILE

- Name — SATO
- Firstname — Takuma
- Nationality — Japanese
- Date of birth — January 28, 1977
- Place of birth — Tokyo (J)
- Lives in — Monaco (MC)
- Marital status — single
- Kids — -
- Hobbies — cyclism, walking, staying with friends
- Favorite music — pop, some japanese groups
- Favorite meal — japanese food
- Favorite drinks — fresh fruits juices
- Height — 164 cm
- Weight — 59 kg
- Web — www.takumasato.com

STATISTICS

- Grands Prix — 91
- Starts — 90
- Best result — 1 x 3rd
- Best qualif. — 1 x 2nd
- Fastest laps — 0
- Podiums — 1
- GP in the lead — 1
- Laps in the lead — 2
- Km in the lead — 10
- Points scored — 44

CAREER

2008	F1	*Super Aguri-Honda, 0 pt, 21st*
2007	F1	*Super Aguri-Honda, 4 pts, 17th*
2006	F1	*Super Aguri-Honda, 0 pt, 23rd*
2005	F1	*B·A·R-Honda, 1 pt, 23rd*
2004	F1	*B·A·R-Honda, 34 pts, 8th*
2003	F1	*B·A·R-Honda, 3 pts, 18th*
2002	F1	*Jordan-Honda, 2 pts, 15th*
2001		*F3 (GB) Champion; F3 International Invitation Challenge √ Winner; F3 Masters Zandvoort Winner; F3 GP Macau Winner; F3 Elf Masters, 3rd • F1 B·A·R tests driver*
2000		*F3 (GB) 3rd*
1999		*F. Opel Euroseries (GB) 6th • F3 (GB) 4th*
1998		*F. Vauxhall Jr.*
1997		*Karting (J) Champion • Driving school Honda*
1996		*Karting (J) Champion*

Aguri Suzuki

19 | Anthony DAVIDSON

DRIVER PROFILE

- Name — DAVIDSON
- Firstname — Anthony Denis
- Nationality — British
- Date of birth — April 18, 1979
- Place of birth — Hemel Hempstead (GB)
- Lives in — Northamptonshire (GB)
- Marital status — married to Carrie
- Kids — -
- Hobbies — informatic, photography, music
- Favorite music — Trance
- Favorite meal — thaï food
- Favorite drinks — no in particular
- Height — 165 cm
- Weight — 56 kg
- Web — www.anthonydavidson.com

STATISTICS

- Grands Prix — 24
- Starts — 24
- Best result — 3 x 11th
- Best qualif. — 2 x 11th
- Fastest laps — 0
- Podiums — 0
- GP in the lead — 0
- Laps in the lead — 0
- Km in the lead — 0
- Points scored — 0

CAREER

2008	F1	*Super Aguri-Honda, 0 pt, 22nd*
2007	F1	*Super Aguri-Honda, 0 pt, 23rd*
2006	F1	*Honda third driver*
2005	F1	*B·A·R-Honda, 0 pt, not classified*
2004	F1	*B·A·R third driver*
2003	F1	*B·A·R tests driver • 12H Sebring 2nd • 24H du Mans • "Petit Le Mans" 2nd*
2002	F1	*Minardi-Asiatech, 0 pt, not classified; B·A·R-Honda third driver*
2001	F1	*B·A·R-Honda tests driver • F3 (GB) 2nd; F3 European Cup Champion; GP Pau and Spa Elf Masters Winner*
2000		*F. Ford Zetec (GB) 2nd; F. Ford Festival World Cup Winner*
1999		*F. Ford Zetec (GB) Champion • Karting (EUR) FSA, 20th*
1998		*Karting (North America) WKA/FMK, 3rd*
1997		*Karting (Oceania) CIK*
1996		*Karting (EUR) CIK; Formule A, 2nd*
1995		*Karting (GB) JICA, RAC/MSA Jr., Champion*
1994		*Karting (GB) JICA, RAC/MSA Jr., Champion*
1992-93		*Karting (GB) Junior, Champion Open*
1987-91		*Karting (GB) Cadet, Multiple 60cc Winner*

Taku-san went from the back of the grid to eleventh place on the opening lap of the opening Grand Prix in Melbourne, but it didn't last. In Barcelona, at least he saw the chequered flag in the Spanish Grand Prix, but he was 13th and last. From there, he went home to Monaco. He was asked to dig out his race suit from the bottom of the laundry basket to test a Toro Rosso, prior to the end of the season and then again in the first post-season test, where he acquitted himself well. Toro Rosso is looking to replace Sebastian Vettel and the Japanese driver could be back on the grid next year. It might well depend on what financial package he brings with him, as much as his performance in testing.

It is hard to make a good impression if you don't have the right equipment and the diminutive Englishman has never really had a car to match his potential talent. How do you notice someone whose greatest achievement in the four races in which he competed this year, was to lap in a time similar to a Force India car? With a maximum of 26 cars allowed to enter a Grand Prix and currently only 20 of those places taken, there are always going to be literally hundreds of deserving drivers who never get a chance to reach the top formula. For Anthony Davidson, it will have been a case of so near and yet so far.

Daniel Audetto

Mark Preston

SUPER AGURI SA08A-HONDA
TAKUMA SATO
SPANISH GRAND PRIX

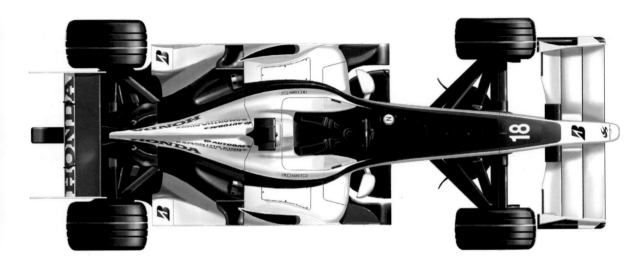

SPECIFICATIONS

- Chassis — *Super Aguri SA08A*
- Type — *Moulded carbon fibre and honeycomb composite structure*
- Suspensions (Front & Rear) — *Wishbones, pushrod operated torsion bars and dampers. Mechanical anti-roll bar*
- Dampers — *Showa*
- Transmission — *SAF1 sequential, longitudinally mounted, semi-automatic /seamless electro hydraulically controlled 7-speed + reverse*
- Clutch — *Sachs*
- Electronic systems — *Honda PGM-IG / Honda PGM-FI + McLaren Electronic Systems-Microsoft SECU*
- Spark plugs / battery — *NGK / 2.5Ah lead acid*
- Engine — *Honda RA808E V8 (90°) of 95 kg*
- Capacity — *2,400cc*
- Horsepower — *more than 700 bhp*
- Max rpm — *19,000 rpm*
- Number of valves — *4 valves per cylinder; pneumatic valve system*
- Fuel / lubricants — *ENEOS / ENEOS*
- Brakes (discs) — *Alcon ventilated carbon-fibre*
- Brakes (calipers) — *Hitco*
- Tyres — *Bridgestone Potenza*
- Wheels dimensions — *13"*
- Wheels — *BBS*
- Wheel base — *3,135 mm*
- Overall length — *4,685 mm*
- Overall width — *1,800 mm*
- Overall height — *950 mm*
- Front track — *1,450 mm*
- Rear track — *1,400 mm*
- Weight — *605 kg, driver + camera + ballast*

TEAM PROFILE

- Address — *Super Aguri F1 Limited Leafield Technical Centre Langley, Witney, Oxfordshire OX29 9EF Great Britain*
- Telephone — *+44 (0)1993 87 1600*
- Fax — *+44 (0)1993 87 1702*
- Web — *www.saf1.co.jp*
- Founded in — *2006*
- First Grand Prix — *Bahrain 2006*
- Official Name — *Super Aguri F1 Team*
- Team Principal — *Aguri Suzuki*
- Managing Director — *Daniel Audetto*
- Technical Director — *Mark Preston*
- Sporting Director — *Graham Taylor*
- Chief Designer — *Peter McCool*
- Head of Aerodynamics — *Ben Wood*
- Chief Race Engineer — *Gerry Hughes*
- Team Manager — *Michael Ainsley-Cowlishaw*
- Race Engineer (Sato) — *Richard Connell*
- Race Engineer (Davidson) — *Richard Lane*
- Chief Mechanic — *Phil Spencer*
- Communication & Medias Manager — *Emma Bearpark*
- Number of employees — *150*
- Partners — *Honda, Metris, Bridgestone, Rodac, Autobacs, Speakerbus, Seiko, Takata, Samantha Thavasa Japan Limited, Nippon Oil Corporation (ENEOS), Four Leaf, NGK, Pioneer, Kinotrope, Nexsan Technologies*

STATISTICS

- Grands Prix — 39
- Best result — 1 x 6th
- Best qualification — 1 x 10th
- Fastest laps — 0
- Podiums — 0
- One-two — 0
- GP in the lead — 0
- Laps in the lead — 0
- Km in the lead — 0
- Points scored — 4
- Best classification in constructors' championship — 9e (2007)
- Best classification in drivers' championship — 17e (2007: Takuma Sato)

POSITION IN CHAMPIONSHIP

2006 *11th, 0 pt*
2007 *9th, 4 pts*
2008 *11th, 0 pt*

2008 TEST DRIVER

- None

SUCCESSION OF DRIVERS 2008

- Takuma SATO (J) — *4 Grands Prix (AUS, MAL, BRN, E)*
- Anthony DAVIDSON (GB) — *4 Grands Prix (AUS, MAL, BRN, E)*

In 2007, they had often embarrassed their parent team, Honda, but this year, the giant Japanese car company pulled the plug on its financial support, based partially on a belief that customer teams would soon be banned and Super Aguri got no further than the paddock entrance in Istanbul, before being told to bring everything home to England. A great shame for a little team that displayed what Honda likes to call "fighting spirit." It was obvious during the winter that the end was in sight and this year's car was the same as last year's but for the modifications to the gearbox which now has to last for four races and some hastily improvised revisions to get the chassis through this year's much stricter crash test regulations. This in itself was a huge handicap, as the only way the team managed to get the cars to pass the higher impact tests was by making the whole thing much heavier. There was a last minute bid from a consortium to take over the operation, but it came to nothing. The team was the first victim of the economic meltdown, well before the words "credit crisis" were on everyone's lips. And so there were ten...

Force India Ferrari

20 | Adrian SUTIL

DRIVER PROFILE

- Name — *SUTIL*
- Firstname — *Adrian*
- Nationality — *German*
- Date of birth — *January 11, 1983*
- Place of birth — *Gräfelfing (D)*
- Lives in — *Munich (D)*
- Marital status — *single*
- Kids — *-*
- Hobbies — *piano, billiards*
- Favorite music — *rock, pop, Phil Collins*
- Favorite meal — *italian food*
- Favorite drinks — *Coca-Cola*
- Height — *183 cm*
- Weight — *75 kg*
- Web — *www.adriansutil.com*

STATISTICS

• Grands Prix	35	• Podiums	0
• Starts	35	• GP in the lead	0
• Best result	1 x 8th	• Laps in the lead	0
• Best qualif.	1 x 16th	• Km in the lead	0
• Fastest laps	0	• Points scored	1

CAREER

2008	F1	*Force India-Ferrari, 0 pt, 20th*
2007	F1	*Spyker-Ferrari, 1 pt, 19th*
2006	F3	*(J) Champion; GP Macau, 3rd • F1 Midland tests driver*
2005	F3	*Euroseries 2nd; Marlboro Masters Zandvoort, 2nd • A1GP 15th*
2004	F3	*Euroseries 17th*
2003		*F. ADAC BMW (D), 6th*
2002		*F. Ford 1800 (CH) Champion*
2001		*Karting (EUR)*
2000		*Karting (D) ICA, 3rd*

21 | Giancarlo FISICHELLA

DRIVER PROFILE

- Name — *FISICHELLA*
- Firstname — *Giancarlo*
- Nationality — *Italian*
- Date of birth — *January 14, 1973*
- Place of birth — *Roma (I)*
- Lives in — *Roma (I) and Monaco (MC)*
- Marital status — *married to Luna*
- Kids — *daughter (Carlotta) & son (Christopher)*
- Hobbies — *football, tennis, stream fishing, pool*
- Favorite music — *Elton John, Madonna, Robbie Williams*
- Favorite meal — *pasta "bucatini alla matriciana"*
- Favorite drinks — *Coca-Cola and orange juice*
- Height — *172 cm*
- Weight — *66 kg*
- Web — *www.giancarlofisichella.com*

STATISTICS

• Grands Prix	214	• Podiums	18
• Starts	212	• GP in the lead	14
• Wins	3	• Laps in the lead	210
• Pole positions	3	• Km in the lead	1093
• Fastest laps	2	• Points scored	267

CAREER

2008	F1	*Force India-Ferrari, 0 pt, 19th*
2007	F1	*Renault, 21 pts, 8th*
2006	F1	*Renault, 72 pts, 4th*
2005	F1	*Renault, 58 pts, 5th*
2004	F1	*Sauber-Petronas, 22 pts, 11th*
2003	F1	*Jordan-Ford, 12 pts, 12th*
2002	F1	*Jordan-Honda, 7 pts, 11th*
2001	F1	*Benetton-Renault, 8 pts, 11th*
2000	F1	*Benetton-Supertec, 18 pts, 6th*
1999	F1	*Benetton-Supertec, 13 pts, 9th*
1998	F1	*Benetton-Mecachrome, 16 pts, 9th*
1997	F1	*Jordan-Peugeot, 20 pts, 8th*
1996	F1	*Minardi-Ford, 0 pts, 19th • ITC 6th • F1 Ferrari tests*
1995		*DTM 15th • ITC 10th • F1 Minardi tests*
1994	F3	*(I) Champion; GP Macau Winner*
1993	F3	*(I) 2nd • Karting (EUR) 3rd*
1992	F3	*(I) 8th*
1991		*Karting (EUR) 2nd • F. Alfa Boxer*
1990		*Karting (World) 2nd*
1989		*Karting (EUR) 2nd; (World) 4th*
1984-88		*Karting (I) Minikart 60cc > Juniors 100cc > KIC 100cc*

Anonymous would be the best word to sum up the lanky German's season. While his best mate in the paddock, Lewis Hamilton pursued his march to glory, Adrian Sutil must have wondered why he was on the grid at all. The best thing one can say about him is that, after completing two full seasons with the Silverstone-based squad, he is learning his trade away from the media spotlight. The only way most people in the paddock knew who he was, was by seeing him chatting to Hamilton during the pre-race Drivers' Parade. He did show signs of progress and in the second half of the year he was pretty much on the same pace as his team-mate. The bitter-sweet highlight of his season came in Monaco, where circumstances in the rain and a good strategy, saw him heading for a fourth place finish, until Kimi Räikkönen drove into him. Tears and more tears...

Giancarlo Fisichella looks like being yet another driver who showed great promise in the early stages of his career — indeed there was talk of him becoming the first Italian driver to be employed by Ferrari for a decade or more — but in the end, he has one win to his name and has been gradually sliding further down the grid, with every passing season. It's a great shame, as he is undoubtedly talented, but this year, you would be hard pressed to see a smile on his face. In 2007, he failed to score a single point, he never made it into Q3 and his best result was tenth place in Barcelona.

Dr. Vijay Mallya

Michiel Mol

Colin Kolles

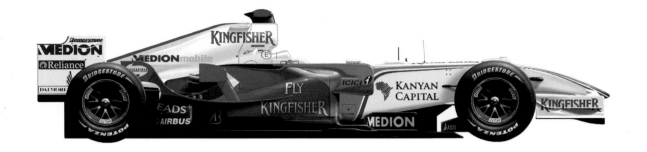

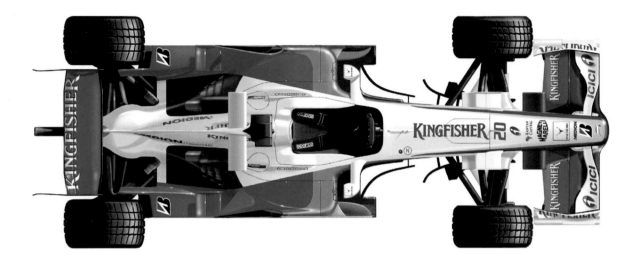

FORCE INDIA VJM01-FERRARI
ADRIAN SUTIL
MONACO GRAND PRIX

SPECIFICATIONS

- Chassis — Force India VJM01
- Type — Carbon-fibre monocoque and honeycomb composite structure
- Suspensions (Front & Rear) — Aluminium alloy uprights, upper and lower carbon wishbones and pushrods, torsion bar springs and anti-roll bars
- Dampers — not revealed
- Transmission — 7-speed + reverse longitudinal gearbox with electrohydraulic sequential gear change
- Clutch — AP Racing
- Electronic systems — McLaren Electronic Systems-Microsoft SECU
- Spark plugs / battery — NGK / not revelated
- Engine — Ferrari Type 056 V8 (90°) of 95 kg
- Capacity — 2,398cc
- Horsepower — more than 700 bhp
- Max rpm — 19,000 rpm
- Number of valves — 32 valves pneumatic distribution
- Fuel / lubricants — Elf / Liqui Moly
- Brakes (discs) — not revelated
- Brakes (calipers) — not revelated
- Tyres — Bridgestone Potenza
- Wheels dimensions — 13"
- Wheels — BBS
- Wheel base — +3,000 mm
- Overall length — 5,000 mm
- Overall width — 1,800 mm
- Overall height — 950 mm
- Front track — 1,480 mm
- Rear track — 1,418 mm
- Weight — 605 kg, driver + camera + ballast

TEAM PROFILE

- Address — Force India Formula One Limited, Dadford Road, Silverstone, Northamptonshire, NN12 8TJ Great Britain
- Telephone — +44 (0)1327 850 800
- Fax — +44 (0)1327 850 866
- Web — www.forceindiaf1.com
- Founded in — 2008
- First Grand Prix — Australia 2008
- Official Name — Force India F1 Team
- Chairman & Managing director — Dr. Vijay Mallya
- Co-Owner — Michiel Mol
- Team Principal — Colin Kolles
- Director of Business Affairs — Ian Philips
- Team Manager — Andy Stevenson
- Chief Technical Officer — Mike Gascoyne
- Technical Director — James Key
- Design Director — Mark Smith
- Projects Leaders — Akio Haga, Ian Hall
- Head of R&D. — Dr. Simon Gardner
- Head of Production — Simon Shinkins
- Head of Aerodynamics — Simon Phillips
- Chief Race and Test Engineer — Dominic Harlow
- Race Engineer (Sutil) — Jody Egginton
- Race Engineer (Fisichella) — Bradley Joyce
- Chief Mechanic — Andy Deeming
- Press Officer — Lucy Nell
- Number of employees — 240
- Partners — Ferrari, Bridgestone, Magneti Marelli
- Sponsors — Medion, UPSDirect, Alpinestars, The Dalmore, AVG Anti-Virus, Rotozip, Kingfisher, Royal Challenge, Bridgestone, Kemppi, Foster Denovo, Samsung, STL, Airbus, Reliance, ICICI Bank, Magneti Marelli

STATISTICS

- Grands Prix disputés — 18
- Best result — 1 x 10th
- Best qualification — 1 x 12th
- Fastest laps — 0
- Podiums — 0
- Doublés — 0
- GP in the lead — 0
- Laps in the lead — 0
- Km in the lead — 0
- Points scored — 0
- Best classification in constructors' championship — 10th (2008)
- Best classification in drivers' championship — 19th (2008: Giancarlo Fisichella)

POSITION IN CHAMPIONSHIP

2008 10th, 0 pt

2008 TEST DRIVER

- Vitantonio LIUZZI (I)

SUCCESSION OF DRIVERS 2008

- Adrian SUTIL (D) — the 18 Grands Prix
- Giancarlo FISICHELLA (I) — the 18 Grands Prix

Bernie Ecclestone and Max Mosley were obviously unhappy about the disappearance of Super Aguri after the first four races of the year. The grid was getting perilously close to fielding the 16 car minimum required to stage a Grand Prix. However, Force India was also dismayed, as the demise of the Anglo-Japanese squad meant that they now had the "honour" of pre-assigned seats on the back of the grid. The arrival of Vijay Mallya and his billions did inject some much needed cash into the project, but it arrived too late to prevent the team running what was effectively a modified version of the previous year's Spyker car, itself based on the even older Midland. Scratch the chassis hard enough and you would probably even find some Jordan DNA lurking under a coat of yellow paint! Mike Gascoyne came on board to oversee the technical side, although Red Bull refugee and former Jordan man, Mark Smith was there as design director. The car could not complain about engine power as Maranello's Prancing Horses were in charge of that end of things. However, by the end of the year, Ferrari were wished a fond farewell, as were Gascoyne and team manager Colin Kolles, as part of a radical shake-up that sees Mallya's money put to good use for 2009, with the purchase of Mercedes engines and a complete McLaren back-end for the cars.

McLaren Mercedes

22 | Lewis HAMILTON

DRIVER PROFILE

- Name — HAMILTON
- Firstname — Lewis Carl
- Nationality — British
- Date of birth — January 7, 1985
- Place of birth — Stevenage (GB)
- Lives in — Geneva (CH)
- Marital status — single
- Kids — -
- Hobbies — playing guitar, remote-controlled machines
- Favorite music — R&B, Reggae, Hip-Hop
- Favorite meal — italian and chinese food
- Favorite drinks — orange juice
- Height — 174 cm
- Weight — 68 kg
- Web — www.lewishamilton.com

STATISTICS

Grands Prix	35	Podiums	22
Starts	35	GP in the lead	23
Wins	9	Laps in the lead	615
Pole positions	13	Km in the lead	2870
Fastest laps	3	Points scored	207

CAREER

2008	F1 McLaren-Mercedes, 98 pts, **World Champion**
2007	F1 McLaren-Mercedes, 109 pts, 2nd
2006	GP2 Series Champion
2005	F3 Euroseries Champion; F3 Masters Winner Zandvoort Pau & Monaco GP
2004	F3 Euroseries 5th; F3 Bahrain Superprix Winner
2003	F. Renault (GB) Champion
2002	F. Renault (GB) 3rd; F. Renault EuroCup, 5th
2001	F. Renault Winter Series (GB), 5th
2000	Karting (EUR) Champion Formule A; World Cup, Champion; Elf Masters Bercy Winner
1999	Karting (I) Champion Intercontinental A; (EUR) Junior ICA, 2nd
1998	Karting (EUR) Junior ICA
1997	Karting (GB) Junior Yamaha, Champion Super One
1996	Karting (GB) Cadet, Champion Sky TV Kart Masters & Champion 5 Nations
1995	Karting (GB) Cadet, Champion Super One & Champion STP

23 | Heikki KOVALAINEN

DRIVER PROFILE

- Name — KOVALAINEN
- Firstname — Heikki
- Nationality — Finnish
- Date of birth — October 19, 1981
- Place of birth — Suomussalmi (FIN)
- Lives in — Oxford (GB)
- Marital status — single
- Kids — -
- Hobbies — skiing, cyclism, golf, viedo games
- Favorite music — Nightwish, rock
- Favorite meal — tomato pasta
- Favorite drinks — mineral water
- Height — 172 cm
- Weight — 66 kg
- Web — www.heikkikovalainen.net

STATISTICS

Grands Prix	35	Podiums	4
Starts	35	GP in the lead	10
Wins	1	Laps in the lead	40
Pole positions	1	Km in the lead	197
Fastest laps	2	Points scored	83

CAREER

2008	F1 McLaren-Mercedes, 53 pts, 7th
2007	F1 Renault, 30 pts, 7th
2006	F1 Renault, third driver
2005	GP2 Series 2nd • F1 Renault tests
2004	World Series by Nissan Champion • F1 Renault tests • "Race of Champions" Winner
2003	World Series by Nissan 2nd • F1 Renault & Minardi tests
2002	F3 (GB) 3rd; GP Macau, 2nd; F3 Masters, 4th
2001	F. Renault (GB) 4th; F3 GP Macau, 8th
2000	Karting (FIN) FA, 2nd; (Scandinavia), FA Champion; (World) Formula Super A, 3rd; Elf Masters Bercy Winner
1999	Karting (FIN) FA, 2nd; (World) FA, 17th
1991-98	Karting

In 2007, he snatched defeat from the jaws of victory, throwing the title away in the last round. This year nearly produced a repeat of that scenario, but in the final few hundred metres at Interlagos, Lewis Hamilton scrabbled past Timo Glock to finish the Brazilian race in fifth place, enough to become the youngest ever F1 world champion. There is no doubt that he is a worthy champion, despite taking only five wins to Felipe Massa's sixth. The youngster matured this season, helped by the lack of politics now that Fernando Alonso had ended his unhappy association with the team. The Englishman's helmet livery reflects his admiration for the late Ayrton Senna and some of his drives in the rain, Silverstone where he won by a minute, Monaco and Spa, had something of the great Brazilian about them. But his was not a perfect season, with that stupid pit lane crash in Montreal, a fluffed start in Bahrain, where he forgot to select launch mode on the grid, a series of errors in France and an over-anxious opening few moments in Japan. At times like these, he reminded us he was only in his second season as a grand prix driver. In 2009, he will no doubt be brimming with self confidence, so maybe he can set aside some time to work on his image in the paddock, where he is not exactly a popular figure, thanks to a somewhat arrogant attitude: but then, isn't that part of the make-up of all great champions?

There's a tendency to think that all Finnish racing drivers are the same in terms of their character. Ron Dennis can tell you different: he has experienced the placid and completely malleable Mika Hakkinen, the taciturn and difficult Kimi Räikkönen and now he has worked with the first Finn who seemed to be content with Number 2 status. Heikki Kovalainen sensibly realised that he was not going to challenge Hamilton's status as the team darling and never made any waves. He also had to deal with the fact that the "pointy" MP4-23 was far more suited to the Englishman's "karting" driving style than his own early corner turn-in technique. He did try and adapt his style and although this helped him look after the tyres more, it also lost him some speed. His one win, in Budapest, owed much to the fact that Massa and Hamilton had problems while running ahead of him, but he should have won in Turkey, but for a puncture after tangling with fellow countryman, Räikkönen. Maybe now that they have delivered Hamilton a world championship title, the team will be able run a more egalitarian set up next season, thus allowing Kovalainen a fairer crack of the whip.

Ron Dennis

Martin Whitmarsh

McLAREN MP4-23-MERCEDES
LEWIS HAMILTON
CHINESE GRAND PRIX

SPECIFICATIONS

- **Chassis** — McLaren MP4-23
- **Type** — McLaren moulded carbon fibre/aluminium honeycomb composite
- **Suspensions (Front & Rear)** — Inboard torsion bar/damper system operated by pushrod and bell crank with a double wishbone arrangement
- **Dampers** — Koni
- **Transmission** — McLaren Isequential, longitudinally mounted, semi-automatic "seamless" electro hydraulically controlled 7-speed + reverse
- **Clutch** — Hand-operated
- **Electronic systems** — McLaren Electronic Systems-Microsoft SECU
- **Spark plugs / battery** — NGK / GS Yuasa Corporation
- **Engine** — Mercedes-Benz FO 108V V8 (90°) of 95 kg
- **Capacity** — 2,400cc
- **Horsepower** — 740 bhp
- **Max rpm** — 19,000 rpm
- **Number of valves** — 32 valves pneumatic distribution
- **Fuel / lubricants** — Mobil Unleaded / Mobil 1 products
- **Brakes (discs)** — Hitco ventilated carbon-fibre
- **Brakes (calipers)** — Akebono
- **Tyres** — Bridgestone Potenza
- **Wheels dimensions** — 13"
- **Wheels** — Enkei ES-071
- **Wheel base** — not revealed
- **Overall length** — not revealed
- **Overall width** — not revealed
- **Overall height** — not revealed
- **Front track** — not revealed
- **Rear track** — not revealed
- **Weight** — 605 kg, driver + camera + ballast

TEAM PROFILE

- **Address** — McLaren Technology Centre Chertsey Road, Woking, Surrey GU21 5JY Great Britain
- **Telephone** — +44 (0) 1483 711 117
- **Fax** — +44 (0) 1483 711 119
- **Web** — www.mclaren.com
- **Founded in** — 1963
- **First Grand Prix** — Monaco 1966
- **Official Name** — Vodafone McLaren Mercedes
- **Team Principal, Chairman et CEO, McLaren Group** Ron Dennis (GB)
- **CEO F1, Chief Operating Officer, McLaren Group** Martin Whitmarsh (GB)
- **Managing Director, McLaren Racing** Jonathan Neale
- **Vice President, Mercedes-Benz Motorsport** Norbert Haug
- **Managing Director, Mercedes-Benz** Ola Källenius
- **Engineering Director** Paddy Lowe
- **Design and Development Director** Neil Oatley
- **Sporting Director** Dave Ryan
- **Head of Aerodynamics** Simon Lacey
- **Chief Engineer MP4-23** Tim Goss
- **Chief Engineer MP4-24** Pat Fry
- **Head of Vehicle Engineering** Mark Williams
- **Operations Director** Simon Roberts
- **Chief Mechanic** Steve Giles
- **Race Engineer (Hamilton)** Phil Prew
- **Race Engineer (Kovalainen)** Mark Slade
- **Press Officer** Steve Cooper
- **Number of employees** — 540
- **Title Partners** Mercedes-Benz, Vodafone • **(Technology)** Exxon Mobil Corporation, Mobil 1, Bridgestone, SAP • **(Corporate)** Johnnie Walker, Aigo, Hugo Boss, Santander, Hilton International, Schüco, TAG Heuer • **(Associate)** Steinmetz Diamond Group • **(Official Suppliers)** FedEx, Olympus, Kenwood, Sonax, GS Yuasa, Enkei, Akebono, Kangaroo TV, Yamazaki Mazak, Belte, Sports Marketing Surveys, Sparco, SGI, Koni, Charmilles, Nescafe

STATISTICS

• Grands Prix	648	• Constructors' World titles	8
• Wins	162	(1974, 1984, 1985, 1988, 1989,	
• Pole positions	141	1990, 1991 et 1998)	
• Fastest laps	137	• Drivers' World titles	12
• Podiums	431	(1974: Emerson Fittipaldi,	
• One-two	44	1976: James Hunt,	
• GP in the lead	282	1984: Niki Lauda,	
• Laps in the lead	9542	1985, 86 & 89: Alain Prost,	
• Km in the lead	44938	1988, 90 & 91: Ayrton Senna,	
• Points scored	3299,5	1998 et 99: Mika Häkkinen,	
	(3310,5)	2008: Lewis Hamilton)	

POSITION IN CHAMPIONSHIP

1966	9th, 2 +1 pts	1977	3rd, 60 pts	1988	1st, 199 pts	1999	2nd, 124 pts
1967	10th, 3 pts	1978	8th, 15 pts	1989	1st, 141 pts	2000	2nd, 152 pts
1968	2nd, 49 +3pts	1979	7th, 15 pts	1990	1st, 121 pts	2001	2nd, 102 pts
1969	4th, 38 (40)pts	1980	7th, 11 pts	1991	1st, 139 pts	2002	3rd, 65 pts
1970	4th, 35 pts	1981	6th, 28 pts	1992	2nd, 99 pts	2003	3rd, 142 pts
1971	6th, 10 pts	1982	2nd, 69 pts	1993	2nd, 84 pts	2004	5th, 69 pts
1972	3rd, 47 (49)pts	1983	5th, 34 pts	1994	4th, 42 pts	2005	2nd, 182 pts
1973	3rd, 58 pts	1984	1st, 143,5 pts	1995	4th, 30 pts	2006	3rd, 110 pts
1974	1st, 73 (75) pts	1985	1st, 90 pts	1996	4th, 49 pts	2007	Excluded (203 pts)
1975	3rd, 53 pts	1986	2nd, 96 pts	1997	4th, 63 pts	2008	2nd, 151 pts
1976	2nd, 74 (75) pts	1987	2nd, 76 pts	1998	1st, 156 pts		

2008 TEST DRIVERS

- Pedro DE LA ROSA (E)
- Gary PAFFETT (GB)

SUCCESSION OF DRIVERS 2008

- Lewis HAMILTON (GB)   the 18 Grands Prix
- Heikki KOVALAINEN (FIN)   the 18 Grands Prix

One has to ask oneself if Ron Dennis is allergic to Kryptonite, because comparisons between the McLaren team boss and Superman are entirely plausible given events of the past year. McLaren had been hit with the biggest fine in the history of sport, paying the FIA one hundred million dollars for the spying scandal. Then the team's engineers had to make a hasty revision to the design of the MP4-23 to remove anything that might conceivably be regarded as derived from a Ferrari. Further personal woes followed for the team boss, with the death of his brother and a split from his wife. Despite these obstacles, the team took its first world championship for nine years – Ferrari won almost everything in the last decade – courtesy of Lewis Hamilton's nail biting last gasp fifth place finish in Brazil. Hamilton might be a child prodigy, but he would not have succeeded without the right equipment. McLaren gave him a chassis built to suit his driving style, which means a preference for oversteer, a la Schumacher. That sort of set up makes the front tyres work hard and this meant the McLaren had the edge over its rivals in qualifying as it worked better in terms of getting tyres up to temperature. The car was a development of the '07 machine, following the trend of increasing its wheelbase and it was generally more user-friendly than its closest rival from Maranello. Matched with the Mercedes V8, possibly the most powerful engine on the grid and combined with an untypical focus on just one of its drivers, McLaren finally got its hands on another World Championship trophy. Could it be the last one before Ron Dennis hands over the reins of the company to his number two, Martin Whitmarsh?

PORTFOLIOS

A great photo can sometimes leave one speechless. Only those who have tried to photograph Formula 1 cars in action know that the technique is so difficult, it becomes an art form. The large format double page spreads of the "Formula 1 Yearbook" mean they can be appreciated even more.

PAINTING

It is very difficult to convey an impression of speed, with a static medium. But sometimes, talent and nerve, combined with a whiff of luck can bring movement to life in a photo. Here is Sebastien Bourdais' Toro Rosso at the British Grand Prix.

THE BLINK OF AN EYE

Those who have seen Kimi Raikkonen smile, are part of an exclusive club. It is even rarer for the event to be immortalised in a photo. Third in the championship, the Finn was not really on the case in 2008…

BYE-BYE DAVID

He represented the age of the gentleman, always smiling, always available. But all good things must come to an end and David Coulthard decided to hang up his helmet and make way for the younger generation. Not many drivers can boast such a great career.

SPOTLIGHTS

Apart from the purely sporting contest between the McLaren and Ferrari teams, the 2008 season also featured plenty of behind the scenes action. The global economic crisis hit F1 at the end of the summer. Beaten to it by the FIA, the teams began to work together to look at reducing costs. For his part, Bernie Ecclestone kicked two Grands Prix into touch. These were some of the themes that cropped up this season. The cancellation of the Canadian Grand Prix, following on the heels of the disappearance of the United States event, seemed like an opportune moment to investigate the difficult marriage between F1 and the world's number one economic power.

Indian billionaire, Vijay Mallya, wants to turn his country on to Formula 1

Vijay Mallya is impossible to miss in the paddock, with his imposing figure, rings on each finger, earrings and a group of lackeys in permanent attendance. An easy man to spot.

Unlike the super-rich who find happiness in anonymity, Mallya isn't afraid to broadcast his success. According to American magazine Forbes, he is the 664th richest man in the world, worth around 1.5 billion dollars, most of it built around his star brand, Kingfisher beer, but now also including an airline company. He rules over an empire of 60,000 employees.

Mallya will only fly on his private Airbus A319 and as a self proclaimed epicurean, he brought his own yacht to Turkey and Monaco for those Grands Prix. One of the five biggest private yachts in the world, the Indian Empress has innumerable lounges, smoking rooms, libraries and fitness areas. In Monaco and Istanbul, Mallya organised "decadent soirees" for a few hundred guests; an orgy of excess accompanied by Indian techno music, with belly dancers and snake charmers as a sideshow.

He loves motor sport and has occasionally been known to have a go at karting. This led him to putting up Kingfisher as a sponsor of the Benetton team in 1994, just so that he could get paddock passes. In 2002, he switched allegiance to Toyota. But after the fun came the return on his investment. Mallya is a shrewd businessman and he proved it. Over the winter of 2007-2008, he bought the Spyker team (formerly Jordan, then Midland) and renamed it "Force India." This was the first step of a plan worked out to the smallest detail, aimed at making Formula 1 one of the major sports in his homeland.

At the moment, Formula 1 does not feature on the Indian sports fans' radar. Last year, a measly 3.5 million watched it on TV over the course of the season, which is less than the average audience for a single Grand Prix in a typical European country. Up until this point, it had only been available on pay-TV channels, but now it can be seen on free to view channels, which should see an explosion in the number of viewers.

India is of course an impressive target. With over a billion inhabitants, with almost half under the age of 25, the potential seems limitless. And Vijay Mallya is counting on being the first man to exploit it, using his degree in economics to manipulate his compatriots. "*Our population is young and will benefit from the current economic boom,*" he explains. "*These people will earn more and will want to spend their money. Of course, F1 has its glamour and sparkle, but who doesn't like that?*"

Mallya knows that sport is one of the best ways to get through to the Indian populace, who for the moment are fanatical only in their following of cricket, which is almost a national religion. Things could soon change. "*Cricket is known to everyone, whereas F1 appeals to the youngsters who aspire to a different more modern lifestyle and who want to follow a unique and high end sport,*" he continues.

In order to get his public on board, Mallya knows that Force India cannot remain indefinitely at the back of the grid.

Over the winter, he invested in technology: the team now has two wind tunnels that operate around the clock, whereas last year, they didn't even have one. The next part of the plan is to set up a school that could bring an Indian driver through to Formula 1, before building a circuit on the outskirts of New Delhi, to host a Grand Prix, as from 2011.

A team, drivers, a circuit: India is building its place in the F1 sun. But there is still a long way to go, even in terms of building up a simple fan base. In Bombay, advertising hoardings give them a chance to find out about "their" team. "Feel the force of a billion hearts" is their clarion call.

And it seems to be working. "Club Force," on the team's internet site, has already attracted over 10,000 members, in just a few weeks. However, there is a need to tread carefully. Three years ago, the Indian Tata group had financed Narain Karthikeyan's 2005 season with Jordan. It was a failure that never attracted the slightest interest from the Indian public, who are only interested in winners.

Therefore, for exactly the same reasons, Vijay Mallya could lose his own business bet, or run into severe difficulties trying to find the young Indian hopeful, which would be the key to attracting interest at home.

For the time being, his competitors seem to think he is taking the right decisions. "*The Indian market is exploding,*" confirmed Toyota managing director, John Howett. "*We might soon see other teams coming from there...F1 will have to reposition itself to take into account this emerging market.*"

In his own unique way, Vijay Mallya is bringing a new beat to Formula 1, which has so far marched to the drum of the European car constructors. His Indian style, a mix of fun and business, could end up bringing millions of his compatriots to the world of F1. As the sport's money man, Bernie Ecclestone suggests, the wind of change in F1 is blowing the sport towards the East, rather than the West.

Fillies, food and fun: Red Bull spares no expense to entertain the paddock

The atmosphere is similar to that in a trendy restaurant or bar, except that there's no need to pay the bill when you leave. Everyday at lunchtime, hundreds of people squeeze into the huge hospitality unit, to feast on a succession of taster plates, concocted by some of the best chefs in the world, brought along by the team to show off their skills.

All the Formula 1 teams now have hospitality units that have nothing in common with the good old motorhome of yesteryear.

The biggest of all is the Red Bull "Energy Station," a real monster, measuring 33 metres by 14. It takes 25 trucks to transport it from one race to another. Built up on three floors, it boasts several offices, four bars, three terraces, a table-football game and it can hold up to 800 people.

The Energy Station is not Red Bull's only extravagance. At each Grand Prix, ten girls from the host country are chosen as "Formula Unas," who get paddock passes to allow them to parade their boredom and pout for the cameras, with one of them selected to take part in a final event at the last race of the season. Further entertainment comes courtesy of the "Red Bulletin," a 24 page, large format, full colour magazine, produced overnight on a printing press brought to each race by truck, which is then distributed free of charge, in the paddock every morning.

Of course, Red Bull also publishes a small guide to local nightlife, highlighting the best restaurants, bars and clubs in the vicinity of the circuit. On top of that, the company also throws several monstrous parties, inviting the entire paddock to a night of excess, attended by thousands who can dance the night away, into the early hours. In Shanghai, in 2005, the drinks manufacturer spent three million dollars on building a bamboo village, for a massive end of season party, with the entire structure pulled down once the event was over.

For whatever bountiful reason, the budget for all this beggars belief, even if the Red Bull bosses see it as part of a well planned commercial strategy.

"I have always loved Formula 1," explains Dietrich Mateschitz, the owner of the Austrian firm. *"Our drink promotes itself as healthy for both mind and body and we support all sorts of activities which highlight individualism, risk taking and a love for life. For us, F1 is a perfect fit with these principals. Unlike other teams, we do not make cars. We don't have a market share to work on or prestige to uphold. We are in F1 for the love of sport and for the pure challenge it represents."*

Reckoning that the paddock was a dull place, the Austrian took ten years to bring his plans to brighten it up to fruition, from the Energy Station to the Formula Unas, aside from supporting young drivers. These include Sebastian Vettel and Sebastien Buemi, who owe their seats in Formula 1 and GP2 to the efforts and expenditure of Red Bull, who also support another twenty or so young and talented drivers.

In true billionaire style, Mateschitz refuses to say how much all this costs. *"At Red Bull, we don't like to talk about money,"* he says. What we do know is that the brand spends 30% of its profits on promotion, around 600 million Euros per year, given that the total business figure is in excess of two billion.

With the arrival of Red Bull, life in the paddock has changed. Everyone can now get something to eat, without having to go begging at one of the other teams, while reading the Red Bulletin has become a morning ritual to go with the cappuccino in the Energy Station.

These little treats for the privileged few are no doubt very costly, for almost no return on the investment. Dietrich Mateschitz doesn't mind and that makes it all the more admirable.

> Max Mosley did not attend many races this season. He made a lightning visit: in Monaco and then again at the Italian Grand Prix.

Max Mosley, the immoveable president and his vision of the future

The whole saga began on Friday 28 March, when Max Mosley had a rendezvous with five prostitutes for a sadomasochistic session, which would have stayed private if the English tabloid, the "News of the World" had not published photos of it, insisting they had Nazi connotations.

These revelations about the oh so respectable FIA president were a bombshell. The following week, several car constructors, including Mercedes and BMW, outraged by the Nazi connotations, as well as the two Japanese giants, Honda and Toyota, along with several motor clubs, including the powerful German ADAC, the American AAA and even the Israeli automobile club, asked for his resignation. Max Mosley has presided over the FIA since 1993. In fifteen years, he has accumulated many enemies. His frequent changes of direction are not much appreciated and he has specifically upset several major constructors, by criticising their management. So far, he had fought them off and managed to push aside all his opponents. Speaking of one of his most vociferous critics, Sir Jackie Stewart, Max Mosley said he was a "certified cretin." As for Ron Dennis, who led a plan to attract the major constructors out of F1, he fined his team 100 million dollars for lying and espionage and this year, relegated them to the cheap end of the paddock next to the toilets.

To date, his enemies had never come off best in any confrontation with Mosley. Seen as a dignified and

respected gentleman, the Englishman lost most of his credibility because of this affair. Afterwards, no politician wanted to be seen in his company. Nevertheless, Mosley managed to get the FIA to give him a vote of confidence at a meeting in early June and thus he avoided having to resign.

Some candidates for the post of president had thought their time had come: Hermann Tomcyk, from the powerful German automobile club, ADAC, Jean Todt the former team principal at Ferrari, who since the start of the year had not denied interest in a job at the FIA, Marco Picchinini, former sporting director at Ferrari and deputy president at the FIA since 1998 and even Ari Vatanen, former world rally champion, now a conservative Finnish member of the Brussels parliament, with an interest in transport matters. These were four serious candidates.

The role of president of the FIA is vital to the survival of motor sport. It is the president who sets the political agenda, who must ensure the sport's future and set its targets.

Max Mosley excelled in this role as a visionary planner. He was one of the first to realise that the 21st century would see an awareness of the finite nature of natural resources and possibly to a ban on watching fast cars racing one another for fun. It would be an age of responsibility, both in terms of safety and the environment.

In 2008, how could one justify F1 cars using 75 litres

of fuel per hundred kilometres, when the cost of a barrel had reached the 150 dollar mark? Why continue an activity that can affect global warming? Some politicians were already of the opinion that such "useless" activities should be banned as soon as possible.

Having seen this coming a long time again, Mosley launched F1 down the "green route." As from 2009, cars would be fitted with an energy recovery system powered by the brakes.

In 2011, engines would have to use a completely different, yet to be defined, technology, which aimed to reduce fuel consumption. Indeed, since 1997, Max Mosley had rendered the F1 championship "carbon neutral" by planting trees in Mexico. These decisions seemed well thought out and aimed at saving motor sport from the threat of a political ban.

So, who could save Formula 1? None of the four potential candidates has the charisma, experience, vision and, above all the intelligence of Max Mosley. It would not be easy to find a replacement.

Max Mosley wants a single engine as a safety net for Formula 1.

Like Robinson Crusoe, Formula 1 lived alone on its island. In 1987 and again a decade later, at the time of the Asian economic crisis, and after 11 September 2001, the economic situation and movement on the stock markets had never affected, not even slowed the increase in F1 budgets.

But now, things were likely to be different. For several months, Max Mosley, the FIA president, was getting F1 ready to face an ecological turning point. At a time when the planet is heating up and the world realises its reserves of petrol are not inexhaustible, Formula 1 could be seen as a useless anachronism, a vestige of an age of consumerism and abundance.

Seeing the danger to motor sport, Mosley decided to put Formula 1 at the forefront of research into hybrid cars, while at the same time, drastically reducing its costs. Since the start of the year, the Englishman had asked the teams to come up with proposals that went in this direction. Given the urgency of the situation and seeing the teams prevaricate, he decided to skip waiting for their opinion and to set out his plans: In Shanghai, the FIA therefore put out to tender the supply of a standard engine and transmission system for the 2010 to 2012 seasons. He had just lobbed a huge rock in the tranquil waters of the little lake which sits in the Shanghai paddock.

Within the teams, no one had expected such a swift reaction from the FIA, especially as the team bosses were due to meet the following week in Geneva, specifically to discuss cost cutting measures.

Reducing costs is Mosley's main concern. "*In the current economic client, as budgets are getting smaller, it is essential to reduce costs in F1,*" he explained. "*For me, it seems quite straightforward. In short, working on elements of F1 that are known - the gearbox and engine - represents a complete waste of time and money. Whatever is spent on these elements is pretty much wasted. For example, developing an engine that revs to 22,000 rpm has no relevance to normal life. It's the same for the gearboxes. Every road car has one, but the teams continue to spend 10 to 15 million Euros per year on its transmission systems. It's madness. Theoretically, engine development is frozen this year, but we know the teams continue to spend between 100 and 150 million each on engines. I've been fighting to reduce costs for ten years now, which is lucky, otherwise it would be a disaster. But now, small measures are not enough. Today, even the teams realise it is a matter of urgency. Because with this crisis, the major constructors in F1 could well take the decision to pull out. And if the FIA says to them: "wait, you can't go, you've signed a contract," these guys will tell us to talk to their lawyers.*"

"Now, the little measures are not enough. Even the teams realise the urgency of the situation."

That is where the danger lies for many of the key players in F1. At the end of 2008, there were 20 cars entered. If one or two of the major manufacturers pulled out, this number would drop to 18 or 16 and the series would lose credibility. To avoid this risk, Mosley wants it to be possible for teams to compete in F1 with budgets one tenth of the current 400 million Euros which the big teams currently spend. "*I can only see one solution and that's a common engine,*" he insisted. "*There is no reason to continue the way we are now. Currently, the whole paddock runs on about a billion Euros each year for engines alone. You could do the same thing for less than 5% of that amount, with a common engine.*"

However, when this proposal was put forward in China, it did not meet with approval from the big constructors. "*Of course, some of them will complain,*" continued Mosley. "*They will want their own engine. But in the real world, the constructors already share technology. I think the gearbox on a Mini is built by Ford. And if VW can buy cheaper engines from Peugeot, they do so and put their badge on it, it's as simple as that.*"

Max Mosley wants to redirect spending to more useful areas. "*Instead of the gearbox and engine, that are commodities, let's spend the research budgets on more useful things. That's why, from 2009, we are launching a system like KERS (Kinetic Energy Recovery System, that recovers energy used in braking, as can already be found on some road-going cars) before moving on to energy recovery from exhaust gases or cooling systems. This is the sort of technology that everyday cars need. The first KERS will provide around 80 horsepower, while weighing under 30 kilos. If one could put such a powerful system in a car, it would be fantastic. After 2011, we'll let the teams increase the power from KERS and recover power form the exhaust system. I am sure the results will be extraordinary.*"

With much cheaper race cars, Mosley thinks Formula 1 could survive economically. In promoting KERS, he believes F1 could even be useful and justify its survival in a world where waste won't be allowed.

In its day, Formula 1 has brought many innovations to road cars, in terms of brakes, chassis strength, materials and even in more efficient engine combustion chambers.

Much of these innovations have never been heard of by the general public. Those days are now over: by concentrating spending on KERS, on-track research will have a direct benefit to road cars and no one will have to ask what use is Formula 1.

< Toyota was one of the teams against the single engine, a Max Mosley project that the teams had every intention of fighting. During the winter of 2008-2009, the teams were due to come up with other means of drastically reducing costs per team. In 2008, many of them employed almost a thousand staff, compared to a decade ago, when the BAR team was set up, with 350 employees. Everyone in the paddock agrees this increase is insane!

Bernie Ecclestone would have preferred to keep the Canadian Grand Prix

At the circuits, he's known simply as "Bernie," or "Mr. E" or sometimes "The Bolt." He reigns supreme over Formula 1, as his company controls the commercial rights of the sport until 2110!

In 2007, Charles Bernard Ecclestone, in an interview published in the "The Formula 1 Yearbook" gave the facilities at the Gilles Villeneuve circuit on the Ile Notre Dame a real tongue lashing, describing them as obsolete. *"Montreal sets a bad example,"* he suggested, with a touch of malice that the Canadian Grand Prix organisers had not come across before.
The Englishman added that the circuit still had potential, that there was enough room on the island "to do something good," but that the city needed to do something about it really quickly. May 2008. A year has passed, which is the equivalent of an eternity in the fast moving world of Formula 1.
Over the past twelve months, the political and economic situation in the sport had changed dramatically.
In this month of May, it was not too clear who would be running the sport: FIA president, Max Mosley, explained that he'd been fighting for months with the F1 commercial rights holder, which meant Bernie, to keep control of the sport in the future. Ecclestone denied this.
The political situation was confused and so was the long term financial future of F1.
In the space of two years, two teams had pulled out (Prodrive, which should have made its debut this season) and Super Aguri. And Toro Rosso was apparently up for sale, but had yet to attract any potential buyer.
In short, morale was not high. As far as the circuits were concerned, Indianapolis had disappeared from the 2008 calendar, having failed to reach a financial agreement with Bernie, who agreed to talk to "The Formula 1 Yearbook" over the Monaco weekend, in his own personal motorhome.
A few small steps to climb, a passageway to negotiate and here you are in Bernie's office, with, as a backdrop, a giant TV screen tuned in to the financial channel, CNBC. Bernie is smiling, as always and in fine form at the age of 77.

- Last year, you criticised the facilities at the Ile Notre Dame. They've been slightly improved, but they cannot match the luxury level of circuits like Shanghai, Valencia or Singapore.
Bernie Ecclestone: But why not? Honestly, I don't see why Montreal couldn't match those venues. I don't understand why our friends over there can't put in a bit of effort. After all, a Grand Prix is shown the world over. The city gets huge publicity value out of Formula 1 and Montreal doesn't make the most of it. While the Grand Prix is on, the circuit symbolises the city for hundreds of millions of TV viewers all over the world.

- Does the disappearance of the United States Grand Prix guarantee the future of a race in Canada?
Bernie Ecclestone: It's true that, for the moment, we don't have a Grand Prix in the United States, but I said, for the moment. But that's got nothing to do with Canada. F1 likes Canada, we've been going to Montreal for a long time and we will go to Canada for as long as we can.

- The American market is very important for the car companies in Formula 1. Is that not enough to ensure there is at least one event in North America?
Bernie Ecclestone: My motto is "Go East" rather than "Go West" and events have proved me right so far. But I'm also working to get a United States Grand Prix back on the calendar, but I don't consider it essential!

- Sometimes, it's difficult to know just how far your power extends in F1. For example, Max Mosley says he's fighting you to keep you from getting total control over the championship. We thought you were best of friends?
Bernie Ecclestone: Oh, that's got nothing to do with friendship (at this point, Mr. E's mobile phone rings, playing the theme tune to the film, "The Good, The Bad And The Ugly." He answers and then continues.) Max and I are still good friends and we are not in conflict.

- Really? But Max Mosley says he is fighting to keep the "classic" Grands Prix on the calendar, like Monaco, France and England, which you

might cancel in favour of more lucrative destinations, such as New Delhi or Moscow...
Bernie Ecclestone: Now, let's be clear on this point: when the European Union's competition commission gave the green light for the acquisition of the F1 commercial rights (rights acquired by Bernie's company up to 2099 Ed.) it separated the powers in strict fashion: the FIA is in charge of the regulations and ensuring that these are respected and we control the rest, the commercial side, the circuit contracts, the television rights and other matters. Therefore, deciding whether or not we have a Monaco Grand Prix is entirely my responsibility. The FIA has nothing to do with it.

- Let's talk a bit about the future of F1. It seems the championship is under threat from several directions, most notably with the loss of some teams. We only have 20 cars on track and two of those seem under threat. What can you do?
Bernie Ecclestone: Honestly, I don't think Formula 1 is under the slightest threat. We have a bigger TV audience than ever. More and more people want to organise a race in their country, so I can't see a single cloud in the sky above F1.

- That's your commercial view of things. The increase in TV viewers is down to countries like India and China. But don't you think that motor sport in general and F1 in particular, risks facing some serious problems, if only for ecological reasons? How can one justify race cars that pollute the environment and waste petrol these days?
Bernie Ecclestone: What threat are you talking about? Who could intervene and ban motor sport?

- Maybe some political power? If natural resources are running out, couldn't some governments ban circuit racing?
Bernie Ecclestone: Honestly, I don't think they'd take that sort of decision. I don't think they want to do that. Anyway, politicians certainly use more fuel going to their offices in Brussels every morning than we use in Formula 1! If they tried something like that, we would fight it with everything we've got. No, really, I don't think F1 is currently under a threat of any kind...

Everyone in the paddock regrets the disappearance of Montreal

For the drivers who travel the globe from Melbourne to Sao Paulo, via Monza and Bahrain, the Grands Prix tend to resemble one another. A unique track in Monaco, the heat and humidity in Malaysia, terminal tedium in Magny-Cours and rain in Spa-Francorchamps: that's about the limit of what they remember from the 18 rounds of the world championship. However, the Canadian Grand Prix stands out because of the unique ambience in Montreal. Neither the track layout on the Ile Notre Dame - straights joined together by slow corners - nor its surface, which breaks up nor even its paddock, floating on a rowing basin, will be missed by the drivers. However, Montreal and its city centre on the other hand, well that's a different matter.

At the Mount Fuji circuit, engineers, mechanics and drivers were all united in lamenting the disappearance of a Grand Prix that they all loved. "*It's bad*," said Toro Rosso driver, Sebastien Bourdais. "*It was a really nice event for everyone. You left the circuit, went for a walk downtown, it was cool.*" "*Where will I buy cheap jeans now?*" asked a Renault mechanic. The drivers felt the same. "*I love Montreal*," commented Jenson Button. "*It's a fantastic city and it's one of the best Grands Prix for nightlife. It's a shame to see it go, but let's say I'll miss the town more than the track itself and what about those steaks. The steaks are excellent!*"

Even the drivers who'd only been to Montreal once, were sad to see it go.

"*The races there have always been very exciting*," reckoned Kazuki Nakajima. "*I'm happy we get a four week break in the summer on the other hand* (this break came about because of the cancellation of Canada Ed.) *but let's say, losing Canada is not the best way to go about it.*"

For Robert Kubica, the Canadian Grand Prix naturally enough holds plenty of special memories: his terrible accident in 2007, when his BMW Sauber smashed full pelt into the concrete barriers and, this year, his first F1 win.

"*I definitely wouldn't have scrubbed this Grand Prix*," commented the Pole. "*I would love to race there again, as I won this year and we were already very quick there last year. I've just heard the news and I'm upset. We will see.*" What with the nostalgia for favourite restaurants, the shopping and the race itself, everyone at Mount Fuji had their reasons for regretting the demise of the Canadian Grand Prix and all had the same final word. "*Let's hope Bernie Ecclestone changes his mind!*"

The teams try to save the race

For the teams, the canning of Canada robbed them of an important shop window in the North American market.

"*I don't know what happened with Montreal*," declared BMW Sauber boss, Mario Theissen. "*We will have to look at the situation, because a constructor like BMW needs the North American market.*" Rumour had it that FOTA wanted to apply pressure to have the Canadian and United States events reinstated on the calendar. "*Today, Formula 1 is a global sport*," explained Honda's Nick Fry. "*It is a world championship. Recently, we have seen new events in Asia and the Middle East. Of course that's a good thing, but we cannot forget North America. Not going there is a serious mistake and a problem which we absolutely must resolve. I don't think we can save the 2009 event, it's too late. But we must find a global solution for 2010. Montreal's case was easier when there was also Indianapolis, because that way, we split the travel costs between two events. Transporting 24 tonnes of equipment and a hundred people per team across the Atlantic is a big expense for just one Grand Prix.*"

< At 77 years of age, Bernie Ecclestone keeps an eye on everything that happens in the paddock. He alone decides who gets to stage a Grand Prix.
In 2009, Canada and France disappear from the calendar, basically for financial reasons.

The new Grand Prix deal

Up to a few years back, Bernie Ecclestone was the only shareholder in Formula 1, through a complex constellation of companies, Formula One Management (FOM,) Allsport Management SA (ASM,) grouped under SLEC Holdings (Slavica Ecclestone Holdings,) which in turn was part of Bambino Holdings. Bernie was the sole master on board the good ship F1. But since 2003, the shares of these companies had all been acquired by the investment company, "CVC Capital Partners" whose sole aim was to increase its investment before selling it on.

Thus Ecclestone's new shareholders were pushing to increase FOM profits as quickly as possible, which could only be done by increasing the number of Grand Prix, therefore increasing revenues from the television rights and the circuit fees.

From a figure of 16 Grands Prix, over the seasons, the calendar has expanded to 17 and then 18 (this year) before moving on initially to 19 for 2009, and 20 in 2010 (see list of new projects below.)

That at least was the plan which was in place in July 2008. But that was when the world financial crisis kicked in, nibbling away at the mood of optimism. In October, the Canadian and French Grands Prix were scrubbed from the provisional calendar. Once the shock had subsided, there was a brief period of trying to save these two races, but they were finally buried for good.

One of the problems is that the cost of buying a place on the calendar, the money the organisers must hand over to FOM to get the F1 circus to turn up, keeps going up and up, so that the price now asked by Bernie Ecclestone, changes the rules of engagement completely.

Singapore has paid FOM 30 million Euros, as did Valencia, while Abu Dhabi is stumping up 40 million for 2009.

Such sums are no longer viable for private companies. Because the only method they have of getting a return on their investment is from the ticket sales at the gate. All other sources of revenue (circuit signage, television rights, merchandise, hospitality suites) slip through their fingers and go to FOM. Ticket sales do not bring in tens of millions, so the only way of writing off the costs is to look at the Grand Prix as a whole, taking into account the revenue from taxes on business, especially hotels and restaurants.

This economic model can only operate if it involves the local authorities, if they put some money up front. This does not work when local or national government does not want to get involved.

This has cost F1 the races in the United States, Canada and France. Bernie Ecclestone does not care. For him and for CVC, profit is all that matters and only countries in the Middle East and Asia or an ambitious city like Valencia can offer him that.

Heading east

The new order in Formula 1 has led to several changes to the traditional Grand Prix calendar. Here's a recap of events that have gone and the circuits hoping to join the party:

- The last five Grands Prix to disappear from the calendar (and the date they were last held):
  - French Grand Prix, 2008
  - Canadian Grand Prix, 2008
  - United States Grand Prix, Indianapolis, 2007
  - San Marino Grand Prix, Imola, 2006
  - Austrian Grand Prix, Zeltweg, 2003

- The five most recent additions to the Grand Prix calendar (and the date they were first held):
  - Bahrain Grand Prix, Sakhir, 2004
  - Chinese Grand Prix, Shanghai, 2004
  - Turkish Grand Prix, Istanbul, 2005
  - European Grand Prix, Valencia, 2008
  - Singapore Grand Prix, 2008

- The four currently planned future Grands Prix (and the year they should appear on the calendar)
  - United Arab Emirates, 2009
  - Korean Grand Prix, Seoul, 2010
  - Indian Grand Prix, New Delhi, 2011
  - Russian Grand Prix, Moscow, 2012

> Watkins Glen, 06/10/68: American Mario Andretti in a Lotus 49-Cosworth thrills the home fans by taking pole position on debut. He sets off ahead of Graham Hill's Lotus 49, which is obscuring Bruce McLaren's McLaren-Ford. In the centre are Jackie Stewart's no.15 Matra-Ford and Chris Amon in the no.8 Ferrari 312B, ahead of Dan Gurney's McLaren (no.14) and Jochen Rindt's Brabham (no.4). Those were the days of strutted wings, cutlawed by the CSI from Monaco 1969.

> Watkins Glen, 04/10/70: chasing Stewart, Clay Regazzoni's Ferrari 312B, third behind team leader Jacky Ickx for some time, had to make two stops, one because of a loose wheel, the other to change the transistor box, which ended any hopes of being classified. With Stewart out and Ickx dropping back, Emerson Fittipaldi scooped the pool for Lotus.

His friend and former BRM rival Graham Hill had joined Team Lotus at the start of the season. The Lotus 49 was on pole position for its very first Grand Prix at Zandvoort, with Clark's car taking the race win. The Scot went on to take another, at Silverstone this time. The Brabham-Repcos of Brabham himself and Hulme won at Monaco, in France, in Germany and in Canada and were in the points often enough to make them favourites to retain the title the Australian driver/constructor had already won in 1966. There were some less-fancied but high-class runners to spice up the 1967 field, such as Dan Gurney's V12 Eagle-Weslake and another V12 in the Honda RA301. Both cars claimed a single victory at Spa and Monza respectively.

A string of problems saw Clark finish third in a Monza race he should have won, while Hill had to retire, so our British friends came to the next round at Watkins Glen thirsting for revenge. Hill was once again on pole as the two monopolised the front row, but they had two serious rivals to contend with in Chris Amon's Ferrari and Gurney's Eagle-Weslake. The Californian driver - whom Clark called his greatest F1 rival - even thrilled the American crowds by insinuating his beautifu Eagle between the two Lotuses for a few laps. It didn't last, Tall Dan having to retire on lap 25 with broken rear suspension. The two Lotuses, Hill leading, ran away with it until Hill slowed with a worn clutch. Clark took over the lead and held on to it despite pressure from Amon, who had slipped into second place. The Ferrari's engine couldn't take the strain, Surtees' Honda and the two BRM H16's retired, and the two Lotuses scored a magnificent 1-2, albeit with Clark's about to lose a rear wheel with a broken universal joint and Hill's engine and gearbox on their last leg. We should add that Hill's lap record of 1:06, an average of 201. 899 km/h, meant the 200 km/h barrier had finally been broken.

The next few years marked the pinnacle of the 3-litre normally-aspirated Formula 1. The Ford-Cosworth DFV was no longer the exclusive plaything of Team Lotus, with McLaren using it from 1968, as did Ken Tyrrell, who entered two Matras, one earmarked for Scotsman Jackie

Stewart, the coming man who had just left BRM. Honda were still there in the shape of Surtees, as of course were Ferrari, who had just signed the brilliant young French Grand Prix winner Jacky Ickx. Missing, sadly never to return, was the great Jim Clark, killed in an F2 race at Hockenheim on April 7. On the 1st of January Clark had done the grand slam - pole, fastest lap and race win - in the South African Grand Prix, leading teammate Graham Hill home by 25.3 seconds.

From Stewart to Rindt

Despite Clark's loss, Lotus were still the ones to beat. His worthy successor Graham Hill took the 49 to victory in Spain and Monaco and led the title race. As for the rest, Bruce McLaren claimed the first win for his own cars at Spa while new McLaren recruit Denny Hulme took the Italian Grand Prix at Monza and the Canadian at Mont-Tremblant. With Stewart driving to an outstanding win on a rain-soaked Nürburgring

and Switzerland's Jo Siffert triumphing in a Rob Walker Lotus 49 in the British GP at Brands Hatch - the last Grand Prix win for a privateer entry, incidentally - and with a solitary success for the V12-engined Ferrari, clearly the Ford-Cosworth was the dominant force in F1. It would be for some time to come. At Watkins Glen this time around Stewart brought the Matra MS10 home in front of Graham Hill's Lotus. The title was decided in Mexico, and it went to Hill. For the first time the Watkins Glen winner took the average race speed past the 200 km/h to 200.988 over the 108 laps, the fastest in 1:05.22 or 204.213. The crowds at the Glen were lucky, too, in that they saw the drivers go by so many times - and carefully-chosen spectator areas meant they had a great view. That would change come 1971 when the circuit, too short now for 440-plus horsepower F1 cars, added a new section that took the overall length to 5.4347 kilometres. The race distance, still 399 km in 1970, was also shortened to 320 km or just 59 laps. In 1970 just 24 cars took the start, of the 27 that took part in practice.

The Ford DFV reigned supreme through to 1974, with Ken Tyrrell's team the dominant force as Stewart took the World Championship for the first time in 1969 in the Matra MS80. It was a year when the Lotus 49's trod water, sometimes losing out to the McLarens and Brabhams as well, also Cosworth-powered. Hill did win Monaco but at Watkins Glen it was Jochen Rindt's turn to come out on top, the Austrian taking his maiden Grand Prix victory in some style, leading Stewart from the start. A small mistake let the Scotsman through, but the persistent Rindt managed to get back in front and after that gripping duel the Lotus gradually left the Matra behind.
Watkins Glen saw the Austrian earn the right to be seen as a title candidate, but sadly he would never be seen at the track again. On September 6th 1970 he was killed in practice for the Italian GP while leading the Championship handsomely in the new Lotus-Ford Type 72. He became the sport's first and only posthumous World Champion.

A trackful of surprises

Thrown off balance by the tragedy, Team Lotus skipped the Canadian GP on October 20 at Mont-Tremblant, reappearing at Watkins Glen with two Lotus 72's, one in the hands of young Swede Reine

Wisell, the other entrusted to an equally youthful Brazilian newcomer from F3, Emerson Fittipaldi. Just as Rindt had done a year earlier, Fittipaldi would produce a dashing win. The script was a little different, though: carrying a heavy responsibility on those young shoulders, the Brazilian debutant was third-fastest in practice behind Ickx (Ferrari) and Stewart (Tyrrell-Ford), and was overtaken by other more experienced drivers in the early stages of the race. Up front there was a ding-dong battle between Stewart's Tyrrell, Pedro Rodriguez in the BRM and the Regazzoni-Ickx Ferraris. At half-distance the front three of Stewart, Ickx and Rodriguez were the only drivers on the same lap. Fittipaldi was driving an immaculate race, lapping consistently and taking advantage of retirements and pit stops to be running fourth behind the three big names, and just in front of teammate Wisell. Then Ickx had to come in to have a fuel leak repaired (he restarted and finished fourth with a gritty

> Long Beach, 28/03/76: a relaxed Clay Regazzoni and a focussed Niki Lauda in the spring California sunshine. That weekend the much-missed Swiss did the hat-trick: pole, race win and fastest race lap in his Ferrari, while the Austrian World Champion, his team leader, was 42 seconds behind him in second place.

comeback drive that earned him a new lap record of 1:02.74 at an average of 212.389 km/h). Stewart, who was running away with it, then had to pull out with an oil leak, which put Rodriguez in the lead from Fittipaldi and Wisell. The race took another dramatic turn on lap 100 when the Mexican had to make a fuel stop, leaving Fittipaldi the leader in only his fourth Grand Prix, which he went on to win from Rodriguez. Wisell, meanwhile, made the podium in his first-ever Grand Prix. Watkins Glen really did throw up some surprise results.

That much was underlined the following year. After starting the season with March chassis while he waited for his own cars to come on-stream, Ken Tyrrell lost the title to Lotus. But in 1971 the Tyrrell-Fords left everyone fighting over the crumbs. The British team's number one driver Jackie Stewart had a new teammate, a lively young Frenchman who was already a race-winner in F3 and F2, by the name of François Cevert. Cevert, brother-in-law of Jean-Pierre Beltoise, was as gifted as he was charming - he was a fine pianist, for one thing - but 1970 had been a rather thankless first year in F1, yielding just a single point despite his obvious talent. But in 1971, under Stewart's benevolent wing, the Frenchman came into his own - as did the Tyrrells. After a hiccup in South Africa, where Stewart was beaten by Andretti's ferrari and Cevert had an off, the rest of the season went much better for Stewart, first and foremost, and for the Tyrrell twosome in general. Stewart won in Monaco, and the French GP at Le Castellet brought the first Stewart-Cevert 1-2 finish. There was another at the Nürburgring in Germany, where the young Frenchman shadowed his team leader, set fastest lap and held off the Ferraris of Regazzoni and Andretti. Third in Monza, sixth in Canada (another Stewart win), Cevert was still waiting for a first win of his own. Watkins Glen would be the place.

Triumph and tragedy
On that third day of October there were 28 F1 cars on the starting-grid. Fifth-fastest in practice, Cevert started from the second row (the grid alternated 3-2-3-2) and was up to third behind Stewart and Hulme by the end of the opening lap. He got past the New Zealander on lap 7, and the

> Las Vegas, 17/10/81: that year's World Champ on Nelson Piquet (Brabham-BMW) was fifth in the season's final Grand Prix, dominated by Alan Jones (Williams-Ford), 20 seconds ahead of Alain Prost (Renault turbo) - as quick in the car park as they were on the cash machines!

<
Detroit, 21/06/87:
France's World Champion
Alain Prost (McLaren-TAG
Porsche) would finish
third in a race dominated
by two Brazilian World
Champions in Honda-
powered cars, Ayrton
Senna (Lotus) and Nelson
Piquet (Williams). So that
made three World
Champions on the
podium!

two Tyrrells were in front. On lap 14 the Frenchman went past his team leader, whose car was struggling for grip, allowing Ickx's Ferrari through into second. A new challenge for Cevert! Stewart was then passed by Siffert as the BRM driver went in pursuit of the Belgian ace. Ickx responded with fastest lap and a new circuit record average of 189.081 km/h. He dropped out on lap 49 with engine failure, but Siffert was still

the danger man for Cevert, who controlled proceedings until the end despite several patches of oil around the track. It was the first French Grand Prix victory since Maurice Trintignant's in a Cooper at Monaco in 1958. Sadly, though, Cevert's maiden win would also be his last. After a lack-lustre 1972, where the only Tyrrell-Ford 1-2 was actually at Watkins Glen, François Cevert deemed destined for great things. In 1973 he had

Stewart's measure, though he always obeyed team orders, and the Tyrrell boys claimed several more 1-2 finishes. On the eve of the United States Grand Prix Stewart, a third world title in his pocket, was ready to announce his retirement. Cevert seemed uneasy: there was talk of another driver coming to Tyrrell in 1974 and François felt his seat was in danger. Was that what led him to overdrive either the car or himself? Trying for the perfect qualifying lap, he went off in the Esses beyond the grandstands; the car was pitched into the 'safety' barriers, and its unfortunate driver was killed on the spot. Tyrrell withdrew from the race as a mark of respect. Jean-Pierre Beltoise, who was then with BRM, found it in him to take part as Ronnie Peterson's Lotus won the Grand Prix.

Watkins Glen's fate hung in the balance, it seemed. On October 6 1974 Australian driver Helmut Koinigg lost control of his Surtees on lap 10 of the race, only his second, at the same spot where Cevert had gone off the previous year. His car speared into the barriers and Koinigg, too, lost his life. The circuit was modified the following year, a chicane cutting the speeds through those notorious Esses. In 1974 Brabhams driven by the two Carloses, Argentine Reutemann and Brazilian Pace, took a 1-2 result, while Niki Lauda was the 1975 winner for Ferrari. Watkins Glen hosted the United States GP through to 1980. The 1979 race went to another French-speaking prodigy in a Ferrari, Quebec's Gilles Villeneuve, who had already taken a convincing win elsewhere in America that year, at Long Beach. Since 1976, in fact, Watkins Glen had become the US GP East. A second, the US GP West, had been created to try and attract the Americans on the other side of the country. Racing through the Long Beach streets on the Pacific coast, the F1 cars passed the once-proud Queen Mary, the liner that was now a floating museum. The 3.25-km track run by Chris Pook would stage eight Grands Prix, the first

<
Detroit, 22/06/86: another high-class podium with winner Ayrton Senna (Lotus-Renault), second-placed man Jacques Laffite (Ligier-Renault) and Alain Prost (McLaren-TAG Porsche). This was Laffite's last visit to the podium: three weeks later, at Brands Hatch, he was injured in a start-line accident at the British GP which brought a halt to his F1 career.

> Phoenix, 11./03/90: surprise package Jean Alesi in the Tyrrell upsets the applecart by holding his own against Ayrton Senna's McLaren-Honda. The Frenchman would have to give best to the Brazilian, but only by 8.6 seconds. Sadly Alesi's F1 career never quite lived up to that early promise.

yielding a 1-2 Ferrari finish for Regazzoni and Lauda. But as Bernie Ecclestone's financial demands grew, Pook finally threw in the towel and Long Beach switched to the CART Championship, formerly known as Indycars, later to become Champcars.

Slippery slope
From then on, it's tempting to wonder if it would not have been best to alternate a Grand Prix East and a Grand Prix West, a duality that was already spreading Americans' debatable interest too thin. Through the 80s and 90s, once Watkins Glen had come and gone (or at least closed its doors to F1 - it was still used for sports prototype and historic racing), a number of artificial circuits came into being in various places, in the hope of bringing F1 to Americans as they didn't seem to be coming to F1. That being the case, there was some sense in choosing Detroit, home of the 'Big 3', from 1982 onward. Sadly, the 4.012-km Motor City circuit had just too many nasty surprises: cracks between the concrete slabs, kerbs and manholes made Monaco look like child's play and were both a danger to the drivers and punishing on the cars. Just as disappointingly, the American crowds were no larger at these pseudo-Grands Prix than they had ever been at Watkins Glen or Long Beach. Nonetheless, and for all the failings of track and surface, the top names prospered there

as they did elsewhere. We were treated to some famous clashes on the Detroit streets. In the era that pitted 1500cc turbos against 3-litre naturally-aspirated cars, Renault and Prost were quickest in practice and race but lost to John Watson's McLaren, Eddie Cheever's Ligier-Matra (much to the delight of the Yankee crowd) and Didier Pironi's Ferrari. The following year, with the 'Grand' Prix reduced to a 'little' 241 km, it was Michele Alboreto who won in a Tyrrell-Ford from the Williams-Ford of Keke Rosberg (father of Nico and 1982 World Champion) and Watson's McLaren-Ford, a top three which proved there was life in the old Ford-Cosworth yet. The Italian driver liked the USA: his first F1 win had come the previous year in the Las Vegas parking lot. From 1984 on, the turbos got the upper hand on the atmospheric cars, as that year's Detroit podium showed: it was a Brabham-BMW sandwich with Nelson Piquet, father of today's driver of that name, first and Teo Fabi third and de Angelis' Lotus-Renault as the filling. Rosberg's Williams-Honda beat the Ferraris of Johansson and Alboreto in 1985, while Senna brooked no argument in 1986 (Lotus-Renault), 1987 (Lotus-Honda) and 1988 (McLaren-Honda).
Taking their questionable cue from Detroit, the Texans wanted a Grand Prix of their own. After all, didn't the centre of the oil industry have as much right to one as Motor City? The Dallas track and lay-out were even worse than Detroit's. In

1984, what passed for a Grand Prix was won by Rosberg in a Williams-Honda from Arnoux (Ferrari) and de Angelis (Lotus-Renault). The spectators were not impressed, though they should have been by the skill of any driver who managed to make it to the end without inflicting damage on his car.

As for Las Vegas, Nevada, they seemed to have got themselves mixed up between car parks and circuits, casinos and Grands Prix. Small wonder when you remember that the race's main sponsor was none other than Caesar's Palace itself. The drivers were as unimpressed as the spectators at two races won there by Jones for Williams in 1981 and Alboreto for Tyrrell in 1982.

Respite and renewal
All these muddleheaded efforts at building circuits in a concrete jungle of sky-scrapers and blind 90-degree corners only accelerated the decline of F1 in the land of Uncle Sam. So it was that in 1989, fans on the west coast were offered a new street circuit at Phoenix, Arizona. The 3.78-km track was as mediocre as its predecessors, though it did have one interesting feature, a hair-pin with a heavy braking area on entry. It was here, in 1990, that French youngster Jean Alesi in his humble Tyrrell bravely led for the first half of the race from His Majesty Ayrton Senna's McLaren-Honda. The

<
Indianapolis, 19/06/05: all-American scenes as the girls eye up a Ferrari on the grid - i.e. one-sixth of the entire field for a race that did F1 enormous harm in the American public's eyes.

Brazilian quickly restored order - though not before the fiery Frenchman had passed him again in that infamous chicane - and went on to win the race by the modest margin of 8.685 seconds from the Tyrrell. It was a rare moment of on-track drama at that circuit, where Senna again came out on top in 1991.

In the end, Phoenix was nothing more than a brief pause in a long process of decline. But after a break of several years, there was good news, it seemed: the return of an F1 race in the United States in 2000, this time using part of the Indianapolis Speedway, running the other way round and embellished, if that was the right word, by a new infield section. Alas, there's many a slip... The story is too fresh in our minds to need recalling in detail. Suffice it to say that after

a hesitant start, and a 2001 race more memorable for the national state of mourning in the aftermath of the World Trade Center attacks than for what happened on track, Indycar spectators seemed at last to be getting the taste for Formula 1. Sadly the business of the tyres and other goings-on at the 2005 event put paid to this brief renaissance. Michelin, you will remember, withdrew from that race, with devastating consequences. It was run with just six cars and drivers, the Bridgestone-shod teams to be precise, which meant seven teams were missing. Ferrari scored a simple 1-2, and the FIA ratified all points scored despite the obviously unrepresentative nature of the Grand Prix. Old suspicions were bound to be revived among the locals, and American consumerism ("I want my money's worth") did the rest. They whistled, they

booed, they threw drink cans from the grandstands, targeting the teams as well as the FIA, and later they demanded a refund or free tickets for the following year. All of that was happenstance; but add in ever-increasing financial demands from Bernie Ecclestone and his partners, which are killing off F1 races one by one (Canada, France... who's next?) to make way for new, artificial but allegedly profitable venues like Valencia and Singapore, and it's hardly surprising that the American race should have disappeared once more. And this time, as other dangers threaten the very survival of motor sport, it could have gone for good.

The author wishes to thank Pierre Ménard for his invaluable help.

<
Indianapolis, 17/06/07: the view from the back of the grid just before the start of the last US GP, won by a masterful Lewis Hamilton (McLaren-Mercedes) from teammate Fernando Alonso. Note the crowd packed into the grandstands on the outside - and the flagrant lack of spectators on the inside terracing.

ATMOSPHERE

A Formula 1 season is so colourful, it is hard to sum up in words. What's needed is a series of photos, in no particular order, to evoke the emotion of the 18 races of the 2008 championship.

What would we do without them?

Formula 1 is a macho world, populated almost exclusively by men. The female touch is rare, but it's hard to imagine F1 surviving without the fairer sex. The danger of course, is that one might fall head over heels in love with one of these beautiful angels, only for them to vanish.
Such sweet pain…

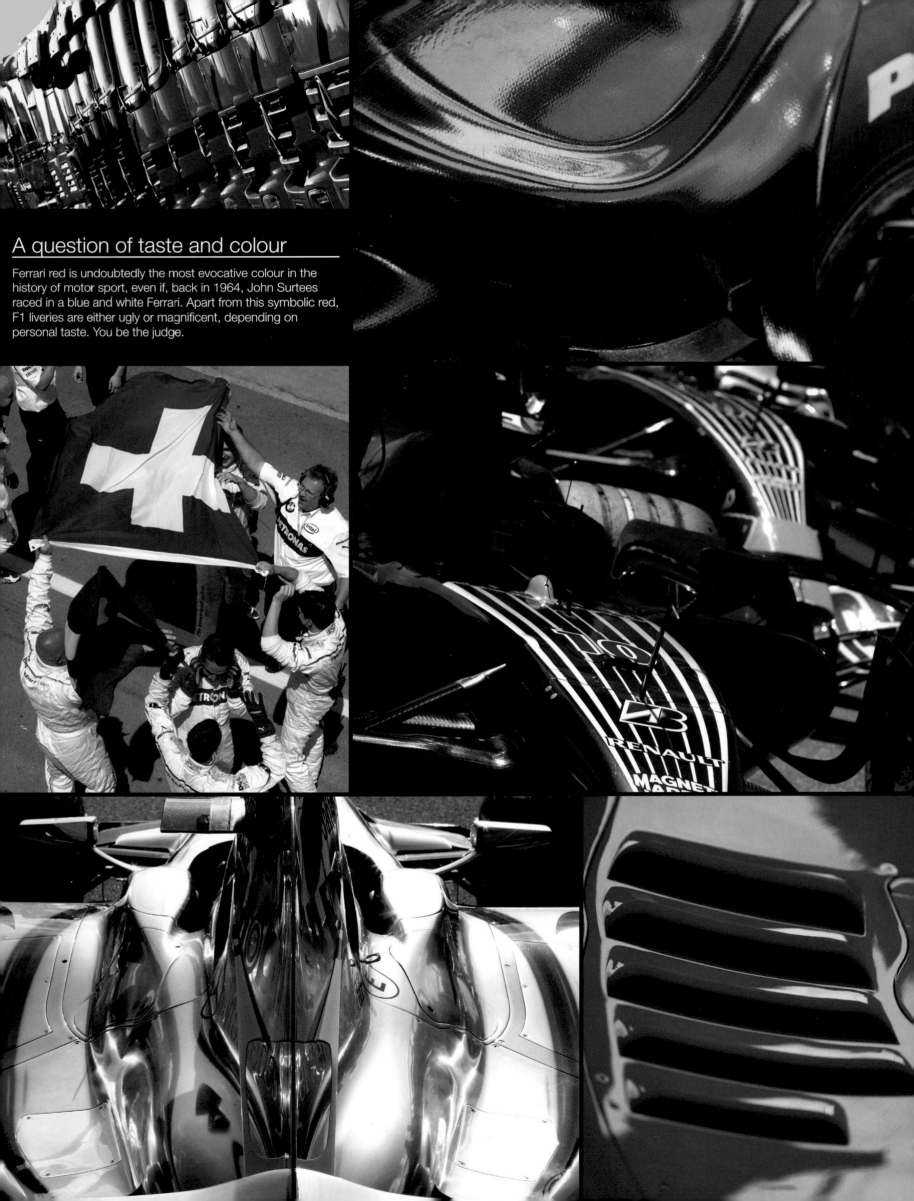

A question of taste and colour

Ferrari red is undoubtedly the most evocative colour in the history of motor sport, even if, back in 1964, John Surtees raced in a blue and white Ferrari. Apart from this symbolic red, F1 liveries are either ugly or magnificent, depending on personal taste. You be the judge.

In action

A Formula 1 season is an explosion of noise, movement and colour. The 2008 season comprised 17 fantastic weekends, each one different, each one new and unique. Much as one can wax lyrical over the effort that goes into this complex world, it's only a bit of fun, as beautiful as it's pointless.

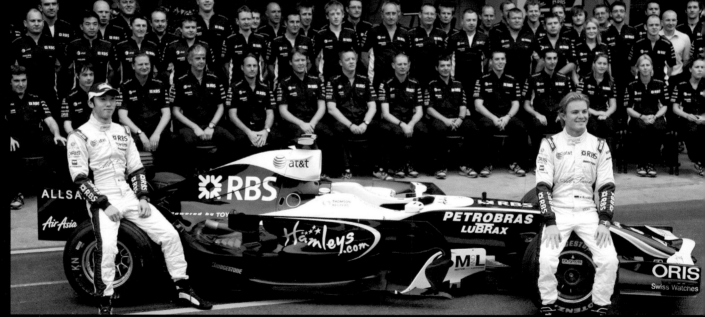

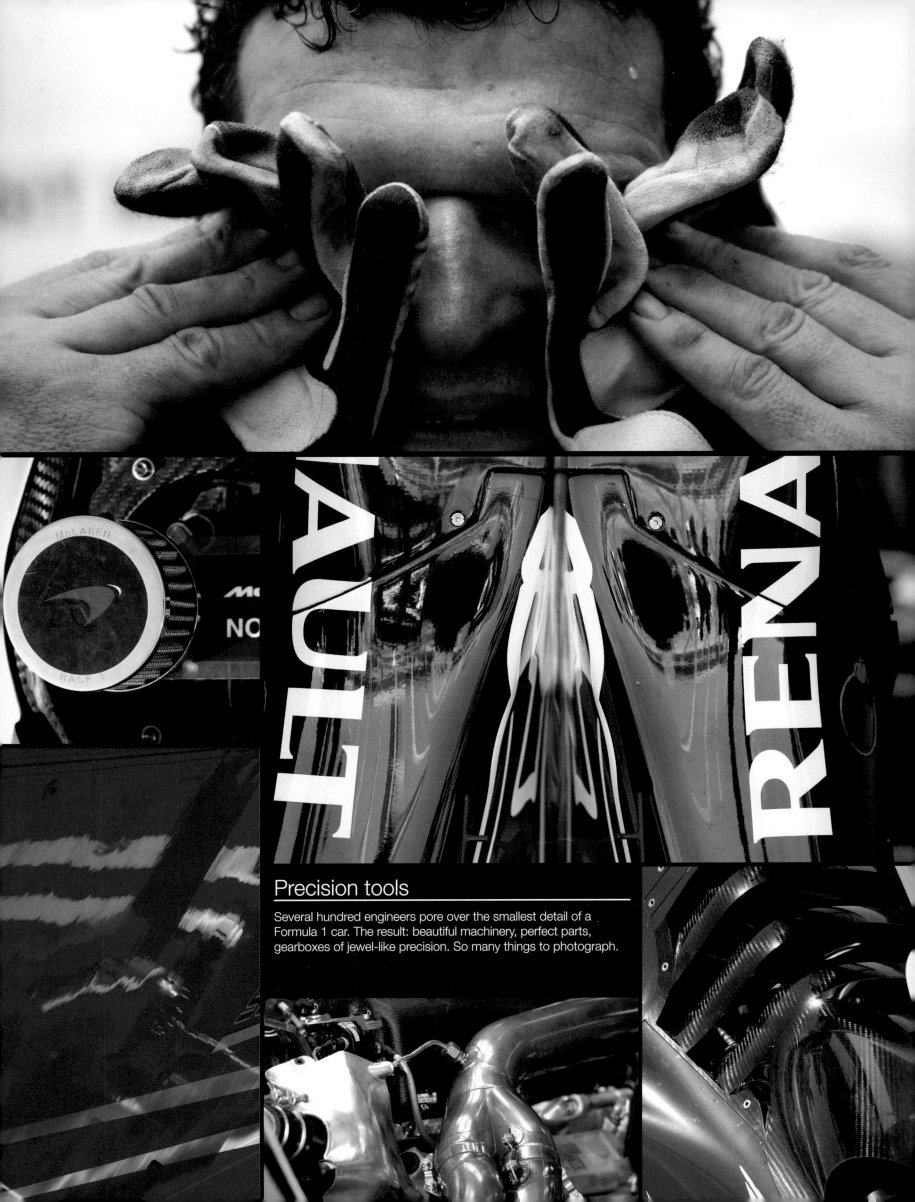

Precision tools

Several hundred engineers pore over the smallest detail of a Formula 1 car. The result: beautiful machinery, perfect parts, gearboxes of jewel-like precision. So many things to photograph.

THE 18 GRANDS PRIX

From Australia to Brazil, the 2008 Formula 1 World
Championship visited 18 countries, each with its own backdrop
and atmosphere. Because, apart from the races themselves, the
venues also contribute to the overall feel of the season.

FORMULA 1 TURNED ON ITS HEAD IN MELBOURNE

Of the twenty two cars that took the start of the Australian Grand Prix, only seven made it to the finish line.
On a very hot day, Lewis Hamilton was one of the few to keep a cool head as he took his first win of the season.
In the Ferrari camp, both cars retired with an unspecified engine problem, in what was a bad start for the favourites.

AFTER 300 METRES

David Coulthard's final season had few satisfying moments. Strangely enough, it started as it would finish, with a tangle at the first corner, which eliminated the Scotsman both in Melbourne and Sao Paulo seven months later.

As for the Australian race, it was a clear case of the car no longer being "fit for purpose."

FRONT AXLE

KIMI'S REVENGE

After posting a retirement in Melbourne, Kimi Raikkonen once again staked his claim as title favourite in Malaysia, taking the win, while team-mate Felipe Massa managed to crash out, all on his own, like a grown-up.
The two Ferrari men didn't know it yet, but this error would cost Felipe Massa the title, while the Finn's win in Sepang would already be his penultimate one of the year. Further back, Lewis Hamilton only picked up four points, having been moved back from fourth on the grid to ninth.

TOYOTA HEADS
FOR ITS DESTINY

The red and white cars were still as anonymous as ever, although they appeared to have made definite progress this year. After a catastrophic 2007 season, 2008 might just turn out to be the best for the German-Japanese team. That at least was Jarno Trulli's opinion and the Italian finished fourth, ahead of Lewis Hamilton who had been unable to get past. "If I don't have problems, it's clear that I can do it," he enthused after the race. "Today, we proved we are the fourth team. We are not yet at the level of Ferrari or McLaren, but we are almost up there with BMW-Sauber. The others, Renault, Williams and Red Bull, will sometimes have the edge at a specific circuit, but we will always be thereabouts."

FINALLY FELIPE!

He had an engine problem in Melbourne, went off the road in Sepang, but this time, Felipe Massa was right on it. In Bahrain, the little Brazilian started from the front row and went on to dominate the race, head and shoulders about the rest, without ever being challenged. His team-mate, Kimi Raikkonen, although none too happy with his car, completed Ferrari's triumph by finishing second.
The Sakhir Surprise was again Robert Kubica, on pole on Saturday and again on the podium on Sunday.

THE PENULTIMATE STAND

The Super Aguri team was going through difficult times in Bahrain, as it would disappear from view after the Spanish Grand Prix, three weeks later. At the Sakhir circuit, the Anglo-Japanese cars qualified on the penultimate row before going on to finish 16th and 17th, albeit ahead of David Coulthard.

FULL ON

Lewis Hamilton doing what he does best, attacking the long corners, be they at Barcelona or elsewhere. The Englishman was in damage limitation mode in the Spanish Grand Prix, finishing third. But he was incapable of following the crushing pace of the merciless red cars.

The wreckage of Heikki Kovalainen's McLaren: the monocoque had not withstood the impact.

The Catalunya circuit seen from an helicopter on race morning.

Lap 22: Heikki Kovalainen, miraculous survivor at turn 9

Lap 22. With the run of pit stops, Heikki Kovalainen, yet to refuel, inherited the lead in the race. Suddenly, on the entry to the super-quick Campsa right-hander, turn 9 at the Catalunya circuit, his left front tyre exploded without warning.

The car went straight on, like a missile, hardly slowing at all and the Finn's car literally buried itself into the tyre wall.

The impact occurred at an estimated speed of 250 km/h.

Extracted from the cockpit by the medics, the Finn was placed on a stretcher and taken to the circuit medical centre, before being transferred to the Catalunya general hospital, at Sant Cugat del Valles where, despite showing no obvious injuries, he was kept in overnight.

A scan showed his brain had not suffered any shock. *"We're not sure exactly what caused the puncture,"* commented McLaren boss Ron Dennis after the race.

"Our telemetry data naturally shows a sudden deflation, but we don't know why. But it would seem probable it could have been due to the rim breaking."

SNAPHSOTS OF THE WEEKEND

+ David Coulthard was hit with a 4000 Euro fine for not having taken part in the customary drivers' parade, in which the 22 F1 drivers do a lap of the track on a flat-bed truck to salute the crowd.
It was definitely not his weekend as the Scotsman qualified a pitiful 17th and he finished the race twelfth and one from last after a duel with Takuma Sato.

+ Qualified on the front row, Fernando Alonso was powerless to fend off Felipe Massa at the first corner. In the early stages, the Renault driver could just about match the pace of the two red cars, before being the first to refuel on lap 16, which partly explained his qualifying performance. Having rejoined the race, the Spaniard's engine let go on lap 35. Nelsinho Piquet retired on lap 7, making it all in all a disastrous weekend for Renault.

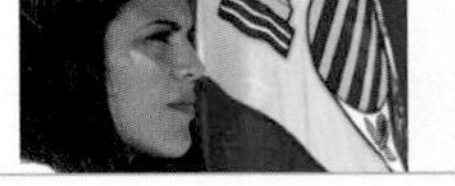

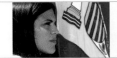

PRACTICE

Date	Weather (AM)	Air temperature	Track temperature	Weather (PM)	Air temperature	Track temperature
Friday April 25, 2008	Sunny	17-21°c	26-30°c	Sunny	25-26°c	36-39°c
Saturday April 26, 2008	Sunny	21-22°c	27-31°c	Sunny	23-24°c	38-39°c

All the time trials

N° Driver	Nat.	N° Chassis- Engine [Nbr. GP]	Pos. Free 1 Friday 10:00-11:30	Laps	Pos. Free 2 Friday 14:00-15:30	Laps	Pos. Free 3 Saturday 11:00-12:00	Laps	Pos. Q1 Saturday 14:00-14:20	Laps	Pos. Q2 Saturday 14:27-14:42	Laps	Pos. Q3 Saturday 14:50-15:00	Laps
1. Kimi Räikkönen	FIN	Ferrari F2008 268 [1]	1. 1:20.649	17	1. 1:21.935	38	13. 1:22.176	18	1. 1:20.701	8	3. 1:20.784	3	1. **1:21.813**	6
2. Felipe Massa	BR	Ferrari F2008 267 [1]	2. 1:20.699	9	5. 1:22.229	32	9. 1:22.075	16	12. 1:21.528	4	1. 1:20.584	6	3. **1:22.058**	6
3. Nick Heidfeld	D	BMW Sauber F1.08-04 [2]	9. 1:22.278	24	13. 1:23.130	40	1. 1:21.269	19	9. 1:21.466	7	5. 1:20.815	7	9. **1:22.542**	6
4. Robert Kubica	PL	BMW Sauber F1.08-03 [1]	4. 1:21.568	20	12. 1:22.788	38	4. 1:21.717	23	6. 1:21.423	4	2. 1:20.597	3	4. **1:22.065**	6
5. Fernando Alonso	E	Renault R28-03 [2]	6. 1:21.933	18	3. 1:22.032	26	3. 1:21.599	16	3. 1:21.347	6	4. 1:20.804	6	2. **1:21.994**	6
6. Nelson Piquet	BR	Renault R28-01 [1]	7. 1:21.936	21	2. 1:22.019	38	7. 1:21.992	18	5. 1:21.409	6	8. 1:20.894	6	10. **1:22.699**	6
7. Nico Rosberg	D	Williams FW30-03 - Toyota [2]	12. 1:23.003	25	7. 1:22.266	33	12. 1:22.174	19	10. 1:21.472	9	15. **1:21.349**	6		
8. Kazuki Nakajima	J	Williams FW30-04 - Toyota [2]	15. 1:23.153	24	4. 1:22.172	35	14. 1:22.189	16	15. 1:21.690	9	12. **1:21.117**	6		
9. David Coulthard	GB	Red Bull RB4 2 - Renault [1]	8. 1:22.118	20	8. 1:22.289	30	2. 1:21.465	16	17. **1:21810**	6				
10. Mark Webber	AUS	Red Bull RB4 4 - Renault [2]	13. 1:23.015	14	6. 1:22.238	36	22.	2	11. 1:21.494	7	10. 1:20.984	6	7. **1:22.429**	6
11. Jarno Trulli	I	Toyota TF108-02 [1]	14. 1:23.141	15	14. 1:23.224	34	5. 1:21.771	21	2. 1:21.158	6	9. 1:20.907	6	8. **1:22.529**	7
12. Timo Glock	D	Toyota TF108-01 [1]	11. 1:23.002	11	20. 1:23.883	40	10. 1:22.081	23	7. 1:21.427	10	14. **1:21.230**	6		
14. Sébastien Bourdais	F	Toro Rosso STR2B-03 - Ferrari [1]	19. 1:23.952	15	19. 1:23.684	37	6. 1:21.942	19	13. 1:21.540	10	16. **1:21.724**	5		
15. Sebastian Vettel	D	Toro Rosso STR2B-04 - Ferrari [2]	20. 1:24.082	15	18. 1:23.661	35	16. 1:22.292	20	18. **1:22.108**	18				
16. Jenson Button	GB	Honda RA108-02 [2]	10. 1:22.632	16	15. 1:23.263	34	8. 1:22.060	17	16. 1:21.757	6	13. **1:21.211**	6		
17. Rubens Barrichello	BR	Honda RA108-04 [2]	18. 1:23.353	14	17. 1:23.415	31	17. 1:22.350	17	14. 1:21.548	6	11. **1:21.049**	6		
18. Takuma Sato	J	Super Aguri SA08A-06 - Honda [2]	21. 1:24.278	14	21. 1:25.110	30	20. 1:23.726	16	22. **1:23.496**	9				
19. Anthony Davidson	GB	Super Aguri SA08A-05 - Honda [2]	22. 1:25.068	10	22. 1:25.163	31	21. 1:23.921	15	21. **1:23.318**	9				
20. Adrian Sutil	D	Force India VJM01/02 - Ferrari [2]	16. 1:23.156	22	10. 1:22.548	38	19. 1:22.689	21	20. **1:23.224**	8				
21. Giancarlo Fisichella	I	Force India VJM01/05 - Ferrari [2]	17. 1:23.196	20	9. 1:22.383	38	18. 1:22.466	22	19. **1:22.516**	11				
22. Lewis Hamilton	GB	McLaren MP4-23 04 - Mercedes [2]	3. 1:21.192	20	11. 1:22.685	33	11. 1:22.094	15	4. 1:21.366	3	7. 1:20.825	5	5. **1:22.096**	6
23. Heikki Kovalainen	FIN	McLaren MP4-23 03 - Mercedes [2]	5. 1:21.758	10	16. 1:23.264	8	15. 1:22.220	16	8. 1:21.430	3	6. 1:20.817	6	6. **1:22.231**	6

Fastest lap overall

F. Massa 1:20.584 (207,956 km/h)

Maximum speed

N° Driver	S1 Qualifs	Pos.	S1 Race	Pos.	S2 Qualifs	Pos.	S2 Race	Pos.	Finish Qualifs	Pos.	Finish Race	Pos.	Radar Qualifs	Pos.	Radar Race	Pos.
1. K. Räikkönen	290,7	3	291,7	4	290,2	1	288,0	1	282,1	2	282,8	2	313,1	1	314,6	1
2. F. Massa	290,6	4	292,0	3	283,7	17	281,6	8	281,6	4	283,8	1	309,1	4	313,8	2
3. N. Heidfeld	288,0	8	288,2	9	286,5	10	282,5	5	279,0	9	279,2	8	308,8	6	312,8	3
4. R. Kubica	288,4	5	291,7	5	286,7	9	283,1	3	279,4	7	280,3	6	310,1	3	312,6	4
5. F. Alonso	288,3	6	288,7	6	284,9	12	276,5	16	280,0	5	280,1	7	307,9	11	308,9	14
6. N. Piquet	288,3	7	288,0	10	286,8	8	266,6	18	279,7	6	281,0	5	308,3	9	308,9	15
7. N. Rosberg	286,3	14	285,1	16	283,9	16	276,9	15	277.7	16	277,6	15	306,4	20	311,8	7
8. K. Nakajima	286,1	16	286,5	14	287,0	7	281.2	9	279,2	8	279,2	10	308,9	5	312,4	5
9. D. Coulthard	286,3	15	286,6	13	284,2	14	279,7	13	278,2	14	278,7	12	308,4	8	310,6	12
10. M. Webber	286,5	13	287,4	11	284,1	15	283,0	4	277,9	15	278,7	13	307,0	16	308,1	18
11. J. Trulli	287,7	10	287,0	12	290,0	3	282,0	7	278,6	11	278,9	11	307,0	17	310,7	10
12. T. Glock	287,8	9	288,5	7	287,5	6	283,3	2	278,5	12	279,2	9	308,7	7	310,5	13
14. S. Bourdais	287,0	11	284,3	18	285,9	11	262,2	20	278,9	10	277,9	14	306,8	19	311,9	6
15. S. Vettel	286,7	12	260,4	22	279,7	19			278,4	13			307,6	14	297,6	22
16. J. Button	284,2	21	284,5	17	287,7	5	282,2	6	274,9	22	275,2	18	301,8	22	304,3	19
17. R. Barrichello	285,4	17	283,2	19	288,2	4	280,5	10	276,0	21	273,6	19	303,6	21	304.0	20
18. T. Sato	284,6	20	286,0	15	276,2	21	278,2	14	276,9	17	277,3	16	308,0	10	310,7	11
19. A. Davidson	283,9	22	280,3	20	280,3	18	262,5	19	276,1	20	272,0	20	307,6	12	308,8	17
20. A. Sutil	285,1	18	273,3	21	274,5	22			276,9	18			307,6	13	302,7	21
21. G. Fisichella	285,1	19	288,3	8	279,4	20	274,1	17	276,3	19	277.2	17	306,8	18	308,9	16
22. L. Hamilton	290,8	2	292,4	1	290,0	2	280,2	11	281.7	3	282.5	4	307,3	15	311,6	8
23. H. Kovalainen	293,4	1	292,0	2	284,6	13	279,8	12	283,3	1	282,7	3	310,7	2	311,6	9

Best sector times

Qualifs	**S1** H. Kovalainen	22.044	**S2** L. Hamilton	30.386	**S3** R. Kubica	27.749	= 1:19.979
Race	**S1** L. Hamilton	22.295	**S2** K. Räikkönen	30.902	**S3** K. Räikkönen	28.218	= 1:21.505

RACE

Date	Weather	Air temperature	Track temperature	Humidity	Wind speed
Sunday April 27, 2008 (14:00)	Sunny	23-22°c	40-35°c	30-40%	1.4 m/s

Classification & retirements

Pos.	Driver	Constructor	Tyres	Laps	Time	Km/h
1.	K. Räikkönen	Ferrari	MMH	66	1:39:19.051	187,415
2.	F. Massa	Ferrari	MMH	66	+ 3.228	187,313
3.	L. Hamilton	McLaren Mercedes	MMH	66	+ 4.187	187,282
4.	R. Kubica	BMW	MMH	66	+ 5.694	187,234
5.	M. Webber	Red Bull Renault	MMH	66	+ 35.938	186,280
6.	J. Button	Honda	MMH	66	+ 53.010	185,746
7.	K. Nakajima	Williams Toyota	MMH	66	+ 58.244	185,583
8.	J. Trulli	Toyota	MMHH	66	+ 59.435	185,546
9.	N, Heidfeld	BMW	MMMH	66	+ 1:03.073	185,432
10.	G. Fisichella	Force India	MMH	65	1 lap	184,268
11.	T. Glock	Toyota	MMHH	65	1 lap	184,137
12.	D. Coulthard	Red Bull Renault	MMHM	65	1 lap	183,017
13.	T. Sato	Super Aguri Honda	MMH	65	1 lap	182,535

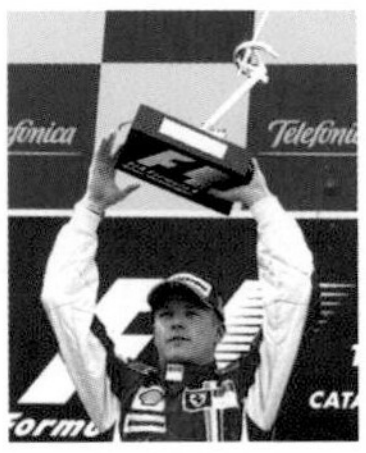

Driver	Constructor	Tyres	Laps	Reason
N. Rosberg	Williams Toyota	MM	41	Blown-up engine
F. Alonso	Renault	MM	34	Engine
R. Barrichello	Honda	MMM	34	Damaged car following collision with Fisichella (pits)
H. Kovalainen	McLaren Mercedes	M	21	Broken left front rim, straight on into tyre wall
A. Davidson	Super Aguri Honda	M	8	Broken radiator
S. Bourdais	STR Ferrari	M	7	Collision with Piquet
N. Piquet	Renault	M	6	Collision with Bourdais
S. Vettel	STR Ferrari	M	0	Front collision with Sutil
A. Sutil	Force India	M	0	Spin following contact with Coulthard, hits Vettel

Tyres H: Hard & M: Medium

Fastest laps

	Driver	Time	Lap	Km/h
1.	F. Räikkönen	1:21.670	46	205,191
2.	R. Massa	1:21.801	45	204,863
3.	L. Hamilton	1:22.017	20	204,323
4.	R. Kubica	1:22.106	20	204,102
5.	J. Button	1:22.353	66	203,489
6.	H. Kovalainen	1:22.453	19	203,243
7.	N. Heidfeld	1:22.519	21	203,080
8.	M. Webber	1:22.564	19	202,969
9.	F. Alonso	1:22.683	15	202,677
10.	J. Trulli	1:22.758	45	202,494
11.	D. Coulthard	1:22.842	57	202,288
12.	T. Glock	1:23.007	57	201,886
13.	N. Rosberg	1:23.319	20	201,130
14.	G. Fisichella	1:23.439	40	200,841
15.	K. Nakajima	1:23.549	48	200,576
16.	R. Barrichello	1:23.858	21	199,837
17.	T. Sato	1:24.617	34	198,045
18.	N. Piquet	1:25.444	6	196,128
19.	S. Bourdais	1:25.999	6	197,862
20.	A. Davidson	1:26.864	6	192,922

Pit stops

	Driver	Lap	Duration	Stop	Total
1.	F. Alonso	16	28.547	1	28.547
2.	F. Massa	19	27.347	1	27.347
3.	K. Räikkönen	20	27.188	1	27.188
4.	M. Webber	20	28.876	1	28.876
5.	J. Trulli	20	26.840	1	26.840
6.	T. Sato	20	38.711	1	38.711
7.	L. Hamilton	21	27.637	1	26.637
8.	R. Kubica	21	26.829	1	26.829
9.	N. Rosberg	22	30.481	1	30.481
10.	N. Heidfeld	24	27.490	1	27.490
11.	R. Barrichello	25	29.517	1	59.517
12.	J. Button	25	34.001	1	34.001
13.	K. Nakajima	25	29.336	1	29.336
14.	G. Fisichella	25	28.110	1	28.110
15.	D. Coulthard	25	27.719	1	27.719
16.	T. Glock	25	27.472	1	27.472
17.	R. Barrichello	26	37.718	2	1:01.235
18.	N. Heidfeld	•33•	29.680	2	57.170
19.	T. Sato	38	34.090	2	1:12.801
20.	G. Fisichella	44	28.012	2	56.122
21.	N. Heidfeld	45	26.433	3	1:23.603
22.	F. Massa	46	26.241	2	53.588
23.	M. Webber	46	26.924	2	55.800
24.	J. Trulli	46	30.542	2	57.382
25.	K. Räikkönen	47	27.999	2	55.187
26.	L. Hamilton	47	26.455	2	54.092
27.	R. Kubica	47	26.156	2	52.985
28.	K. Nakajima	51	26.446	2	55.782
29.	T. Glock	51	25.324	2	55.796
30.	D. Coulthard	52	27.266	2	54.985
31.	J. Trulli	53	16.796	3	1:14.178
32.	T. Glock	53	27.655	3	1:20.451
33.	J. Button	54	25.413	2	59.414
34.	D. Coulthard	54	32.360	3	1:27.345

•• Stop-go penalty (10 sec.): Heidfeld.
For pitting before the pit lane opening,

Race leader

Driver	Laps in the lead	Nbr of laps
K. Räikkönen	1 > 20	20
L. Hamilton	21	1
N. Heidfeld	22 > 24	3
K. Räikkönen	25 > 66	42

Driver	Nbr of laps	Kilometers
K. Räikkönen	62	288,484 km
N. Heidfeld	3	13,965 km
L. Hamilton	1	4,655 km

Lap chart

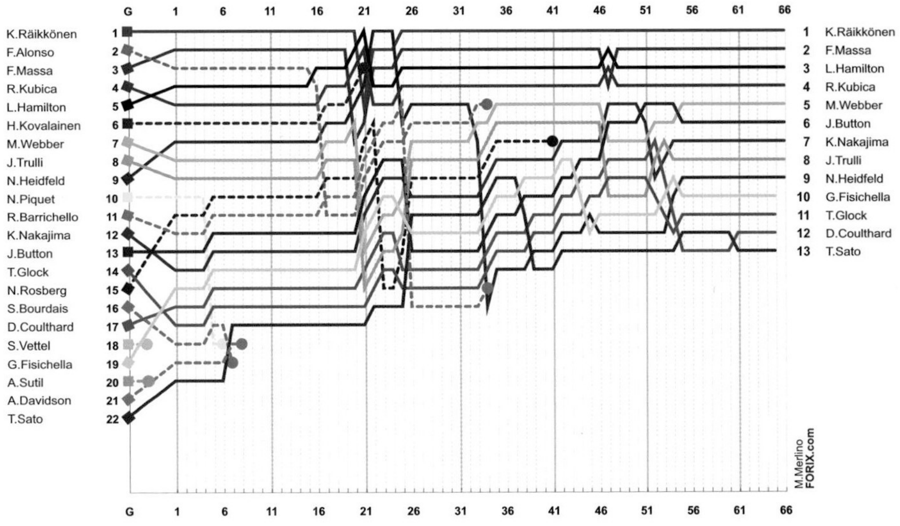

Gaps on the lead board

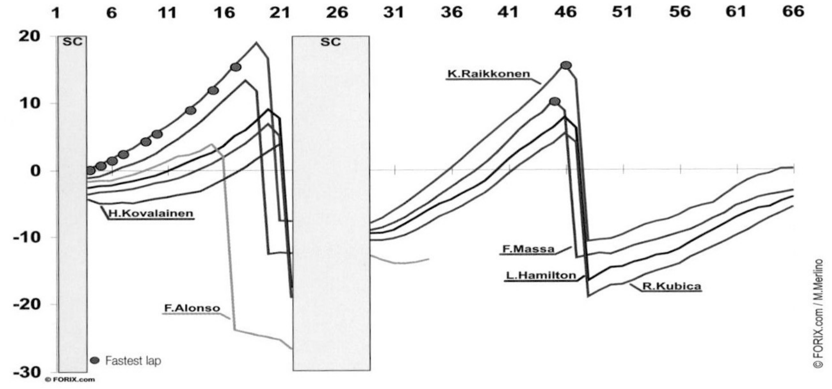

CHAMPIONSHIPS 4/18

Drivers

	Driver	Constructor	Wins	Points
1.	K. Räikkönen	Ferrari	2	29
2.	L. Hamilton	McLaren Mercedes	1	20
3.	R. Kubica	BMW		19
4.	F. Massa	Ferrari	1	18
5.	N. Heidfeld	BMW		16
6.	H. Kovalainen	McLaren Mercedes		14
7.	J. Trulli	Toyota		9
8.	M. Webber	Red Bull Renault		8
9.	N. Rosberg	Williams Toyota		7
10.	F. Alonso	Renault		6
11.	K. Nakajima	Williams Toyota		5
12.	J. Button	Honda		3
13.	S. Bourdais	STR Ferrari		2
14.	T. Glock	Toyota		0
15.	D. Coulthard	Red Bull Renault		0
16.	G. Fisichella	Force India		0
17.	R. Barrichello	Honda		0
18.	N. Piquet	Renault		0
19.	T. Sato	Super Aguri Honda		0
20.	A. Davidson	Super Aguri Honda		0
21.	A. Sutil	Force India		0
	S. Vettel	STR Ferrari		

Constructors

	Constructor	Wins	Points
1.	Scuderia Ferrari Marlboro	3	47
2.	BMW Sauber F1 Team		35
3.	Vodafone McLaren Mercedes	1	34
4.	AT&T Williams		12
5.	Panasonic Toyota Racing		9
6.	Red Bull Racing		8
7.	ING Renault F1 Team		6
8.	Honda Racing F1 Team		3
9.	Scuderia Torro Rosso		2
10.	Force India F1 Team		0
11.	Super Aguri F1 Team		0

THE CIRCUIT

Name Circuit de Catalunya; Montmelò, Barcelona
Lenght 4655 m
Distance 66 laps, 307,104 km

Latitude 41°34'12.00"N
Longitude 2°15'40.00"E

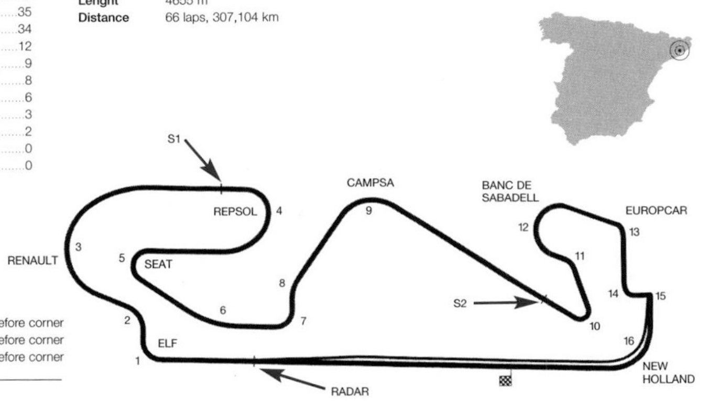

S1 60m before corner
S2 85m before corner
Radar 250m before corner

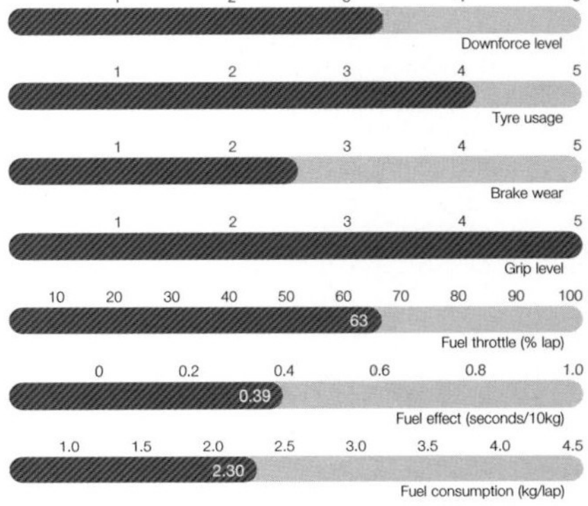

All results: © 2008 Formula One Administration Ltd, 6 Princes Gate, London, SW7 1QJ, England

FELIPE MASSA
HAPPY FOR NOW

It was an incident packed weekend in Turkey.
On the celebration front, Rubens Barrichello
was very proud of celebrating his 257th Grand
Prix, which meant he beat the record for the
greatest number of Grand Prix starts, held until
now by Riccardo Patrese.
On the down side, this event took place
without the Super Aguri team, a victim of the
first signs of an economic crisis that was just
beginning to make itself felt.
On track, a strange tyre tale robbed Lewis
Hamilton of an almost guaranteed win, as his
team put him on a three stop strategy to save
his rubber.
That meant a win for Felipe Massa, who thus
moved back up to second in the world
championship, equal on points to Hamilton and
seven points behind his team-mate, Kimi
Raikkonen.

OVER THE TOP

Won't work down the inside, but it will over the top! Giancarlo Fisichella's Force India mounts Kazuki Nakajima's Williams in somewhat cavalier style at the first corner of the Grand Prix. The first corner saw a spectacular crash between the two men as the Italian was simply unable to brake and rammed the back of the Japanese driver's car. "I wanted to pit to change the wing, but there was too much damage and I had to retire," explained Nakajima.

BATTLE OF THE
BARRICADES

The cars rushing between the barriers at
Monaco at over 200 km/h is a real spectacle,
which one can never tire of watching. Heikki
Kovalainen was particularly adept at the
exercise, qualifying his McLaren on the front row.

MAY THE FORCE BE WITH YOU

After the terrible disappointment of Monaco, where Adrian Sutil
was crashed into by Kimi Raikkonen, who'd lost control of his
Ferrari, just as the German was heading for a miraculous fourth
place, the season was back on course in Montreal: 17th on the
grid, Sutil retired on lap 14 with a gearbox problem.

FERRARI BACK IN CHARGE

Having stumbled in Monaco and Montreal, just as it did the previous year, the Ferraris demonstrated in Magny-Cours that they are definitely the best on a quick circuit.
By winning the French Grand Prix, Felipe Massa retook the lead in the drivers' classification from Robert Kubica, who could do no better than fifth in the Nievre region of France.
Lewis Hamilton's situation was still not getting any better, as once again he failed to score and dropped to fourth in the classification.

> Only tenth on the grid for Fernando Alonso, because of an inopportune gearbox problem. "It couldn't have come at a worse time," lamented the Spaniard. "Now, all I can do is hope the rain they predict will arrive. I'll pray all night long for it. Or maybe I should sing, that might work better."

200th pole for Ferrari, outright favourite on the quick tracks

Scuderia Ferrari had failed to shine in the previous two rounds in Monaco and Montreal, but it definitely intended catching up in the French Grand Prix.
On a track made to measure for their chassis, the two red cars monopolised the front row, never giving their rivals a chance. *"We were not that quick in the first two parts of qualifying, but that's normal,"* explained Kimi Raikkonen. *"During all the practice sessions, we set up the car with a heavy fuel load*

and then suddenly we find ourselves with a very light car. Of course, it doesn't handle quite as we expect. But it all came good in the final part, when we were back on full tanks again."
Felipe Massa was a mere four hundredths slower than the Finn, to ensure his place on the front row. "I'm not too disappointed," commented the Brazilian. "I'm at the front which is what matters. The car is fantastic, the team is ready...every-

thing is fine."
And it was all the finer because Ferrari's main rivals in the McLaren camp were a long way back.
Lewis Hamilton had set the third fastest time, but was dropped down to thirteenth, because of the penalty imposed after his mistake in Canada, while Heikki Kovalainen, who was sixth quickest, would start tenth for having impeded Mark Webber on his quick lap.

> The rain dance had been an illusion, given the cloudless sky over Magny-Cours. But Kimi Raikkonen's delight at the end of qualifying was good to see. It was the Finn's first pole position since Spain.

IN BRIEF

+ F1 commercial rights holder Bernie Ecclestone was in France and confirmed he had a contract with the FFSA (the French motor sport authority) which went up to and including 2011. "There will therefore be a French Grand Prix up until then, but not necessarily at Magny-Cours. The choice of venue is down to the FFSA," specified Bernie, thus contradicting what he had always said up until then, which was that 2008 would be the last French Grand Prix here.

+ The BMW Sauber team didn't look likely to repeat its Canadian one-two finish. Nick Heidfeld was knocked out in Q2, as he still struggled to get the most out of his tyres on a first flying lap and Robert Kubica could do no better than seventh. Thanks to the penalties for the two McLaren drivers, the Pole finally ended up fifth on the grid. "We knew this would be a difficult weekend and that's how it's turning out. We're finding it very difficult to set the car up for this circuit," he admitted.

+ Lewis Hamilton's father, Anthony, evidently doesn't have his lad's talent at the wheel. Driving a friend's Porsche GT3, Hamilton Senior crashed 200 metres from his home, after a rather brutal getaway followed by a spin. No damage, except to his self esteem.

+ The previous week, the F1 drivers complained about the attitude of the FIA, which had declared it planned a price hike for a superlicense, which is compulsory if you want to race in Formula 1. The cost was due to rise from 1725 Euros to 10,000 Euros per year.
On top of that, for each point scored, a driver would have to pay a further 2000 Euros, rather than the existing 456 Euros. Furious with this increase, claimed to be made in the name of covering the costs of safety, the drivers contemplated going on strike at Silverstone, although Lewis Hamilton had already declared he wanted no part of it. The Englishman still categorically refused to join the GPDA.

STARTING GRID

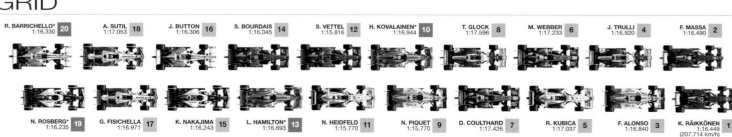

R. BARRICHELLO* 1:16.330 **20**	A. SUTIL 1:17.053 **18**	J. BUTTON 1:16.306 **16**	S. BOURDAIS 1:16.045 **14**	S. VETTEL 1:15.816 **12**	H. KOVALAINEN* 1:16.944 **10**	T. GLOCK 1:17.596 **8**	M. WEBBER 1:17.233 **6**	J. TRULLI 1:16.920 **4**	F. MASSA 1:16.490 **2**
N. ROSBERG* 1:16.235 **19**	G. FISICHELLA 1:16.971 **17**	K. NAKAJIMA 1:16.243 **15**	L. HAMILTON* 1:16.693 **13**	N. HEIDFELD 1:15.770 **11**	N. PIQUET 1:15.770 **9**	D. COULTHARD 1:17.426 **7**	R. KUBICA 1:17.037 **5**	F. ALONSO 1:16.840 **3**	K. RÄIKKÖNEN 1:16.449 **1** (207.714 km/h)

<
Kimi Raikkonen's exhaust problems allowed Felipe Massa to pocket another win, his third of the season.

Felipe Massa the Magny-ficent and Kimi Raikkonen the Unlucky

What is happening with Kimi Raikkonen? Five years ago, when driving for McLaren, the Finn had gone through such a bad patch that he was known as the unluckiest driver ever. Back then, it cost him the world title that went to Michael Schumacher, driving a Ferrari that was not as quick as the McLaren, but more reliable.

Two years later, in 2005, it was Fernando Alonso who profited from the Finn's misfortune to take the title crown which should have gone to Raikkonen, but for another run of retirements.

Lastyear however, the Finn finally made it. When Lewis Hamilton looked a certainty for the title, Raikkonen snaffled it from him at the final round, by one little point, which could have been seen as a sign that his rotten luck had finally deserted him.

But this season, it's back. The Finn seemed to have more talent and skill than his team-mate, but it was the latter who was heading the points table.

In Magny-Cours, Raikkonen appeared to be on course for victory: having taken pole position, he was cruising along in the lead, with a comfortable gap to Felipe Massa, until a broken exhaust slowed his pace. The problem had never manifested itself before on the Ferrari F2008. "*We still don't know what happened,*" commented the Team Principal of the Scuderia, Stefano Domenicali, after the race. "*When it happened, we advised Kimi to reduce the revs as much as possible.*"

Fortunately, the Scuderia was way ahead of the opposition at this circuit and, even in economy mode, the Finn managed to finish second. "*I had hardly any power,*" he recounted. "*But our car is really strong, because with a problem like that, I would have expected to retire in any other car. It's very disappointing, but on the positive side, at least I still scored 8 points.*"

In the meantime, Felipe Massa made the most of it to win and lead the world championship for the first time in his career. It was also the first time a Brazilian had topped the points table since a certain Ayrton Senna, fifteen years earlier.

Lewis Hamilton 10th

Lewis Hamilton faced a difficult task: 13th on the grid, he absolutely had to go flat out if he was to get into the points.

He would certainly have managed it, if he hadn't cut the "Nurburgring" chicane on the opening lap, which saw the stewards give him a drive-through penalty.

The Englishman finally finished tenth, with no points to his name, losing more ground in the championship. "*That's the third race this season where I haven't scored any points. But there are still ten to go!*" said the McLaren man philosophically.

His team-mate Heikki Kovalainen finished fourth, having started tenth.

"*It shows we went for an excellent strategy,*" commented the Finn. In the Ferrari camp, the team would have to change Kimi Raikkonen's engine for the forthcoming British Grand Prix, thus playing the driver's "joker."

Lastyear, such a change would have led to a ten place grid penalty. But the drivers felt this was too severe and so the 2008 rules included a "joker" which allowed the first engine change to be penalty-free.

<
And a little kiss for the winner's trophy handed to Felipe Massa. A cup that would end up at Ferrari, as is always the case in F1, with the drivers getting a copy for their collection.

Jarno on the podium

It must have seemed like a long time to the Toyota team, which hadn't seen one of its drivers on the podium since the 2006 Australian Grand Prix, over two years ago.

Jarno Trulli's third place in Magny-Cours thus put an end to this drought. "*Yes, it's an amazing result. The whole team worked very hard to get here, because we really wanted to dedicate this result to Ove Andersson (the former Toyota team boss, who had died a few days earlier on a rally in South Africa) who did so much for our marque.*"

At the end of the race, Heikki Kovalainen, who was right behind, tried all he knew to pass the Toyota, but without success. "*His chances of getting past were nil,*" continued Trulli. "*I had to fight with a lot of cars that were quicker than mine, but that's what I'm known for. Towards the end, it had begun to rain again and I was very cautious, because it is hard to tell how slippery the track is when you're in front. I fought with Heikki and it was like a karting race, but I wasn't going to let him by.*"

As for whether or not another podium was in the offing, Trulli was less sure. "*There is still a lot to do, but today we can finally be happy with our work. The team put in a lot of effort. The car is finally competitive and we are all motivated. Things are moving.*"

GP2: Brilliant Buemi

Fabulous, amazing, fantastic: observers in the paddock were running out of words to describe Sebastien Buemi's drive in the GP2 race held on Sunday morning, as a curtain raiser to the Grand Prix.

Having started from down in 21st place on the grid, at a circuit where overtaking is known to be difficult, the 19 year old Swiss managed to carve his way through the entire field, to win the race.

To do so, he needed a good deal of bravery, which saw him take the start on slick tyres, while the track was still damp.

But it also required an amazing level of talent to stay on the black stuff and overtake everyone on a track transformed into an ice rink. It was so slippery that several of his rivals got it wrong, especially when the racing line began to dry out and they chopped in their rain tyres for slicks.

Buemi never put a foot wrong.

"*It's the best win of my career,*" said Red Bull Racing's F1 reserve driver.

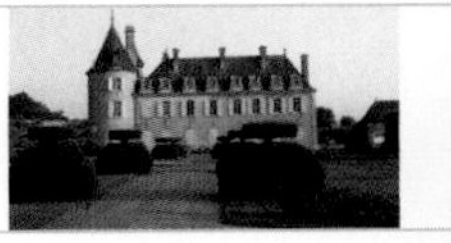

PRACTICE

Date	Weather (AM)	Air temperature	Track temperature	Weather (PM)	Air temperature	Track temperature
Friday June 20, 2008	Some clouds	18-20°c	18-25°c	Sunny	22-24°c	39-41°c
Saturday June 21, 2008	Sunny	26°c	34-37°c	Sunny	27-29°c	40-48°c

All the time trials

N° Driver	Nat.	N° Chassis- Engine [Nbr. GP]	Pos. Free 1 Friday 10:00-11:30	Laps	Pos. Free 2 Friday 14:00-15:30	Laps	Pos. Free 3 Saturday 11:00-12:00	Laps	Pos. Q1 Saturday 14:00-14:20	Laps	Pos. Q2 Saturday 14:27-14:42	Laps	Pos. Q3 Saturday 14:50-15:00	Laps
1. Kimi Räikkönen	FIN	Ferrari F2008 270 [1]	4. 1:16.073	21	3. 1:15.999	42	5. 1:16.003	16	2. 1:15.133	8	2. 1:15.161	3	1. **1:16.449**	5
2. Felipe Massa	BR	Ferrari F2008 267 [1]	1. 1:15.306	22	2. 1:15.854	24	9. 1:16.256	17	1. 1:15.024	8	1. 1:15.041	3	2. **1:16.490**	6
3. Nick Heidfeld	D	BMW Sauber F1.08-07 [2]	9. 1:16.870	21	8. 1:16.458	43	18. 1:16.687	19	12. 1:16.006	8	12. **1:15.786**	6		
4. Robert Kubica	PL	BMW Sauber F1.08-03 [1]	5. 1:16.377	19	6. 1:16.317	35	14. 1:16.617	20	5. 1:15.687	7	10. 1:15.723	6	7. **1:17.037**	6
5. Fernando Alonso	E	Renault R28-02 [1]	6. 1:16.400	23	1. 1:15.778	37	12. 1:16.437	20	7. 1:15.754	6	5. 1:15.483	6	4. **1:16.840**	6
6. Nelson Piquet	BR	Renault R28-01 [1]	11. 1:17.063	31	9. 1:16.543	39	1. 1:15.750	19	9. 1:15.848	6	11. **1:15.770**	6		
7. Nico Rosberg	D	Williams FW30-05 - Toyota [2]	14. 1:17.394	30	11. 1:16.682	42	4. 1:15.974	17	15. 1:16.085	6	15. **1:16.235**	6		
8. Kazuki Nakajima	J	Williams FW30-04 - Toyota [2]	17. 1:17.696	25	14. 1:17.002	32	15. 1:16.644	16	16. **1:16.243**	9				
9. David Coulthard	GB	Red Bull RB4 3 - Renault [2]	12. 1:17.234	21	10. 1:16.572	36	10. 1:16.282	18	8. 1:15.802	7	9. 1:15.654	6	9. **1:17.426**	6
10. Mark Webber	AUS	Red Bull RB4 4 - Renault [2]	13. 1:17.269	22	16. 1:17.106	38	2. 1:15.759	14	13. 1:16.020	6	6. 1:15.488	6	8. **1:17.233**	6
11. Jarno Trulli	I	Toyota TF108-05 [1]	7. 1:16.758	32	12. 1:16.743	43	6. 1:16.147	20	3. 1:15.521	7	4. 1:15.362	6	5. **1:16.920**	6
12. Timo Glock	D	Toyota TF108-06 [1]	10. 1:16.886	31	15. 1:17.092	39	11. 1:16.344	20	6. 1:15.727	10	7. 1:15.558	6	10. **1:17.596**	8
14. Sébastien Bourdais	F	Toro Rosso STR3-01 - Ferrari [1]	16. 1:17.683	27	13. 1:16.758	42	8. 1:16.235	18	14. 1:16.072	11	14. **1:16.045**	6		
15. Sebastian Vettel	D	Toro Rosso STR3-03 - Ferrari [1]	8. 1:16.838	27	5. 1:16.298	42	3. 1:15.827	21	10. 1:15.918	10	13. **1:15.816**	7		
16. Jenson Button	GB	Honda RA108-02 [2]	18. 1:17.928	21	17. 1:17.244	37	16. 1:16.651	20	17. **1:16.306**	9				
17. Rubens Barrichello	BR	Honda RA108-04 [2]	15. 1:17.491	25	19. 1:17.591	27	17. 1:16.658	17	18. **1:16.330**	6				
20. Adrian Sutil	D	Force India VJM01/02 - Ferrari [2]	20. 1:18.673	13	20. 1:17.868	33	20. 1:17.365	23	20. **1:17.053**	9				
21. Giancarlo Fisichella	I	Force India VJM01/05 - Ferrari [1]	19. 1:18.072	27	18. 1:17.394	42	19. 1:17.365	23	19. **1:16.971**	10				
22. Lewis Hamilton	GB	McLaren MP4-23 04 - Mercedes [2]	2. 1:16.002	22	4. 1:16.232	29	7. 1:16.182	16	4. 1:15.634	3	3. 1:15.293	6	3. **1:16.693**	6
23. Heikki Kovalainen	FIN	McLaren MP4-23 05 - Mercedes [2]	3. 1:16.055	20	7. 1:16.340	36	13. 1:16.545	16	11. 1:15.965	6	8. 1:15.639	6	6. **1:16.944**	6

Fastest lap overall
F. Massa 1:15.024 (211,660 km/h)

Maximum speed

N° Driver	S1 Qualifs	Pos.	S1 Race	Pos.	S2 Qualifs	Pos.	S2 Race	Pos.	Finish Qualifs	Pos.	Finish Race	Pos.	Radar Qualifs	Pos.	Radar Race	Pos.
1. K. Räikkönen	306,2	3	305,8	8	280,0	1	279,4	3	164,4	1	157,9	1	306,4	4	305,0	2
2. F. Massa	304,3	5	308,2	4	279,5	5	281,6	1	162,8	7	156,4	5	307,6	1	307,6	1
3. N. Heidfeld	299,7	11	302,2	11	274,3	14	276,4	11	160,0	16	156,5	4	301,6	10	301,0	9
4. R. Kubica	299,0	13	302,5	10	275,2	9	276,2	10	162,8	5	157,8	2	302,0	8	299,5	15
5. F. Alonso	308,1	2	309,1	2	279,6	4	279,1	5	161,8	5	153,8	14	306,9	3	304,2	5
6. N. Piquet	308,5	1	308,5	3	279,7	3	278,9	6	159,9	17	155,2	11	307,6	2	304,9	3
7. N. Rosberg	304,9	4	307,8	5	279,5	6	279,2	4	163,5	3	156,8	3	305,4	5	299,5	14
8. K. Nakajima	304,3	7	305,6	9	278,9	8	278,5	7	161,9	8	153,6	16	303,3	7	304,3	4
9. D. Coulthard	300,3	10	299,0	17	273,2	16	272,4	18	160,6	13	153,4	17	301,0	13	300,5	10
10. M. Webber	298,5	15	300,2	16	274,5	12	273,9	14	160,0	15	155,5	10	301,5	11	301,1	8
11. J. Trulli	297,6	17	297,8	19	273,0	17	271,3	20	162,8	6	155,7	9	299,8	15	298,6	17
12. T. Glock	297,2	18	298,3	18	272,1	20	273,3	16	163,5	2	156,1	8	299,4	17	299,7	13
14. S. Bourdais	298,1	16	301,7	12	274,3	13	276,7	9	160,4	14	152,1	19	301,6	9	299,2	16
15. S. Vettel	301,2	9	301,1	14	275,0	10	275,7	12	161,3	11	154,4	13	301,5	12	300,0	11
16. J. Button	296,7	20	300,6	15	272,8	18	271,3	19	158,5	18	148,9	20	298,5	18	290,7	20
17. R. Barrichello	297,0	19	297,1	20	272,7	19	273,2	17	161,2	12	155,1	12	298,0	19	297.5	18
20. A. Sutil	304,3	6	307,1	7	274,7	11	275,4	13	157,2	19	153,7	15	298,0	20	300,0	12
21. G. Fisichella	299,2	12	301,7	13	273,2	15	273,8	15	156,2	20	152,4	18	299,6	16	297,4	19
22. L. Hamilton	302,9	8	311,8	1	279,8	2	280,1	2	163,4	4	156,2	7	305,1	6	302,4	7
23. H. Kovalainen	299,0	14	307,2	6	276,9	8	278,2	8	161,6	10	156,4	6	300,9	14	303,2	6

Best sector times

Qualifs	**S1** L. Hamilton	21.742	**S2** F. Massa	28.818	**S3** F. Massa	24.198	= 1:14.758
Race	**S1** K. Räikkönen	22.003	**S2** K. Räikkönen	29.464	**S3** K. Räikkönen	24.916	= 1:16.383

RACE

Date	Weather	Air temperature	Track temperature	Humidity	Wind speed
Sunday June 22, 2008 (14:00)	Cloudy, drizzle	25°c	31-25°c	70%	3.3 m/s

Classification & retirements

Pos.	Driver	Constructor	Tyres	Laps	Time	Km/h
1.	F. Massa	Ferrari	MMS	70	1:31.50.245	201,608
2.	K. Räikkönen	Ferrari	MMS	70	+ 17.984	200,952
3.	J. Trulli	Toyota	MMS	70	+ 28.250	200,579
4.	H. Kovalainen	McLaren Mercedes	MMS	70	+ 28.929	200,555
5.	R. Kubica	BMW	MMS	70	+ 30.512	200,497
6.	M. Webber	Red Bull Renault	MMS	70	+ 40.304	200,144
7.	N. Piquet	Renault	MMS	70	+ 41.033	200,117
8.	F. Alonso	Renault	MMS	70	+ 43.372	200,033
9.	D. Coulthard	Red Bull Renault	MMS	70	+ 51.072	199,756
10.	L. Hamilton	McLaren Mercedes	SSMS	70	+ 54.521	199,632
11.	T. Glock	Toyota	MMS	70	+ 57.738	199,517
12.	S. Vettel	STR Ferrari	MMS	70	+ 58.065	199,505
13.	N. Heidfeld	BMW	MMS	70	+ 1:02.079	199,361
14.	R. Barrichello	Honda	MMS	69	1 lap	198,178
15.	K. Nakajima	Williams Toyota	SMM	69	1 lap	198,054
16.	N. Rosberg	Williams Toyota	SM	69	1 lap	198,029
17.	S. Bourdais	STR Ferrari	MMS	69	1 lap	198,006
18.	G. Fisichella	Force India	MMS	69	1 lap	197,053
19.	A. Sutil	Force India	SMM	69	1 lap	196,347

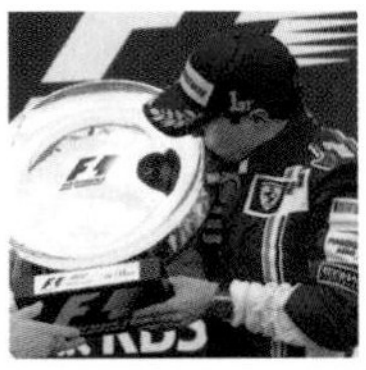

Driver	Constructor	Tyres	Laps	Reason
J. Button	Honda	MM	16	Contact with Bourdais

Tyres M: Medium & S: Soft

Fastest laps

	Driver	Time	Lap	Km/h
1.	K. Räikkönen	1:16.630	16	207,224
2.	F. Massa	1:16.729	20	206,956
3.	H. Kovalainen	1:17.134	46	205,870
4.	R. Kubica	1:17.172	16	205,768
5.	L. Hamilton	1:17.453	40	205,022
6.	M. Webber	1:17.507	22	204,879
7.	J. Trulii	1:17.567	12	204,721
8.	F. Alonso	1:17.641	39	204,525
9.	N. Heidfeld	1:17.716	46	204,328
10.	N. Piquet	1:17.758	24	204,218
11.	S. Vettel	1:17.760	36	204,212
12.	D. Coulthard	1:17.818	23	204,060
13.	T. Glock	1:17.836	45	204,013
14.	R. Barrichello	1:17.969	54	203,665
15.	K. Nakajima	1:18.054	60	203,443
16.	S. Bourdais	1:18.216	28	203,022
17.	N. Rosberg	1:18.311	38	202,776
18.	A. Sutil	1:18.462	41	202,385
19.	G. Fisichella	1:18.557	53	202,141
20.	J. Button	1:20.876	15	196,345

Pit stops

	Driver	Lap	Duration	Stop	Total
1.	J. Button	5	28.958	1	28.958
2.	L. Hamilton	•13•	14.559	1	14.559
3.	F. Alonso	15	25.117	1	25.117
4.	L. Hamilton	19	25.864	2	40.423
5.	J. Trulli	20	25.888	1	25.888
6.	R. Kubica	20	24.901	1	24.901
7.	A. Sutil	20	24.766	1	24.766
8.	K. Räikkönen	21	25.714	1	25.714
9.	T. Glock	21	26.655	1	26.655
10.	F. Massa	23	26.068	1	26.068
11.	M. Webber	23	24.886	1	24.886
12.	N. Piquet	25	25.269	1	25.269
13.	H. Kovalainen	25	26.121	1	26.121
14.	D. Coulthard	26	26.127	1	26.127
15.	S. Bourdais	26	26.203	1	26.203
16.	S. Vettel	29	24.261	1	24.261
17.	N. Heidfeld	29	22.988	1	22.988
18.	G. Fisichella	32	24.871	1	24.871
19.	R. Barrichello	34	24.767	1	24.767
20.	K. Nakajima	35	24.950	1	24.950
21.	N. Rosberg	40	26.519	1	26.519
22.	N. Rosberg	40	26.519	1	26.519
23.	F. Alonso	42	26.310	2	51.427
24.	A. Sutil	43	26.485	2	51.251
25.	R. Kubica	46	24.839	2	49.740
26.	S. Bourdais	46	24.384	2	50.587
27.	S. Vettel	48	24.241	2	48.502
28.	N. Heidfeld	48	23.889	2	46.887
29.	M. Webber	49	23.864	2	48.750
30.	T. Glock	49	25.578	2	52.233
31.	J. Trulli	50	23.848	2	49.736
32.	N. Piquet	50	23.540	2	48.809
33.	K. Räikkönen	52	25.075	2	50.789
34.	H. Kovalainen	52	23.304	2	49.425
35.	D. Coulthard	52	23.811	2	49.938
36.	L. Hamilton	52	23.625	3	1:04.048
37.	F. Massa	54	23.983	2	50.051
38.	G. Fisichella	54	25.161	2	50.032
39.	R. Barrichello	56	23.550	2	48.317
40.	K. Nakajima	58	24.545	2	49.495

•• Drive-through penalty: Hamilton.
Missing the apex of T7 and gaining an advantage.

Race leader

Driver	Laps in the lead	Nbr of laps
K. Räikkönen	1 > 21	21
F. Massa	22 > 23	2
K. Räikkönen	24 > 38	15
F. Massa	39 > 70	32

Driver	Nbr of laps	Kilometers
K. Räikkönen	36	158,612 km
F. Massa	34	149,974 km

Lap chart

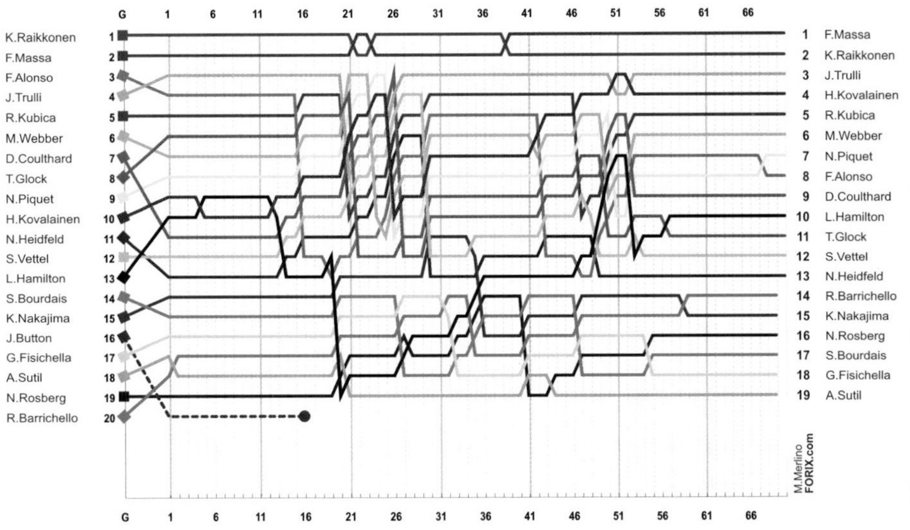
G 1 6 11 16 21 26 31 36 41 46 51 56 61 66
K.Raikkonen 1
F.Massa 2
F.Alonso 3
J.Trulli 4
R.Kubica 5
M.Webber 6
D.Coulthard 7
T.Glock 8
N.Piquet 9
H.Kovalainen 10
N.Heidfeld 11
S.Vettel 12
L.Hamilton 13
S.Bourdais 14
K.Nakajima 15
J.Button 16
G.Fisichella 17
A.Sutil 18
N.Rosberg 19
R.Barrichello 20
1 F.Massa
2 K.Raikkonen
3 J.Trulli
4 H.Kovalainen
5 R.Kubica
6 M.Webber
7 N.Piquet
8 F.Alonso
9 D.Coulthard
10 L.Hamilton
11 T.Glock
12 S.Vettel
13 N.Heidfeld
14 R.Barrichello
15 K.Nakajima
16 N.Rosberg
17 S.Bourdais
18 G.Fisichella
19 A.Sutil
M.Merlino
FORIX.com

Gaps on the lead board

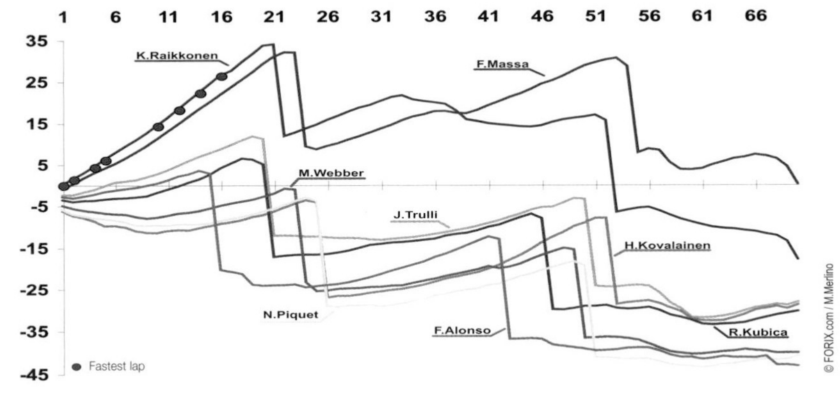
1 6 11 16 21 26 31 36 41 46 51 56 61 66
35
25
15
5
-5
-15
-25
-35
-45
K.Raikkonen
F.Massa
M.Webber
J.Trulli
H.Kovalainen
N.Piquet
F.Alonso
R.Kubica
Fastest lap
© FORIX.com / M.Merlino

CHAMPIONSHIPS 8/18

Drivers

	Driver	Constructor	Wins	Points
1.	F. Massa	Ferrari	3	48
2.	R. Kubica	BMW	1	46
3.	K. Räikkönen	Ferrari	2	43
4.	L. Hamilton	McLaren Mercedes	2	38
5.	N. Heidfeld	BMW		28
6.	H. Kovalainen	McLaren Mercedes		20
7.	J. Trulli	Toyota		18
8.	M. Webber	Red Bull Renault		18
9.	F. Alonso	Renault		10
10.	N. Rosberg	Williams Toyota		8
11.	K. Nakajima	Williams Toyota		7
12.	D. Coulthard	Red Bull Renault		6
13.	T. Glock	Toyota		5
14.	S. Vettel	STR Ferrari		5
15.	R. Barrichello	Honda		5
16.	J. Button	Honda		3
17.	N. Piquet	Renault		2
18.	S. Bourdais	STR Ferrari		2
19.	G. Fisichella	Force India		0
20.	T. Sato	Super Aguri Honda		0
21.	A. Davidson	Super Aguri Honda		0
22.	A. Sutil	Force India		0

Constructors

	Constructor	Wins	Points
1.	Scuderia Ferrari Marlboro	5	91
2.	BMW Sauber F1 Team	1	74
3.	Vodafone McLaren Mercedes	2	58
4.	Red Bull Racing		24
5.	Panasonic Toyota Racing		23
6.	AT&T Williams		15
7.	ING Renault F1 Team		12
8.	Honda Racing F1 Team		8
9.	Scuderia Torro Rosso		7
10.	Force India F1 Team		0
11.	Super Aguri F1 Team		0

THE CIRCUIT

Name	Circuit de Nevers Magny-Cours; Magny-Cours	**Latitude**	46°51'50.70"N
Lenght	4411 m	**Longitude**	3°09'48.50"E
Distance	70 laps, 308,586 km		

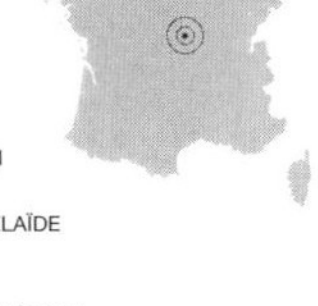

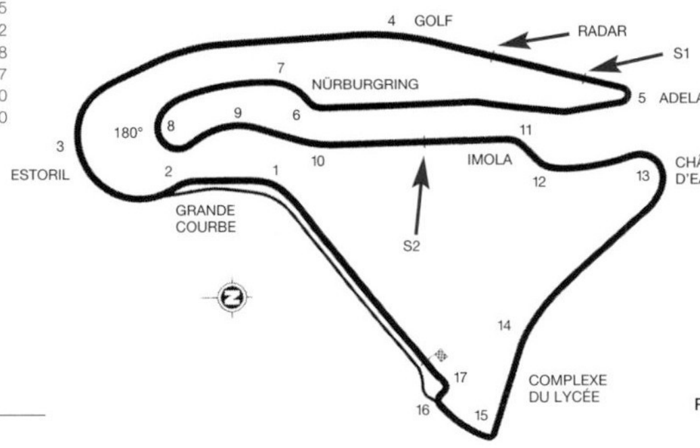
4 GOLF
RADAR
S1
7
NÜRBURGRING
5 ADELAÏDE
180°
8
9
6
11
3
ESTORIL
2
1
10
IMOLA
12
13
CHÂTEAU D'EAU
GRANDE COURBE
S2
14
17
16
15
COMPLEXE DU LYCÉE

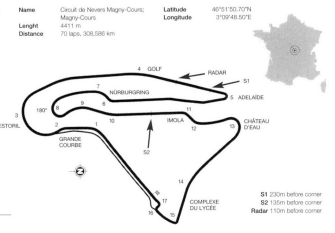

S1 230m before corner
S2 135m before corner
Radar 110m before corner

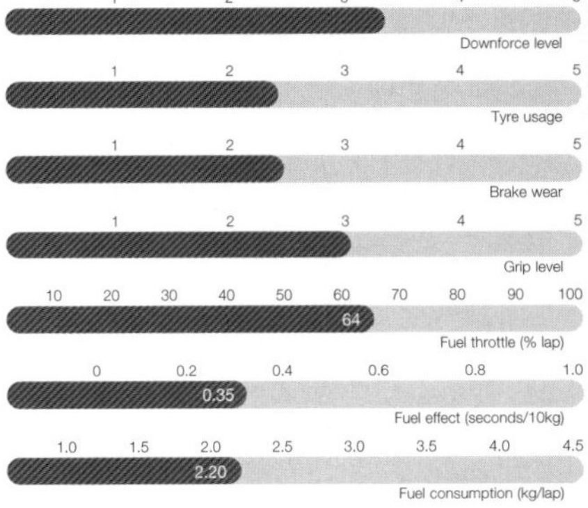
Downforce level
Tyre usage
Brake wear
Grip level
64
Fuel throttle (% lap)
0.35
Fuel effect (seconds/10kg)
2.20
Fuel consumption (kg/lap)

A PROPHET IN HIS OWN LAND

Having failed to score in Canada and France, Lewis Hamilton was back to his winning ways in front of a crowd that only had eyes for him. At Silverstone, through a series of downpours, the Englishman was majestic, finishing over a minute ahead of all his pursuers.

In the Ferrari camp it was a complete debacle, with neither driver finishing in the points.

After the British Grand Prix, the top three in the championship classification were equal on points with 48 apiece. An historic moment.

> Heikki Kovalainen took his maiden pole at Silverstone.

First pole for Heikki ahead of Mark Webber

The Ferrari camp was stupefied after qualifying. The Scuderia had approached the British Grand Prix in confident manner, fresh off the back of its supremacy at the French Grand Prix and its fine form at the test at this circuit a week earlier. However, Kimi Raikkonen was only on the second row of the grid, while Felipe Massa, hindered by a sticking wheel nut towards the end of the session, was only ninth. "*On Friday, the car wasn't working at all,*" said Raikkonen by way of explanation. "*Our engineers worked on the problem over night and it's better now. But there's a lot of wind and the car's handling is unstable.*"

At the front, to everyone's surprise, was Heikki Kovalainen, who took pole position ahead of Mark Webber in the Red Bull. It was a very unusual front row, as this was also the Finn's first ever F1 pole.

His lead over his pursuers, at over half a second, made it even more remarkable. "*It's fabulous,*" conceded Kovalainen after the session. "*Everything's gone well this weekend and I have to say our engineers have done some incredible work on the car. They modified it after last week's test session and it's definitely quicker now, especially in the slow sections.*" The Finn, while very happy about his first pole position, was keeping his cool. "*Pole doesn't bring any points and the most important thing is the race,*" he reasoned. "*And it's going to be a tough race, looking at the drivers around me on the start grid.*"

For Lewis Hamilton, it had been a disappointing

afternoon. Fourth quickest, the Englishman would start from the second row, in front of a crowd that only had eyes for him. "*Of course it's a shame, but probably I pushed a bit too hard!*" he admitted. "*I wanted to go too quickly and I ran a bit wide at Priory, which cost me a place on the front row. But at least I feel very comfortable in the car. And if it rains, my settings will work very well.*"

> David Coulthard has just announced his imminent retirement and the news seems to go down well with his compatriots, Lewis Hamilton and Jenson Button.

David Coulthard will retire at the end of the season

In Monaco, he still insisted he had no plans to retire. "*I'm the oldest driver on the grid? That's a good thing isn't it?,*" laughed David Coulthard, when he was reminded he would soon be 38 years old. "*In any case, no way am I thinking of stopping,*" he continued. "*I love this as much as my first day, I'm still as quick and I'm better because of my experience. In any case, if you start thinking about retirement, it's because you've already turned the page in your head and then it's best to stop immediately.*"

Just six weeks later, he turned his remarks on their head. "*I think the time has come for me to stop,*" declared the Scotsman on Thursday at Silverstone. "*Recently, that feeling has been getting stronger and stronger. It was not a difficult decision to take, especially as, barring any surprises, I'm unlikely to win any races in the next few weeks. I don't want to wake up one morning feeling I no longer want to drive...*"

Coulthard stated he would stay on with the Red Bull team as a consultant, similar to Michael Schumacher's role at Ferrari, adding that he might have a look at other forms of motor sport - he was seen attending a NASCAR race prior to the Canadian Grand Prix.

Mark Webber was already confirmed for 2009, but there was no decision yet about the second Red Bull seat. "*We still have time,*" claimed team boss Christian Horner. "*Sebastian Vettel is one possibility, but there are others. I was very impressed by Sebastien Buemi's drive in Magny-Cours and he has huge potential.*"

STARTING GRID

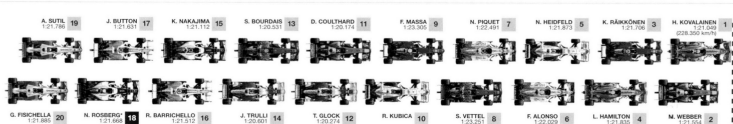

* N. ROSBERG starts from the pit lane.

A. SUTIL 19 1:21.786	J. BUTTON 17 1:21.631	K. NAKAJIMA 15 1:21.112	S. BOURDAIS 13 1:20.531	D. COULTHARD 11 1:20.174	F. MASSA 9 1:23.305	N. PIQUET 7 1:22.491	N. HEIDFELD 5 1:21.873	K. RÄIKKÖNEN 3 1:21.706	H. KOVALAINEN 1 1:21.049 (228.350 km/h)
G. FISICHELLA 20 1:21.885	N. ROSBERG* 18 1:21.668	R. BARRICHELLO 16 1:21.512	J. TRULLI 14 1:20.601	T. GLOCK 12 1:20.274	R. KUBICA 10 1:22.492	S. VETTEL 8 1:23.251	F. ALONSO 6 1:22.029	L. HAMILTON 4 1:21.835	M. WEBBER 2 1:21.554

< Lewis Hamilton shines as the sun returns to Silverstone. The Englishman was brilliant in the difficult conditions affecting this Grand Prix.

∧ Lewis Hamilton charges off right from the start, while Heikki Kovalainen maintains his pole position. The Finn would lead the race for four laps.

The rain never stops and Scuderia Ferrari drowns

In the space of four days, Scuderia Ferrari went from heaven to hell. On Thursday, when they arrived at Silverstone, the management was in confident mood. The previous week, testing here had confirmed the superiority of the F2008. After a one-two finish in Magny-Cours, it seemed that nothing could stop the progress of the Italian steamroller.

However, right from Friday, the situation turned nasty. At the end of the afternoon's free practice session, the two Ferraris were only 8th and 12th. On Saturday morning, it was worse still and the Maranello engineers had no answers for this poor showing. But the worst was yet to come: in infernal race conditions, the Scuderia could barely keep its head above water. At the start of the race, Kimi Raikkonen was able to match Lewis Hamilton's pace, but it all unravelled after the first pit stops. *"We opted to stay on the same tyres, which was a big mistake,"* confessed team principal, Stefano Domenicali. *"Our weather forecast prediced an improvement, which meant the best option was to stay with the same rubber."*

Unfortunately, Ferrari forecaster, Meteo France had got it wrong...again. Instead of sunshine, another downpour hit the track. On almost slick tyres, the two Ferrari drivers began losing a lot of ground, up to 5 second per lap. *"And that was another mistake we made. Instead of calling in our drivers, we continued to wait for an improvement,"* continued Domenicali.

It was even worse for Felipe Massa. Starting from ninth, the Brazilian had an unbelievable number of spins. *"We are not going to blame Felipe,"* added the boss. *"His car was very difficult to drive, as the settings were apparently too stiff for the rain. On top of that, we made the same mistake as with Kimi, leaving him on the same set of tyres at the pit stop. I must admit we have to improve the way we run things in wet races. It's a Grand Prix to forget, but at the same time we have to take note and make sure we don't make the same mistakes again."*

< Felipe Massa fights the awful conditions at Silverstone. The Brazilian finished 13th. A poor showing which would cost him dear in the championship.

Sliding spectacular

The rain never stopped falling throughout the race and that meant the track was the stage for an incredible number of cars flying off the track. A brief resume of the slide and spin show, driver by driver:

1. Raikkonen: laps 37 and 38
2. Mass: laps 1, 3, 36, 47 and 49
3. Kubica: laps 36 and 40 (retires)
6. Piquet: lap 36 (retires)
7. Rosberg: lap 40, accident with Glock
8. Nakajima: lap 23
9. Coulthard: lap 1, accident with Vettel
10. Webber: laps 1 and 38
11. Glock: laps 35 and 43
15. Vettel: lap 1, hit by Coulthard
16. Button: lap 39 (retires)
20. Sutil: Lap 11 (retires)
22. Hamilton: Lap 36
23. Kovalainen: laps 10 and 49

Winning by miles

Lewis Hamilton won with real style. He demonstrated an impressive mastery of the wet conditions, finishing the race with over a minute in hand over his closest pursuer, Nick Heidfeld. And he did it in front of a Silverstone crowd entirely devoted to his cause: 90,000 fans meant there were 180,000 arms raised every time he drove past. *"It was fantastic,"* confirmed the winner. *"The crowd and my country deserved this win. To be honest, it was the toughest race of my career. Conditions were awful, as there were times when the first sector was dry and the second soaking wet. I couldn't see anything and I had to clear my visor every lap. I told myself that, if I managed to win, it would be the nicest of all my wins. So I prayed, then prayed some more that everything would work out well."* And God evidently heard his prayers and indulged them, to such an extent that Lewis Hamilton eventually had over a minute in hand, when he crossed the line.

So why the need for such a big gap? *"Everything was going fine. At one point, I was lapping 6 seconds quicker than the second placed guy and my engineer told me I had a lead of over 60 seconds. At that point, I said to myself, "watch out, I mustn't go off and retire with such a lead." If that had happened, I'd never forgive myself, I would have to retire...But on the other hand, I didn't want to slow too much and lose concentration. Actually, at one point, I did go on the grass at Brooklands. I had two very busy weeks before this Grand Prix (read further on.) This morning, when I got up, I didn't feel too great, I felt empty. Nothing serious, just one of those things. My brother restored my energy and here we are."*

MAGIC SILVERSTONE

As usual the arm wrestling continues between Bernie Ecclestone and the BRDC, the drivers' club that owns the circuit. And also as usual, you'd have to bet on Bernie, as Silverstone loses the Grand Prix contract as from 2010.

> Once again it was time to see Rubens Barrichello's famous smile on the podium. After a catastrophic practice, which saw both Hondas out of qualifying in the first session, the Brazilian stood on the third step of the podium, making the most of the unusual circumstances in the race. "It seems I'm definitely a wet weather specialist," said the amused Brazilian. "Anyway, it felt like an easy race for me. My engineer, Jock Cleare told me to slow down to take fewer risks, but I was under the impression I was driving slowly!" Barrichello was one of only a handful of drivers not to make a single mistake during the race.

Lewis Hamilton advised to tone down his celebrity lifestyle

He'd done it now: having signed a five year contract with footwear firm Reebok, Lewis Hamilton was Britain's best paid sportsman. His new deal was worth ten million pounds over five years, to add to the 75 million McLaren would be paying over the same period.

However, these lucrative deals and the star lifestyle that went with them, risked distracting Hamilton from the actual job of driving. Or at least, that's what Jackie Stewart felt. *"To win races, you must not make any mistakes,"* reckoned the three times world champion. *"Because, to finish first, first you have to finish. Drivers should not do too much and that's probably what cost Lewis the title in 2007. He has to calm down!"*

Hamilton did not seem keen on heeding the advice of his illustrious elder. Since the French Grand Prix, he had met Nelson Mandela at the former South African president's 90th birthday. He then took part in testing for McLaren at Silverstone circuit. Once the two days of testing were over, he went to Amsterdam for a Reebok promotional event.

The next day, he took part in a demo day for historic Mercedes cars at Brooklands circuit. Then, he went home to Switzerland to take part in a kayak race for a McLaren sponsor. Phew!

It was a crazy timetable that risked exhausting the young Englishman. However, Hamilton claimed he could take it all in his stride and he underlined the importance of meeting Nelson Mandela.

"For me, seeing him was like meeting God. He

was so nice to me. For the first time in my life, I was speechless. I was very honoured to be invited. During the meal, I sat next to Chelsea Clinton, opposite Bill Clinton and close to Elton John and Oprah Winfrey. It was one of the best nights of my life. If I had to choose between winning the British Grand Prix and meeting

Nelson Mandela, I would definitely choose Mandela."

So, not too many regrets then if the McLaren driver didn't manage to beat the Ferraris this weekend, as Jackie Stewart feared. The celebrity lifestyle risked being more important than the driving.

SNAPSHOTS OF THE WEEKEND

+ For years now, the BRDC (British Racing Drivers Club) that owns Silverstone circuit, has been fighting with Bernie Ecclestone, the F1 commercial rights holder, to keep its race on the calendar.

Therefore, it came as a surprise to everyone when Bernie announced at Silverstone that he had signed a ten year deal with Donington Park circuit to host the British Grand Prix, as from 2010.

F1 had been to the circuit near Nottingham, back in 1993, for a memorable wet race won by Ayrton Senna.

+ Lewis Hamilton has decided to invest some money: his father-manager advised him to buy a hotel on the Grand Anse beach in Grenada in the Carribean, the island from which his family originates.

The hotel complex, valued at more than 10 million pounds, should allow the McLaren driver to embark on new ventures when the time comes.

+ For the first time this season, neither Toyota driver

made it into the top ten in qualifying. The disappointment came hot on the heels of Jarno Trulli's podium finish in France. "It's completely unbelievable," admitted the Italian. "We haven't changed the car since Magny-Cours, so there's no reason for us to be this slow."

The two Toyotas opted for a wet weather set-up, hoping the race would be run in the wet.

+ During the Monaco weekend, the McLaren team put up for auction a visit to its factory, pompously referred to as "The Technology Centre," for four people.

Against all the odds, it was David Coulthard who placed the winning bid of a thousand pounds sterling.

The visit took place on the Monday prior to the British Grand Prix and the Scotsman turned up with Adrian Newey, Red Bull's chief technical officer, Christian Horner, the team boss and Martin Brundle, now a commentator on British TV. Needless to say, all the top secret stuff was kept well out of the way during the visit.

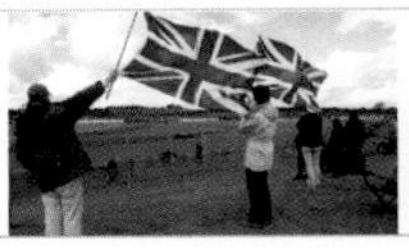

PRACTICE

Date	Weather (AM)	Air temperature	Track temperature	Weather (PM)	Air temperature	Track temperature
Friday July 4, 2008	Sunny, some clouds	17-19°c	21-26°c	Sunny, some clouds	21-23°c	33-35°c
Saturday July 5, 2008	Some clouds	20-22°c	23-25°c	some clouds, wind gusts	19-20°c	28-30°c

All the time trials

N° Driver	Nat.	N° Chassis- Engine [Nbr. GP]	Pos. Free 1 Friday 10:00-11:30	Laps	Pos. Free 2 Friday 14:00-15:30	Laps	Pos. Free 3 Saturday 10:00-11:00	Laps	Pos. Q1 Saturday 13:00-13:20	Laps	Pos. Q2 Saturday 13:27-13:42	Laps	Pos. Q3 Saturday 13:50-14:00	Laps
1. Kimi Räikkönen	FIN	Ferrari F2008 270 [1]	4. 1:19.948	16	12. 1:21.275	31	9. 1:22.355	20	4. 1:20.370	6	6. 1:19.971	6	3. **1:21.706**	6
2. Felipe Massa	BR	Ferrari F2008 267 [2]	1. 1:19.575	8	8. 1:20.943	18	12. 1:22.461	20	7. 1:20.676	6	8. 1:20.086	6	9. **1:23.305**	4
3. Nick Heidfeld	D	BMW Sauber F1.08-07 [1]	13. 1:21.107	18	13. 1:21.453	36	15. 1:22.916	22	12. 1:21.022	7	5. 1:19.802	3	5. **1:21.873**	6
4. Robert Kubica	PL	BMW Sauber F1.08-03 [2]	5. 1:20.367	11	11. 1:21.023	33	19. 1:23.282	20	5. 1:20.444	7	4. 1:19.788	3	10. **DNF**	2
5. Fernando Alonso	E	Renault R28-02 [2]	6. 1:20.436	7	15. 1:21.511	27	1. 1:20.740	16	11. 1:20.998	3	7. 1:19.992	6	6. **1:22.029**	6
6. Nelson Piquet	BR	Renault R28-01 [2]	8. 1:20.653	16	18. 1:21.642	45	6. 1:21.786	14	8. 1:30.818	7	10. 1:20.115	6	7. **1:22.491**	6
7. Nico Rosberg	D	Williams FW30-05 - Toyota [1]	10. 1:20.744	27	5. 1:20.748	43	13. 1:22.544	18	18. **1:21.668**	6				
8. Kazuki Nakajima	J	Williams FW30-04 - Toyota [1]	16. 1:21.282	21	9. 1:20.985	18	16. 1:23.028	17	15. 1:21.407	7	15. **1:21.112**	7		
9. David Coulthard	GB	Red Bull RB4 3 - Renault [1]	9. 1:20.698	16	4. 1:20.589	36	20. 1:32.119	6	14. 1:21.224	8	11. **1:20.174**	6		
10. Mark Webber	AUS	Red Bull RB4 4 - Renault [1]	11. 1:20.892	10	2. 1:20.520	32	2. 1:20.988	18	10. 1:20.982	4	3. 1:19.710	6	2. **1:21.554**	6
11. Jarno Trulli	I	Toyota TF108-05 [2]	15. 1:21.265	22	20. 1:22.196	23	14. 1:22.556	20	13. 1:21.145	7	14. **1:20.601**	6		
12. Timo Glock	D	Toyota TF108-06 & 02 [2]	12. 1:21.102	22	14. 1:21.472	18	8. 1;22.183	21	9. 1:20.893	8	12. **1:20.274**	6		
14. Sébastien Bourdais	F	Toro Rosso STR3-01 - Ferrari [2]	14. 1:21.166	17	17. 1:21.634	39	7. 1:22.059	21	6. 1:20.584	10	13. **1:20.531**	6		
15. Sebastian Vettel	D	Toro Rosso STR3-03 - Ferrari [2]	7. 1:20.588	18	6. 1:20.805	43	4. 1:21.277	19	3. 1:20.318	7	9. 1:20.109	6	8. **1:23.251**	3
16. Jenson Button	GB	Honda RA108-02 [1]	17. 1:21.901	7	7. 1:20.929	39	11. 1:22.440	19	17. **1:21.631**	11				
17. Rubens Barrichello	BR	Honda RA108-04 [1]	20. 1:24.123	4	10. 1:21.002	34	10. 1:22.387	17	16. **1:21.512**	9				
20. Adrian Sutil	D	Force India VJM01/02 - Ferrari [1]	18. 1:22.169	16	19. 1:21.756	30	17. 1:23.049	22	19. **1:21.786**	9				
21. Giancarlo Fisichella	I	Force India VJM01/05 - Ferrari [2]	19. 1:22.219	19	16. 1:21.520	42	18. 1:23.112	21	20. **1:21.885**	8				
22. Lewis Hamilton	GB	McLaren MP4-23 02 & 04 - Mercedes [1]	3. 1:19.623	13	3. 1:20.543	31	5. 1:21.668	14	2. 1:20.288	4	1. 1:18.537	3	4. **1:21.835**	6
23. Heikki Kovalainen	FIN	McLaren MP4-23 05 - Mercedes [1]	2. 1:19.587	15	1. 1:19.989	35	3. 1:21.266	14	1. 1:19.957	6	2. 1:19.597	3	1. **1:21.049**	6

Fastest lap overall
L. Hamilton 1:19.537 (232,691 km/h)

Maximum speed

N° Driver	S1 Qualifs	Pos.	S1 Race	Pos.	S2 Qualifs	Pos.	S2 Race	Pos.	Finish Qualifs	Pos.	Finish Race	Pos.	Radar Qualifs	Pos.	Radar Race	Pos.
1. K. Räikkönen	293,6	4	293,2	1	270,3	9	230,1	7	289,0	2	281,7	2	301,1	1	244,6	17
2. F. Massa	292,0	10	291,6	3	271,7	5	229,1	9	288,7	3	281,9	1	297,2	9	258,1	11
3. N. Heidfeld	292,6	6	285,9	11	274,3	1	237.9	1	287,5	5	278,4	6	297,2	8	271.5	2
4. R. Kubica	292,4	8	289,1	4	273,0	2	230,5	5	286,2	11	278,2	8	297,4	7	244,6	18
5. F. Alonso	292,4	9	286,7	7	268,9	12	220,9	17	286,3	9	278,2	7	298,6	3	247,1	16
6. N. Piquet	293,9	2	286,6	9	267,1	15	225,8	13	287,4	6	277,2	12	298.0	6	259,6	9
7. N. Rosberg	287,1	19	286,3	10	265,0	19	221,8	16	283,1	19	275,7	14	293,2	18	260,2	7
8. K. Nakajima	290,1	17	284,6	13	265,2	18	227,3	11	286,7	8	275,7	15	295,5	13	252,4	14
9. D. Coulthard	290,4	15	274,5	19	267,0	16	194,0	19	285,3	13			296,1	11	212,0	19
10. M. Webber	293,7	3	285,6	12	272,5	3	236,5	2	286,3	10	277,2	11	295,0	15	267,5	4
11. J. Trulli	287,6	18	282,9	16	269,4	10	226,7	12	282,5	20	275,2	16	292,6	20	259,8	8
12. T. Glock	292,0	11	286,6	8	270,9	7	229,1	10	284,8	14	277,6	10	295,1	14	274,2	1
14. S. Bourdais	290,5	14	288,3	5	271,5	6	225,8	14	286,8	7	280,2	5	298,5	4	251,9	15
15. S. Vettel	292,6	5	273,6	20	272,3	4	184,3	20	285,9	12			297,0	10	196,8	20
16. J. Button	290,2	16	283,3	15	261,6	20	232,5	4	283,7	16	276,0	13	293,7	17	259,3	10
17. R. Barrichello	291,8	12	284,5	14	266,0	17	229,2	8	284,1	15	277,7	9	293,1	19	262,1	6
20. A. Sutil	290,5	13	278,4	18	267,9	14	218,3	18	283,6	17	269,3	18	295,6	12	262,3	5
21. G. Fisichella	285,4	20	282,1	17	269,3	11	230,3	6	283,4	18	273,4	17	293,8	16	253,6	12
22. L. Hamilton	295,8	1	287,9	6	270,6	8	236,0	3	288,4	4	280,8	4	299,5	2	271,0	3
23. H. Kovalainen	292,5	7	292,6	2	267,9	13	222,5	15	291.1	1	281,1	3	298,0	5	253,4	13

Best sector times

Qualifs	**S1** L. Hamilton	25.200	**S2** R. Kubica	34.259	**S3** H. Kovalainen	19.735	= 1:19.194
Race	**S1** L. Hamilton	27.527	**S2** K. Räikkönen	40.289	**S3** K. Räikkönen	23.687	= 1:31.503

RACE

Date	Weather	Air temperature	Track temperature	Humidity	Wind speed
Sunday July 6, 2008 (13:00)	Intermittent rain	18-21°c	17-24°c	81%	6.1 m/s

Classification & retirements

Pos.	Driver	Constructor	Tyres	Laps	Time	Km/h
1.	L. Hamilton	McLaren Mercedes	WWW	60	1:39:09.440	186,585
2.	N. Heidfeld	BMW	WWW	60	+ 1:08.577	184,459
3.	R. Barrichello	Honda	WWEW	60	+ 1:22.273	184,040
4.	K. Räikkönen	Ferrari	WWW	59	1 lap	183,287
5.	H. Kovalainen	McLaren Mercedes	WWW	59	1 lap	183,059
6.	F. Alonso	Renault	WWW	59	1 lap	182,970
7.	J. Trulli	Toyota	WWW	59	1 lap	182,937
8.	K. Nakajima	Williams Toyota	WWE	59	1 lap	182,900
9.	N. Rosberg	Williams Toyota	WWEW	59	1 lap	182,873
10.	M. Webber	Red Bull Renault	WWW	59	1 lap	182,467
11.	S. Bourdais	STR Ferrari	WWE	59	1 lap	182,130
12.	T. Glock	Toyota	WWW	59	1 lap	181,350
13.	F. Massa	Ferrari	WWWW	58	2 laps	179,262

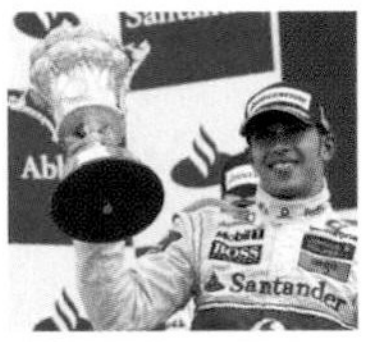

Driver	Constructor	Tyres	Laps	Reason
R. Kubica	BMW	WWW	39	Aquaplaned off, spin and went off
J. Button	Honda	WWE	38	Aquaplaned off, went off
N. Piquet	Renault	WW	35	Aquaplaned off, went off
G. Fisichella	Force India	W	26	Aquaplaned off, went off
A. Sutil	Force India	W	10	Aquaplaned off, spin and went off
S. Vettel	STR Ferrari	W	0	Hit by Coulthard
D. Coulthard	Red Bull Renault	W	0	Hits Vettel

Tyres W: Wet & E: Extreme Wet

Fastest laps

	Driver	Time	Lap	Km/h
1.	K. Räikkönen	1:32.150	18	200,842
2.	N. Heidfeld	1:32.719	21	199,609
3.	L. Hamilton	1:32.817	16	199,398
4.	M. Webber	1:32.952	17	199,109
5.	H. Kovalainen	1:33.130	17	198,728
6.	F. Alonso	1:33.133	17	198,722
7.	N. Piquet	1:33.203	21	198,573
8.	F. Massa	1:33.257	19	198,458
9.	S. Bourdais	1:33.367	21	198,224
10.	J. Button	1:33.376	21	198,205
11.	R. Barrichello	1:33.386	21	198,183
12.	R. Kubica	1:33.539	22	197,859
13.	J. Trulli	1:33.808	22	197,292
14.	K. Nakajima	1:34.277	21	196,310
15.	T. Glock	1:34.610	19	195,619
16.	N. Rosberg	1:34.797	21	195,234
17.	G. Fisichella	1:34.930	21	194,960
18.	A. Sutil	1:38.160	5	188,545

Pit stops

	Driver	Lap	Duration	Stop	Total
1.	M. Webber	18	25.861	1	25.861
2.	H. Kovalainen	19	26.529	1	26.529
3.	F. Alonso	20	26.703	1	26.703
4.	L. Hamilton	21	26.340	1	26.340
5.	K. Räikkönen	21	26.242	1	26.242
6.	F. Massa	21	26.770	1	26.770
7.	N. Heidfeld	22	26.562	1	26.562
8.	N. Piquet	22	27.714	1	27.714
9.	R. Kubica	23	27.349	1	27.349
10.	R. Barrichello	24	26.681	1	26.681
11.	N. Rosberg	24	26.842	1	26.842
12.	T. Glock	25	26.280	1	26.280
13.	J. Button	25	26.439	1	26.439
14.	K. Nakajima	25	25.817	1	25.817
15.	J. Trulli	26	25.926	1	25.926
16.	F. Alonso	26	26.558	2	53.261
17.	S. Bourdais	27	30.488	1	30.488
18.	M. Webber	28	28.312	2	54.173
19.	K. Räikkönen	30	28.218	2	54.460
20.	F. Massa	30	26.680	2	53.450
21.	H. Kovalainen	34	25.595	2	52.124
22.	R. Barrichello	35	47.461	2	1:14.142
23.	J. Button	35	48.083	2	1:14.522
24.	N. Rosberg	35	29.122	2	55.964
25.	K, Nakajima	35	36.232	2	1:02.049
26.	S. Bourdais	35	26.850	2	57.338
27.	L. Hamilton	38	25.638	2	51.978
28.	N. Heidfeld	38	25.783	2	52.345
29.	R. Kubica	38	29.443	2	56.792
30.	N. Rosberg	40	31.520	3	1:27.484
31.	T. Glock	43	24.726	2	51.006
32.	R. Barrichello	46	26.864	3	1:41.006
33.	J. Trulli	47	24.088	2	50.014
34.	F. Massa	49	24.643	3	1:18.093

Race leader

Driver	Laps in the lead	Nbr of laps
H. Kovalainen	1 > 4	4
L. Hamilton	5 > 21	17
N. Heidfeld	22	1
L. Hamilton	23 > 60	38

Driver	Nbr of laps	Kilometers
L. Hamilton	55	282,755 km
H. Kovalainen	4	20,459 km
N. Heidfeld	1	5,141 km

Gaps on the lead board

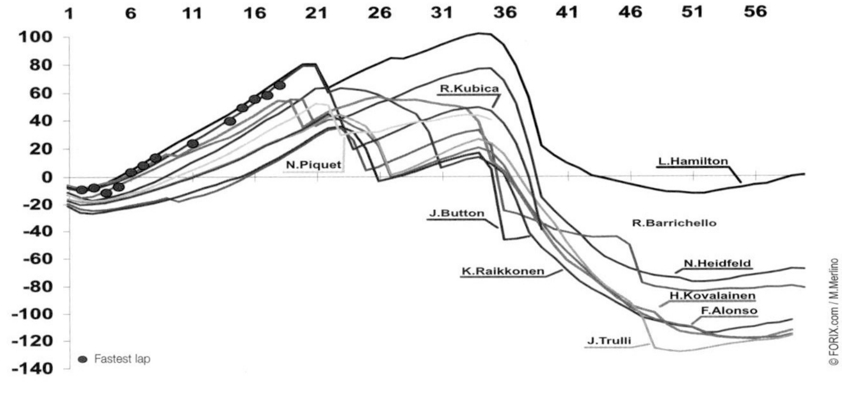
1 6 11 16 21 26 31 36 41 46 51 56
100 80 60 40 20 0 -20 -40 -60 -80 -100 -120 -140
R.Kubica
N.Piquet
L.Hamilton
J.Button
R.Barrichello
N.Heidfeld
K.Raikkonen
H.Kovalainen
F.Alonso
J.Trulli
Fastest lap
© FORIX.com / M.Merlino

Lap chart

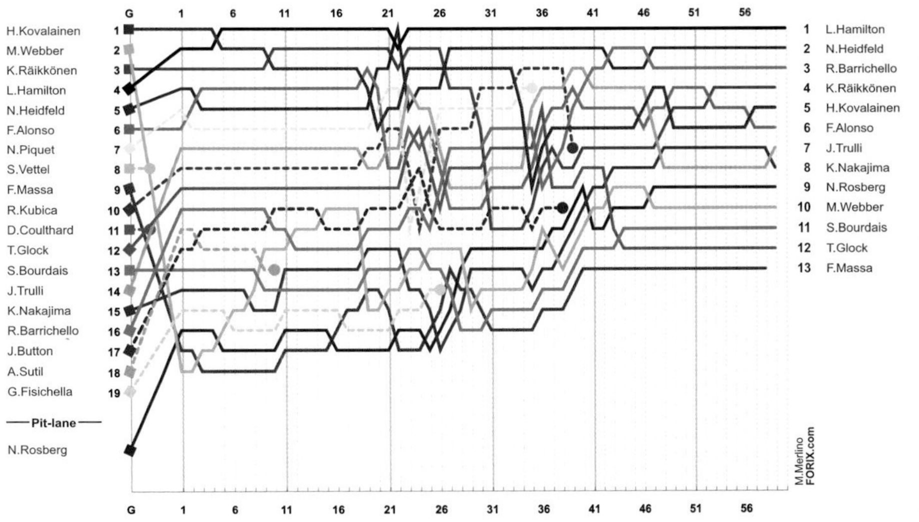
G 1 6 11 16 21 26 31 36 41 46 51 56
H.Kovalainen 1
M.Webber 2
K.Räikkönen 3
L.Hamilton 4
N.Heidfeld 5
F.Alonso 6
N.Piquet 7
S.Vettel 8
F.Massa 9
R.Kubica 10
D.Coulthard 11
T.Glock 12
S.Bourdais 13
J.Trulli 14
K.Nakajima 15
R.Barrichello 16
J.Button 17
A.Sutil 18
G.Fisichella 19
Pit-lane
N.Rosberg
1 L.Hamilton
2 N.Heidfeld
3 R.Barrichello
4 K.Räikkönen
5 H.Kovalainen
6 F.Alonso
7 J.Trulli
8 K.Nakajima
9 N.Rosberg
10 M.Webber
11 S.Bourdais
12 T.Glock
13 F.Massa
M.Merlino
FORIX.com

CHAMPIONSHIPS 9/18

Drivers

	Driver	Team	Wins	Points
1.	L. Hamilton	McLaren Mercedes	3🏆	48
2.	F. Massa	Ferrari	3🏆	48
3.	K. Räikkönen	Ferrari	2🏆	43.
4.	R. Kubica	BMW	1🏆	46
5.	N. Heidfeld	BMW		36
6.	H. Kovalainen	McLaren Mercedes		24
7.	J. Trulli	Toyota		20
8.	M. Webber	Red Bull Renault		18
9.	F. Alonso	Renault		13
10.	R. Barrichello	Honda		11
11.	N. Rosberg	Williams Toyota		8
12.	K. Nakajima	Williams Toyota		8.
13.	D. Coulthard	Red Bull Renault		6
14.	T. Glock	Toyota		5
15.	S. Vettel	STR Ferrari		5
16.	J. Button	Honda		3
17.	S. Bourdais	STR Ferrari		2
18.	N. Piquet	Renault		2
19.	G. Fisichella	Force India		0
20.	T. Sato	Super Aguri Honda		0
21.	A. Davidson	Super Aguri Honda		0
22.	A. Sutil	Force India		0

Constructors

	Constructor	Wins	Points
1.	Scuderia Ferrari Marlboro	5🏆	96
2.	BMW Sauber F1 Team	1🏆	82
3.	Vodafone McLaren Mercedes	3🏆	72
4.	Panasonic Toyota Racing		25
5.	Red Bull Racing		24
6.	AT&T Williams		16
7.	ING Renault F1 Team		15
8.	Honda Racing F1 Team		14
9.	Scuderia Torro Rosso		7
10.	Force India F1 Team		0
11.	Super Aguri F1 Team		0

S1 400m before corner
S2 100m before corner
Radar 100m before corner

THE CIRCUIT

Name Silverstone Circuit; Silverstone
Lenght 5141 m
Distance 60 laps, 308,355 km
Latitude 52°04'43.70"N
Longitude 1°00'55.60"O

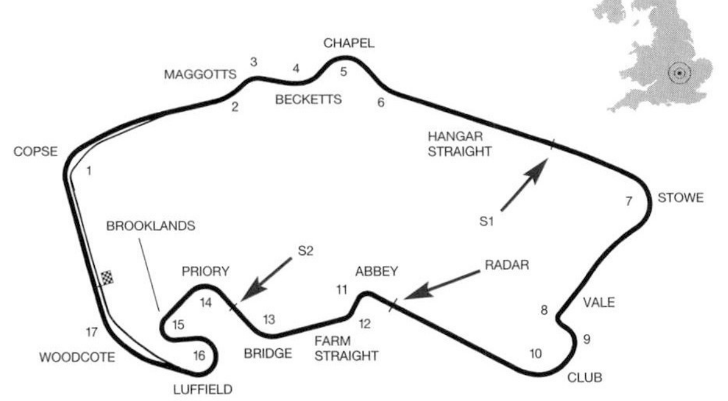
CHAPEL
MAGGOTTS
BECKETTS
COPSE
HANGAR STRAIGHT
STOWE
BROOKLANDS
S1
S2
PRIORY
ABBEY
RADAR
VALE
WOODCOTE
BRIDGE
FARM STRAIGHT
CLUB
LUFFIELD
1 2 3 4 5 6 7 8 9 10 11 12 13 14 15 16 17

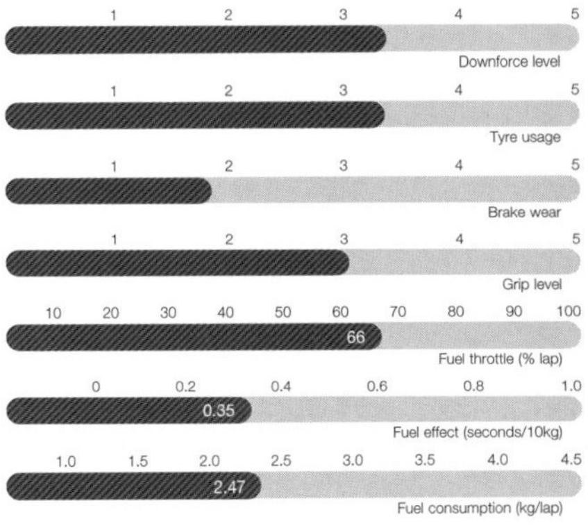
Downforce level
Tyre usage
Brake wear
Grip level
66
Fuel throttle (% lap)
0.35
Fuel effect (seconds/10kg)
2.47
Fuel consumption (kg/lap)

All results: © 2008 Formula One Administration Ltd, 6 Princes Gate, London, SW7 1QJ, England

ADVANTAGE LEWIS

Lewis Hamilton arrived at Hockenheim equal on points with his two main rivals but got the upper hand on them in Germany.

Clearly in the quickest car, he came out on top despite a disastrous strategy call by his team, insisting that he stay out while the Safety Car was controlling the race.

Fifth on the restart, he regained the lead with eight laps remainng.

Behind him, Nelsinho Piquet took full advantage of the Safety Car to finish on the second step of the podium and claim his best result of the season.

The Ferrari drivers were both unhappy with their cars, though unable to pinpoint where the trouble lay. It looked like being a long, hard finish to the season for the Scuderia.

> Lewis on pole, Heikki third on the grid: the McLaren pair had good reason to be happy with their qualifying performance.

Advantage Lewis!

Hockenheim, Saturday, 3 pm. Qualifying had left us with an enthralling prospect: everything was set for a superb battle between McLaren-Mercedes and Ferrari. At the halfway stage of the Championship, three drivers - Lewis Hamilton, Felipe Massa and Kimi Räikkönen - were on absolutely level pegging with 48 points apiece.

It couldn't have been more thrillingly poised, especially as it was so hard to separate the McLarens and the Ferraris.

The fight at the front continued through qualifying, top spot changing hands several times before Hamilton snatched the fastest time from Massa right at the end of the session. "*It was quite a lap,*" the British driver acknowledged. "*In fact my first run wasn't that bad either, but my very last lap was absolutely perfect - in fact I thought the time might have been even better.*"

Massa didn't seem too disappointed to be second, certainly not as much as teammate Räikkönen. He was only sixth on the grid and a tough race was in prospect.

"*We've been struggling to find the right set-up since the weekend started,*" said the Finn. "*Last night I thought we'd found the answer, but we're still too slow on a full fuel load. Obviously I'm not too happy about starting sixth, but it's not the end of the world. It's going to be a long race, and they only give points at the end...*"

The reigning World Champion's main problem would be getting past Fernando Alonso and Jarno Trulli, who had both qualified ahead of him and were likely to be slower in the race. Unless, that is, both men owed their grid positions to empty tanks, which meant they would be coming in early - and leaving the Finn's Ferrari with a clear track...

IN BRIEF...

+ During a sponsor appearance Fernando Alonso - rumoured to be on the brink of signing for Ferrari - was asked about his tastes in cooking.
"Which do you prefer, French or Italian?"
"Spanish," was the answer.
"But if you're talking about anything else, then I'd go for Italian."

+ This was the first weekend where the Toro Rossos seemed to be on the pace of their sister cars at Red Bull, with Sebastian Vettel splitting Mark Webber and David Coulthard in qualifying. "This car doesn't suit our car all that well," said Vettel, "but I know the place so well that I'm able to get the maximum out of it."

> Jarno Trulli had an excellent session, qualifying on the second row.

STARTING GRID

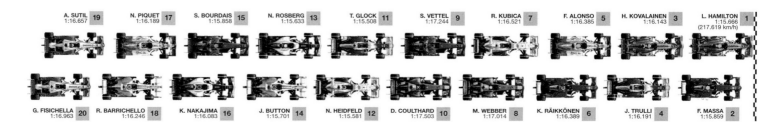

A. SUTIL 19 1:16.657	N. PIQUET 17 1:16.189	S. BOURDAIS 15 1:15.858	N. ROSBERG 13 1:15.633	T. GLOCK 11 1:15.508	S. VETTEL 9 1:17.244	R. KUBICA 7 1:16.521	F. ALONSO 5 1:16.385	H. KOVALAINEN 3 1:16.143	L. HAMILTON 1 1:15.666 (217.619 km/h)
G. FISICHELLA 20 1:16.963	R. BARRICHELLO 18 1:16.246	K. NAKAJIMA 16 1:16.083	J. BUTTON 14 1:15.701	N. HEIDFELD 12 1:15.581	D. COULTHARD 10 1:17.503	M. WEBBER 8 1:17.014	K. RÄIKKÖNEN 6 1:16.389	J. TRULLI 4 1:16.191	F. MASSA 2 1:15.859

<
Victory was no gimme for Lewis Hamilton. Well down in fifth place after his second stop, the British driver had to battle his way back into the lead.

Hamilton wins - despite team tactics

Lewis Hamilton had the air of a man determined to exact revenge for the previous year's debacle. No-one at Hockenheim could get close to the Hamilton machine.

"*I hope things will improve at the next few circuits,*" said Felipe Massa after finishing the race third for Ferrari. "*The car was really hard to drive today, and we don't know why. Early in the race Lewis got away easily and in the closing stages I had brake problems.*"

The Brazilian couldn't have said much else - if everything had gone to plan for McLaren, Hamilton would have had a very straightforward race indeed, with a huge lead by the end. "*I was putting half a second on my opponents, I felt great, it was like sitting at home,*" the British driver explained. "*It was just a matter of keeping my driving nice and smooth. Then all of a sudden, the Safety Car wiped out my lead completely.*"

Timo Glock's accident (see below) was the danger point for Hamilton. While the Scuderia took advantage of the race being neutralised to refuel both cars, McLaren opted to leave their star driver out there.

"*I came on the radio and asked them if they were sure we shouldn't be stopping like everyone else,*" added Hamilton, "*but they told me they knew what they were doing - the guys who were stopping would be heavily fuelled*" and I would be able to open up a gap. But then when the track was clear I had to build a 23-second gap in seven laps! I gave it all I had but it didn't work out.*"

Rejoining in fifth after his second pit stop, Hamilton still managed to overtake his rivals and take the race win.

"*It was very tough,*" he said. "*I don't understand why my engineers took that decision, but as I said to Ron Dennis, that's the kind of race he pays me for!*"

It meant Hamilton had opened up a small lead in the Championship. "*Too soon to draw any conclusions in terms of the title,*" he insisted. "*In F1 things can change so quickly.*"

< As the race starts Hamilton holds on to the front position he earned in qualifying.

< Tough at the top: after his second stop Hamilton had to wrest first place back from Massa. "I was a second a lap faster than him at that stage," said the Briton. "I just tried to keep my pace up. I got into his slipstream and left my braking very late. He was very clean…"

Second in the German Grand Prix was a magnificent effort from Nelsinho Piquet. "I don't know what to say," he stammmered at the finish.
"At the end I was pushing, concentrating on not making a mistake - I wasn't even looking at my pit board. I didn't want to know how many laps there were to go."

Timo Glock unhurt in huge pit straight accident

Lap 35: Timo Glock is lying ninth when his Toyota's right rear suspension suddenly collapses on the last corner, catapulting the race-car into the concrete wall.

The impact is so severe that the car explodes - only the survival cell around the driver stands up to the shock.

After crossing the track backwards, the wrecked Toyota slides to a halt a few metres further on.

The dazed German is extracted by marshals but is unable to walk without support. He sits, stunned, for several minutes, unable to describe the way he feels.

"*He looked distraught and he was struggling to get his words out,*" said one witness on the spot. "*He was obviously having to make a huge effort. He kept pointing to the back of his head as if it was all going round in there, and that's when the ambulance arrived.*"

Taken to the circuit Medical Centre for a preliminary examination, he was then moved to hospital in Mannheim and kept overnight for observation. "*Timo should be back with us for Hungary,*" said Toyota managing director Tadashi Yamashina.

After the race his engineers still couldn't explain the failure.

SNAPSHOTS OF THE WEEKEND

+ "His problem is he can't find the accelerator…" Following private testing in the week leading up to the German Grand Prix, Toro Rosso boss Franz Tost stuck a verbal knife in Sébastien Bourdais.

+ After the 'spygate' saga that left such a blemish on 2007, Ferrari took out a number of civil actions against McLaren in England. This week the teams decided to bury the hatchet and close the distressing case once and for all, provided the English team met the Scuderia's legal costs.

+ The bankrupt Super Aguri team were getting ready to hold a fire sale at their Leafield premises in the UK and on eBay. Among the items up for sale: one SA06, Takuma Sato's 2006 car.

+ Ferrari announced possible plans to introduce an F1-type KERS system on their production cars.

+ Signed, sealed and delivered: Bernie Ecclestone approved a Grand Prix in the suburbs of New Delhi, India, for 2011. Work has already begun, with the aim of building the world's finest circuit.

> The Hockenheim campground is almost as much of a legend as the circuit itself. The local restaurants certainly knew how to bring the crowds in…

>> David Coulthard and Sébastien Bourdais fight it out - for 12th place. The Scotsman eventually had to give best to the French driver.

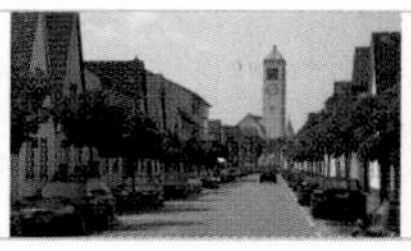

PRACTICE

Date	Weather (AM)	Air temperature	Track temperature	Weather (PM)	Air temperature	Track temperature
Friday July 18, 2008	Cloudy, wet track	17-18°c	16-19°c	Cloudy	22-24°c	24-32°c
Saturday July 19, 2008	Some clouds	22-23°c	25-28°c	Sunny	24-25°c	35-30°c

All the time trials

N° Driver	Nat.	N° Chassis- Engine (Nbr. GP)	Pos. Free 1 Friday 10:00-11:30	Laps	Pos. Free 2 Friday 14:00-15:30	Laps	Pos. Free 3 Saturday 11:00-12:00	Laps	Pos. Q1 Saturday 14:00-14:20	Laps	Pos. Q2 Saturday 14:27-14:42	Laps	Pos. Q3 Saturday 14:50-15:00	Laps
1. Kimi Räikkönen	FIN	Ferrari F2008 270 [2]	5. 1:15.537	22	3. 1:15.760	34	9. 1:16.380	19	2. 1:15.201	10	5. 1:14.949	3	6. **1:16.389**	6
2. Felipe Massa	BR	Ferrari F2008 269 [1]	3. 1:15.796	22	2. 1:15.722	31	2. 1:15.693	21	1. 1:14.921	7	2. 1:14.747	3	2. **1:15.859**	6
3. Nick Heidfeld	D	BMW Sauber F1.08-07 [2]	8. 1:16.606	27	9. 1:16.377	40	16. 1:16.906	24	8. 1:15.596	9	12. **1:15.581**	5		
4. Robert Kubica	PL	BMW Sauber F1.08-05 [1]	19. 1:18.779	8	8. 1:16.363	36	20. 1:17.469	15	14. 1:15.985	8	6. 1:15.109	6	7. **1:16.521**	6
5. Fernando Alonso	E	Renault R28-02 [1]	4. 1:16.163.	22	6. 1:16.230	38	4. 1:15.943	18	11. 1:15.917	7	4. 1:14.943	6	5. **1:16.385**	6
6. Nelson Piquet	BR	Renault R28-01 [1]	10. 1:17.063	26	15. 1:16.734	42	7. 1:16.161	21	17. **1:16.083**	10				
7. Nico Rosberg	D	Williams FW30-05 - Toyota [2]	6. 1:16.606	27	7. 1:16.355	41	10. 1:16.405	20	9. 1:15.863	10	13. **1:15.633**	6		
8. Kazuki Nakajima	J	Williams FW30-04 - Toyota [2]	9. 1:16.821	26	17. 1:16.829	21	13. 1:16.530	18	16. **1:16.083**	10				
9. David Coulthard	GB	Red Bull RB4 3 - Renault [2]	11. 1:17.108	18	10. 1:16.378	35	12. 1:16.515	19	13. 1:15.975	7	8. 1:15.338	6	10. **1:17.503**	7
10. Mark Webber	AUS	Red Bull RB4 4 - Renault [2]	14. 1:17.268	11	5. 1:16.017	25	8. 1:16.196	19	10. 1:15.900	7	10. 1:15.481	6	8. **1:17.014**	7
11. Jarno Trulli	I	Toyota TF108-05 [1]	17. 1:17.556	29	12. 1:16.530	45	6. 1:16.133	25	6. 1:15.560	7	7. 1:15.122	6	4. **1:16.191**	8
12. Timo Glock	D	Toyota TF108-02 [1]	13. 1:17.185	28	16. 1:16.781	44	14. 1:16.636	27	7. 1:15.560	10	11. **1:15.508**	7		
14. Sébastien Bourdais	F	Toro Rosso STR3-01 - Ferrari [1]	20. 1:21.506	16	18. 1:16.860	14	15 1:16.808	23	12. 1:15.927	10	15. **1:15.858**	5		
15. Sebastian Vettel	D	Toro Rosso STR3-03 - Ferrari [1]	7. 1:16.618	25	11. 1:16.422	41	5. 1:16.037	24	5. 1:15.532	10	9. 1:15.420	6	9. **1:17.244**	6
16. Jenson Button	GB	Honda RA108-02 [1]	12. 1:17.131	28	13. 1:16.542	38	11. 1:16.447	22	15. 1:15.993	9	14. **1:15.701**	6		
17. Rubens Barrichello	BR	Honda RA108-04 [2]	16. 1:17.500	24	14. 1:16.677	28	18. 1:17.189	20	18. **1:16.246**	10				
20. Adrian Sutil	D	Force India VJM01/02 - Ferrari [2]	18. 1:17.784	29	19. 1:17.008	39	17. 1:16.938	20	19. **1:16.657**	10				
21. Giancarlo Fisichella	I	Force India VJM01/05 - Ferrari [1]	15. 1:17.471	30	20. 1:17.047	37	19. 1:17.312	22	20. **1:16.963**	10				
22. Lewis Hamilton	GB	McLaren MP4-23 06 - Mercedes [2]	1. 1:16.537	22	1. 1:15.025	37	3. 1:15.839	21	3. 1:15.218	4	1. 1:14.603	3	1. **1:15.666**	6
23. Heikki Kovalainen	FIN	McLaren MP4-23 05 - Mercedes [2]	2. 1:15.666	19	4. 1:15.990	37	1. 1:15.624	18	4. 1:15.476	5	3. 1:14.855	6	3. **1:16.143**	6

Fastest lap overall
L. Hamilton 1:14.603 (220,720 km/h)

Maximum speed

N° Driver	S1 Qualifs	Pos.	S1 Race	Pos.	S2 Qualifs	Pos.	S2 Race	Pos.	Finish Qualifs	Pos.	Finish Race	Pos.	Radar Qualifs	Pos.	Radar Race	Pos.
1. K. Räikkönen	215,6	6	214,8	4	265,7	2	263,4	4	271,9	3	269,1	4	318,6	2	318,6	4
2. F. Massa	214,6	7	215,2	3	265,2	3	263,9	3	272,6	2	270,6	1	319,2	1	319,1	1
3. N. Heidfeld	215,6	5	216,8	2	262,4	7	263,9	2	268,6	7	267,8	5	315,8	6	318,0	3
4. R. Kubica	215,8	4	213,8	7	262,9	6	261,8	7	269,0	6	267,4	7	316,4	4	316,5	10
5. F. Alonso	216,3	3	214,5	6	264,9	4	262,9	5	270,3	5	269,6	3	313,3	14	313,1	18
6. N. Piquet	213,1	13	213,7	8	262,0	9	261,3	10	268,3	9	267,4	8	312,7	15	312,6	20
7. N. Rosberg	212,3	16	210,3	18	260,3	17	260,1	12	266,7	14	265,1	15	316,2	5	318,7	3
8. K. Nakajima	213,5	10	212,3	10	258,9	19	259,6	14	265,5	19	266,0	10	313,4	12	317,2	8
9. D. Coulthard	213,8	9	211,0	14	261,9	11	259,4	16	268,4	8	265,5	13	313,3	13	314,5	14
10. M. Webber	211,1	19	209,3	20	260,4	16	259,1	18	266,9	12	266,1	9	310.7	19	314,3	15
11. J. Trulli	213,2	11	212,8	9	262,0	10	259,3	17	268,3	10	263,8	17	312,0	18	313,7	17
12. T. Glock	213,8	8	210,5	17	261,6	12	261,5	9	267,7	11	263,1	20	313,6	11	312,8	19
14. S. Bourdais	212,7	15	211,6	13	260,4	15	261,2	11	266,5	15	265,9	11	312,5	16	315,6	12
15. S. Vettel	211,8	18	211,8	12	262,0	8	261,8	8	266,2	16	265,6	12	313,8	10	316,9	9
16. J. Button	213,1	12	210,7	16	261,1	14	259,6	15	266,7	13	265,5	14	310,5	20	315,2	13
17. R. Barrichello	213,1	14	212,0	11	261,4	13	259,7	13	265,6	18	263,8	18	312,5	17	316,5	11
20. A. Sutil	211,9	17	211,0	15	258,8	20	257,8	19	265,6	17	263,9	16	316,8	3	317,7	6
21. G. Fisichella	210,6	20	210,2	19	259,3	18	257,6	20	265,4	20	263,7	19	314.0	9	317,3	7
22. L. Hamilton	216,5	2	217,1	1	264,3	5	265,3	1	272,6	1	270,1	2	315,2	8	318,9	2
23. H. Kovalainen	217,4	1	214,6	5	265,8	1	261,8	6	270,9	3	267,7	6	315,6	7	314,3	16

Best sector times

Qualifs	**S1** L. Hamilton	16.276	**S2** L. Hamilton	35.669	**S3** L. Hamilton	22.615	= 1:14.056
Race	**S1** N. Heidfeld	16.578	**S2** L. Hamilton	36.118	**S3** L. Hamilton	23.068	= 1:15.756

RACE

Date	Weather	Air temperature	Track temperature	Humidity	Wind speed
Sunday July 20, 2008 (14:00)	Some clouds	23-25°c	27-29°c	40-37%	5.4 m/s

Classification & retirements

Pos.	Driver	Constructor	Tyres	Laps	Time	Km/h
1.	L. Hamilton	McLaren Mercedes	HHM	67	1:31:203.874	201,290
2.	N. Piquet	Renault	HM	67	+ 5.586	201,085
3.	F. Massa	Ferrari	HMH	67	+ 9.339	200,948
4.	N. Heidfeld	BMW	MMH	67	+ 9.825	200,930
5.	H. Kovalainen	McLaren Mercedes	HHM	67	+ 12.411	200,835
6.	K. Räikkönen	Ferrari	HMM	67	+ 14.483	200,760
7.	R. Kubica	BMW	MMH	67	+ 22.603	200,463
8.	S. Vettel	STR Ferrari	MMH	67	+ 33.282	200,075
9.	J. Trulli	Toyota	MMH	67	+ 37.199	199,933
10.	N. Rosberg	Williams Toyota	MMH	67	+ 37.658	199,917
11.	F. Alonso	Renault	HMH	67	+ 38.625	199,882
12.	S. Bourdais	STR Ferrari	HMH	67	+ 39.111	199,864
13.	D. Coulthard	Red Bull Renault	MMH	67	+ 54.971	199,291
14.	K. Nakajima	Williams Toyota	MMH	67	+ 1:00.003	199,110
15.	A. Sutil	Force India	HHM	67	+ 1:09.488	198,770
16.	G. Fisichella	Force India	HMM	67	+ *1:24.093	198,248
17.	J. Button	Honda	MHMM	66	1 lap	196,834

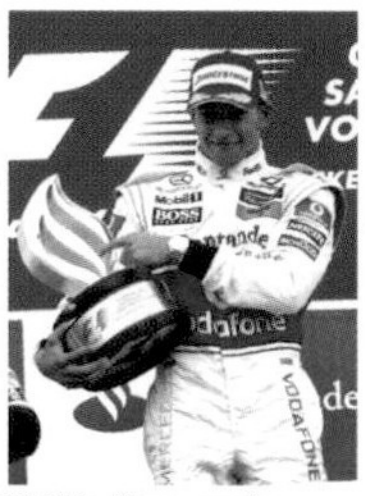

*59.093 + 25 sec. penalty

Driver	Constructor	Tyres	Laps	Reason
R. Barrichello	Honda	MMH	50	Contact with Coulthard
M. Webber	Red Bull Renault	MMH	40	Oil radiator damaged by debris from Glock's crash
T. Glock	Toyota	MM	35	Right rear suspension failure, hit pit wall hard

Tyres H: Hard & M: Medium

Fastest laps

	Driver	Time	Lap	Km/h
1.	N. Heidfeld	1:15.987	52	216,700
2.	L. Hamilton	1:16.039	17	216,552
3.	K. Räikkönen	1:16.342	66	215,692
4.	H. Kovalainen	1:16.495	63	215,261
5.	F. Massa	1:16.502	19	215,241
6.	R. Kubica	1:16.610	17	214,937
7.	T. Glock	1:16.712	24	214,652
8.	S. Vettel	1:16.772	20	214,484
9.	N. Piquet	1:16.910	66	214,099
10.	S. Bourdais	1:16.969	63	213,935
11.	D. Coulthard	1:16.994	18	213,866
12.	J. Trulli	1:17.023	17	213,785
13.	F. Alonso	1:17.115	17	213,530
14.	M. Webber	1:17.206	20	213,278
15.	N. Rosberg	1:17.380	34	212,799
16.	J. Button	1:17.636	56	212,097
17.	K. Nakajima	1:17.691	23	211,947
18.	A. Sutil	1:17.889	66	211,408
19.	R. Barrichello	1:17.986	30	211,145
20.	G. Fisichella	1:18.208	67	210,546

Pit stops

	Driver	Lap	Duration	Stop	Total
1.	S. Vettel	21	24.893	1	24.893
2.	D. Coulthard	21	25.247	1	25.247
3.	K. Räikkönen	22	24.352	1	24.352
4.	M. Webber	23	24.769	1	24.769
5.	S. Bourdais	23	24.841	1	24.841
6.	A. Sutil	25	24.655	1	24.655
7.	N. Heidfeld	27	24.602	1	24.603
8.	J. Button	27	25.145	1	25.145
9.	G. Fisichella	27	22.850	1	22.850
10.	N. Rosberg	28	24.015	1	24.015
11.	T. Glock	29	24.490	1	24.490
12.	K. Nakajima	29	24.011	1	24.011
13.	R. Barrichello	31	24.069	1	24.069
14.	N. Piquet	35	28.375	1	28.375
15.	J. Button	35	24.327	2	49.472
16.	F. Massa	38	25.622	1	25.622
17.	G. Fisichella	37	25.896	2	48.746
18.	R. Kubica	38	24.419	1	24.419
19.	J. Trulli	38	25.043	1	25.043
20.	S. Vettel	38	24.639	2	49.532
21.	F. Alonso	38	24.270	1	24.270
22.	M. Webber	38	24.919	2	49.688
23.	D. Coulthard	38	36.101	2	1:01.348
24.	S. Bourdais	38	33.428	2	58.269
25.	N. Rosberg	38	29.361	2	53.376
26.	A. Sutil	39	24.986	2	49.641
27.	K. Nakajima40	40	23.280	2	47.291
28.	R. Barrichello	49	34.314	2	58.383
29.	L. Hamilton	50	22.952	1	22.952
30.	N. Heidfeld	53	22.263	2	46.865
31.	J. Button	54	23.000	3	1:12.472

*25 seconds time penalty for having unlapped himself under safety car.

Race leader

Driver	Laps in the lead	Nbr of laps
L. Hamilton	1 > 18	18
F. Massa	19 > 20	2
H. Kovalainen	21	1
L. Hamilton	22 > 37	16
F. Massa	38	1
L. Hamilton	39 > 50	12
N. Heidfeld	51 > 53	3
N. Piquet	54 > 59	6
L. Hamilton	60 > 67	8

Driver	Nbr of laps	Kilometers
L. Hamilton	54	246,996 km
N. Piquet	6	27,444 km
F. Massa	3	13,722 km
N. Heidfeld	3	13,722 km
H. Kovalainen	1	4,574 km

Gaps on the lead board

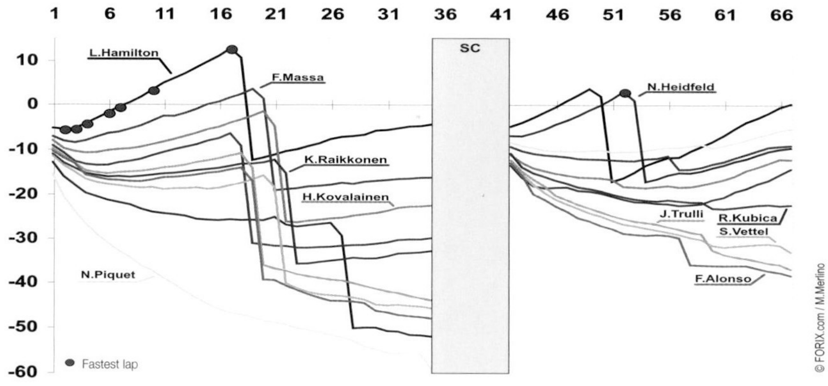
1
6
11
16
21
26
31
36
41
46
51
56
61
66
10
0
-10
-20
-30
-40
-50
-60
SC
L.Hamilton
F.Massa
K.Raikkonen
H.Kovalainen
N.Piquet
N.Heidfeld
J.Trulli
R.Kubica
S.Vettel
F.Alonso
Fastest lap
© FORIX.com / M.Merlino

Lap chart

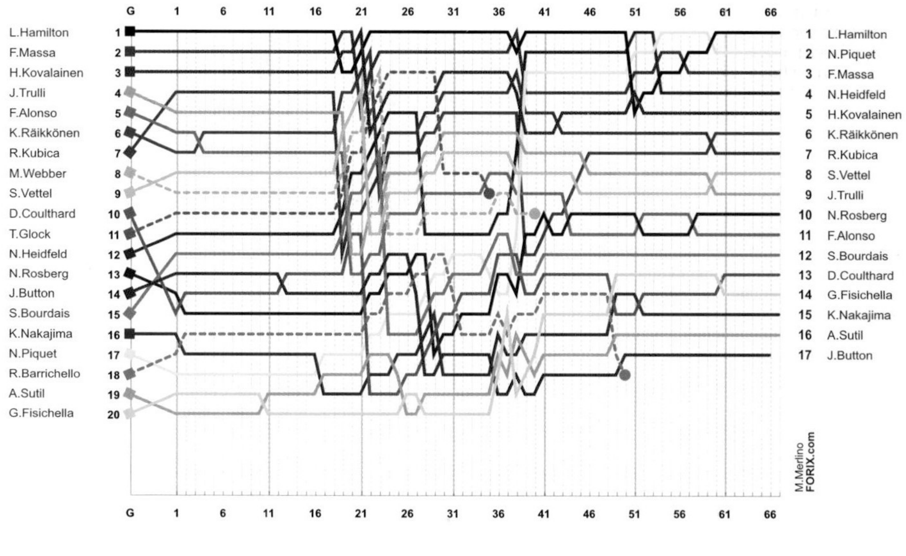
G
1
6
11
16
21
26
31
36
41
46
51
56
61
66
L.Hamilton 1
F.Massa 2
H.Kovalainen 3
J.Trulli 4
F.Alonso 5
K.Räikkönen 6
R.Kubica 7
M.Webber 8
S.Vettel 9
D.Coulthard 10
T.Glock 11
N.Heidfeld 12
N.Rosberg 13
J.Button 14
S.Bourdais 15
K.Nakajima 16
N.Piquet 17
R.Barrichello 18
A.Sutil 19
G.Fisichella 20
1 L.Hamilton
2 N.Piquet
3 F.Massa
4 N.Heidfeld
5 H.Kovalainen
6 K.Räikkönen
7 R.Kubica
8 S.Vettel
9 J.Trulli
10 N.Rosberg
11 F.Alonso
12 S.Bourdais
13 D.Coulthard
14 G.Fisichella
15 K.Nakajima
16 A.Sutil
17 J.Button
M.Merlino
FORIX.com

CHAMPIONSHIPS 10/18

Drivers

	Driver	Constructor	Wins	Points
1.	L. Hamilton	McLaren Mercedes	4	58
2.	F. Massa	Ferrari	3	54
3.	K. Räikkönen	Ferrari	2	51
4.	R. Kubica	BMW	1	48
5.	N. Heidfeld	BMW		41
6.	H. Kovalainen	McLaren Mercedes		28
7.	J. Trulli	Toyota		20
8.	M. Webber	Red Bull Renault		18
9.	F. Alonso	Renault		13
10.	R. Barrichello	Honda		11
11.	N. Piquet	Renault		10
12.	N. Rosberg	Williams Toyota		8
13.	K. Nakajima	Williams Toyota		8.
14.	D. Coulthard	Red Bull Renault		6.
15.	S. Vettel	STR Ferrari		6
16.	T. Glock	Toyota		5
17.	J. Button	Honda		3
18.	S. Bourdais	STR Ferrari		2
19.	G. Fisichella	Force India		0
20.	T. Sato	Super Aguri Honda		0
21.	A. Davidson	Super Aguri Honda		0
22.	A. Sutil	Force India		0

Constructors

	Constructor	Wins	Points
1.	Scuderia Ferrari Marlboro	5	105
2.	BMW Sauber F1 Team	1	89
3.	Vodafone McLaren Mercedes	4	86
4.	Panasonic Toyota Racing		25
5.	Red Bull Racing		24
6.	ING Renault F1 Team		23
7.	AT&T Williams		16
8.	Honda Racing F1 Team		14
9.	Scuderia Torro Rosso		8
10.	Force India F1 Team		0
11.	Super Aguri F1 Team		0

THE CIRCUIT

Name Hockenheimring; Hockenheim
Lenght 4574 m
Distance 67 laps, 306,458 km
Latitude 49°19'40.00"N
Longitude 8°33'57.00"E

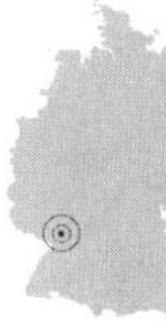

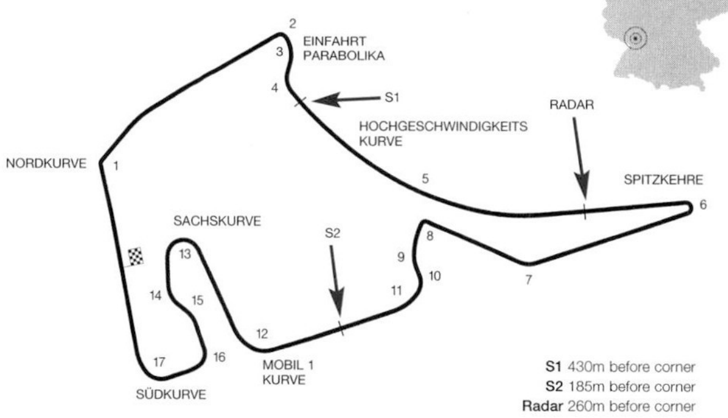
EINFAHRT PARABOLIKA
S1
HOCHGESCHWINDIGKEITS KURVE
RADAR
NORDKURVE
SPITZKEHRE
SACHSKURVE
S2
MOBIL 1 KURVE
SÜDKURVE
1
2
3
4
5
6
7
8
9
10
11
12
13
14
15
16
17

S1 430m before corner
S2 185m before corner
Radar 260m before corner

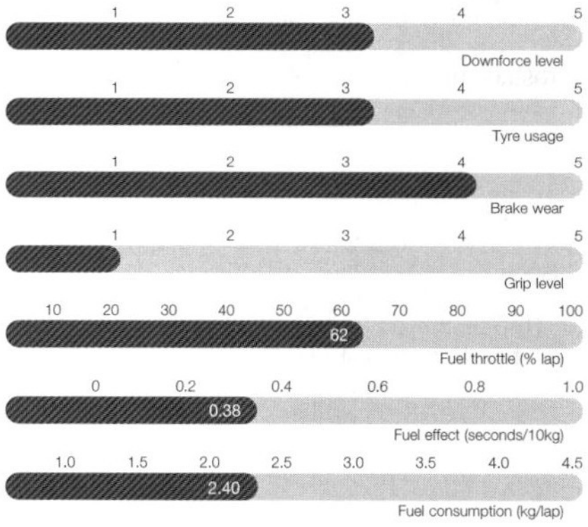
1 2 3 4 5
Downforce level
1 2 3 4 5
Tyre usage
1 2 3 4 5
Brake wear
1 2 3 4 5
Grip level
10 20 30 40 50 60 70 80 90 100
62
Fuel throttle (% lap)
0 0.2 0.4 0.6 0.8 1.0
0.38
Fuel effect (seconds/10kg)
1.0 1.5 2.0 2.5 3.0 3.5 4.0 4.5
2.40
Fuel consumption (kg/lap)

HEIKKI IN
SEVENTH HEAVEN

Teammate Lewis Hamilton slowed by a puncture, Felipe Massa's hopes dashed by a blown engine: Heikki Kovalainen saw bad luck sideline his rivals, but he still had to be in the right place at the right time. And Kovalainen duly was, picking up the first win of his F1 career. In his wake, no points for Massa, though Hamilton picked up four for fifth to limit the damage. He would need them by season's end…

> Dust, nothing but dust on the Hungaroring. Nestling in the countryside to the north of Budapest, the track often has a layer of the local sand on it - but that didn't stop Lewis Hamilton taking his fourth pole of the year and his second in a row since Hockenheim.

Lewis looking for a hat-trick - and a knock-out blow

At season's start the Ferrari was clearly the car to beat. On fast circuits in Malaysia, Bahrain, Spain and Turkey no-one could come close to performances based on a blend of road-holding and stability.

But since late May the wheel of fortune seemed to have turned the McLaren MP4-23's way. Hamilton had flourished in the wet to win at Silverstone, but it was the car itself that took him to victory in Germany a fortnight before the Hungarian event.

And this weekend a new McLaren-Mercedes aerodynamic package was making the cars stronger than ever. On Saturday Hamilton and

Budapest has been a regular staging-post on the F1 calendar since 1986, in the days of the Iron Curtain. The city centre has changed a lot since then but remains a firm favourite with F1 folk.
∨

Kovalainen simply got on with it and monopolised the front row of the grid.

On a circuit where passing can be as tricky as in Monaco, that was virtually game over for the McLaren team. *"Things are looking good this weekend,"* Hamilton agreed. *"The team have done a fantastic job with the car. And speaking personally, I don't think I've ever enjoyed a better time. I feel right on top of things, both professionally and in my personal life. But I know I can still do better, and that's my goal from now on."*

There was no panic at Ferrari, though. *"We weren't very strong in Germany, or yesterday,"*

said third-fastest qualifier Felipe Massa. *"But since this morning's practice things seem to be really improving. For the first two phases of qualifying I was on the McLarens' pace, and I think I can give them a hard time in the race."*

Kimi Räikkönen in the second Ferrari was finding life a little harder. The World Champion was sixth on the grid and apparently not in the hunt: *"This is not an easy time, but we just have to get through it,"* he said reassuringly. *"I made a mistake on my quick lap, that's why I'm so far back. The good results will start coming again soon."* But too late, maybe, for his Championship chances?

IN BRIEF...

+ *"No more excuses: now he needs to start getting some results."* Sébastien Bourdais was in the hot seat at Toro Rosso, it seemed, if team boss Gerhard Berger's words were anything to go by.

+ Fifth on the grid was Timo Glock's best qualifying effort of the season - but there was disappointment at Toyota. *"We're a bit dismayed,"* said technical director Pascal Vasselon, *"because Timo did his time on worn tyres and should have been half a second quicker at least on new ones. We expected to see him on the front row."*

+ Currently living at Mont-sur-Rolle above Lake Geneva, in Switzerland, Fernando Alonso was apparently looking for a new home in Ticino, in the Italian-speaking part of the country, to be closer to Maranello should the need arise. Rumour had it that the Spaniard was in talks with Ferrari and the

Italian team, for whom Kimi Räikkönen had seemed detuned since the onset of summer, were getting ready to announce his early retirement.

+ F1 commercial rights-holder Bernie Ecclestone and Hungary's sports minister Istvan Gyenesei announced on Saturday that the Hungarian GP's contract had been extended by a further five years to 2016.

+ A 53-year-old engineer, William Millar, took his own life on Wednesday in the Renault team's factory at Enstone in England.
The F1 fanatic had joined the team at 27 in 1981, when it was still known as Toleman, and was in charge of research and development. The enormous pressure on engineers was cited as the reason for the tragic incident, the first of its kind in F1 history.

STARTING GRID

* S. BOURDAIS relegated of 5 positions for having blocking HEIDFELD in his fast lap on Q1.

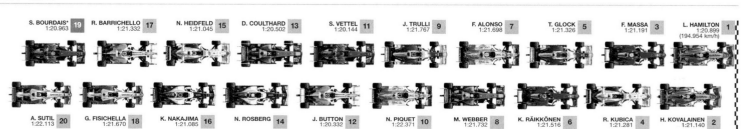

Pos	Driver	Time
19	S. BOURDAIS*	1:20.963
17	R. BARRICHELLO	1:21.332
15	N. HEIDFELD	1:21.045
13	D. COULTHARD	1:20.502
11	S. VETTEL	1:20.144
9	J. TRULLI	1:21.767
7	F. ALONSO	1:21.698
5	T. GLOCK	1:21.326
3	F. MASSA	1:21.191
1	L. HAMILTON	1:20.899 (194.954 km/h)
20	A. SUTIL	1:22.113
18	G. FISICHELLA	1:21.670
16	K. NAKAJIMA	1:21.085
14	N. ROSBERG	
12	J. BUTTON	1:20.332
10	N. PIQUET	1:22.371
8	M. WEBBER	1:21.732
6	K. RÄIKKÖNEN	1:21.516
4	R. KUBICA	1:21.281
2	H. KOVALAINEN	1:21.140

Heikki inherits win as Lewis blows out and Felipe blows up

The sign of a good team is being able to cope with unusual circumstances. If one driver has a problem, his teammate has to be able to step into the breech. That's exactly how McLaren handled things in Budapest. With both cars on the front row, the British team were expecting podium places as well. At the start, though,

Felipe Massa astonished everyone with the way he took the lead on the first corner. Rocketing away from the second row, the Brazilian caught Hamilton out by going the long way round. "*On Saturday we went through all the possible scenarios for the first corner,*" Massa explained, "*and attacking round the outside was the one*

we thought might work."
Settling into the lead, the Ferrari man then controlled the race, helped when Hamilton, running a few seconds behind, suffered a deflating front left tyre at the start of lap 41. Limping back to the pits, he could only manage fifth at the finish. "*I think I could have had a go at passing Felipe in the closing stages,*" was all Hamilton said after the race as the Bridgestone engineers tried to fathom out what had gone wrong.
Up front Massa was cruising serenely to victory when his engine went up in smoke just three laps from the chequered flag.
That left a delighted Heikki Kovalainen to reap the reward for playing a waiting game with the first win of his F1 career.
For Ferrari, Räikkönen spent most of his race stuck behind Fernando Alonso, but got the Spaniard's Renault out of the way in the second round of stops and was closing in on Timo Glock's Toyota before slowing dramatically to avoid possible suspension failure.
McLaren may not have managed to take Hamilton to the race win, but their number two driver was on hand to step in.
The sign of a great team...

Domenicali hints at new approach

Although the Scuderia Ferrari cars only qualified on the second and third rows, they would have won the Hungarian Grand Prix but for Felipe Massa's engine blow-up just three short laps from the end.
"*I think today showed the quality of our team, our drivers and our engineers,*" said Stefano Domenicali after the race. "*We were very competitive - I think Felipe drove the best race of his career. He made an outstanding start, he controlled every stage of the race and he was cruising to what would have been a wonderful win. Unfortunately our reliability let us down. With Kimi's car we were worried about a suspension problem, and asked him to slow down towards the finish. But before that,*

once he got Alonso out of the way, Kimi was the quickest man on the track."
The lack of reliability was a mystery. "*We will have to analyse what happened very carefully,*" added Domenicali. "*I can assure you we will react the way we know best, working together wth determination and tenacity.*"
It was all about approaching the Grand Prix weekend in a different way: "*We need to change our approach to race weekends. We realise that where you are on the grid is absolutely fundamental, so we will be doing what we can to avoid qualifying sixth, as Kimi did here. And that means we will be changing the way we go into race weekends.*"

VALENCIA ASPIRES TO BE THE MONACO OF SPAIN

The contract with the town of Valencia had been signed a year earlier. The city was looking to exploit the marina built to accommodate the 2007 Americas Cup (centre of photo,) and they decided on staging a Grand Prix.
It was an onerous task, but it ended up as a qualified success. The weather was good, but the race turned out to be very dull. Despite a track layout that appeared to offer the excitement of overtaking, the dust that is a permanent feature of Valencia, meant the drivers daren't put a wheel off the racing line. Starting from pole position, Felipe Massa won it comfortably from Lewis Hamilton and Robert Kubica and if proof was needed that it was a monotonous affair, the top three finishers were the top three starters off the grid.

> Sun, sea and big yachts: Valencia had all the elements to seduce the world of Formula 1. But not the drivers, who complained of an insipid track, which they regarded as just one long tunnel lined with concrete walls. Robert Kubica (photo) set the third fastest time in qualifying.

Too soon forgotten, Felipe gets his revenge

At first, the little world of Formula 1 praised the Valencia circuit, acknowledging the effort involved in producing a circuit around the Americas Cup port. But that first wave of enthusiasm soon

Valencia: rough edges to smooth

Those in charge of safety at the Valencia circuit spent a bad night on Friday, because of the teething troubles that affected the first day of practice. In the morning, several spectators were calmly leaning on a concrete wall alongside the track, without anyone telling them to move on. In the afternoon, one of them climbed over the wall onto the track, just a few metres from the passing cars.

> Felipe Massa down the main straight (in fact a long curve.) Pole position awaits.

There were several off track moments too that day, most notably in GP2, when practice had to be stopped twice, as the marshals were clearly incapable of removing stricken cars. This also highlighted the lack of cranes: with the track surrounded by concrete blocks with fencing on top, cranes were essential to clear the narrow track, and there just weren't enough of them.

Comments from the drivers however were generally positive, even if they couldn't see much of the décor with those concrete walls. "*It could do with some high speed corners,*" regretted Robert Kubica. "*The designers tried to include some, but in fact, they're all completely flat, which means the circuit involves just some heavy braking and acceleration...*"

passed and criticism began to rain down, especially from the drivers. The main complaint was the same fault raised by the Alinghi management when the town was selected as the venue for the 33rd Americas Cup: the Valencia port is very dusty.

The problem is caused chiefly by the commercial port situated alongside the circuit. On Thursday for example, the organisers put the finishing touches to painting blue and white highlights on a parking zone. On Friday, the colours had practically disappeared under a layer of white dust.

This meant the racing line was the only clean thing about the circuit, which made any attempted overtaking move very risky. "*Looking at a plan of the circuit, it seems as though there are several*

opportunities to overtake," explained Robert Kubica, who qualified third in the BMW-Sauber. "*But in fact, it will be very difficult because of the dust off line.*" These conditions gave qualifying an added importance and therefore, Felipe Massa was especially pleased to have taken pole position, three weeks after the disappointment of Hungary. "*When you have the race won and you retire with a technical problem, it's really hard. In these situations, you would like to immediately do another race to forget your disappointment, but I had to wait three weeks. I tried to turn my frustration into motivation, but it wasn't easy.*" Alongside him on the grid, Lewis Hamilton would be trying to get his revenge for that first corner in Hungary, where he was passed by the very same Felipe Massa.

STARTING GRID

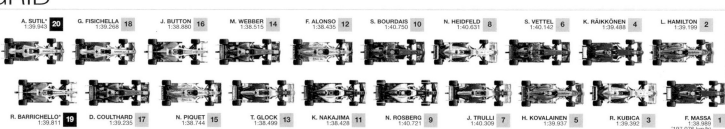

* R. BARRICHELLO
starts from the pit lane.

A. SUTIL
modification on his gearbox, starts from the pit lane.

| A. SUTIL* 1:39.943 **20** | G. FISICHELLA 1:39.268 **18** | J. BUTTON 1:38.880 **16** | M. WEBBER 1:38.515 **14** | F. ALONSO 1:38.435 **12** | S. BOURDAIS 1:40.750 **10** | N. HEIDFELD 1:40.631 **8** | S. VETTEL 1:40.142 **6** | K. RÄIKKÖNEN 1:39.488 **4** | L. HAMILTON 1:39.199 **2** |

| R. BARRICHELLO* 1:39.811 **19** | D. COULTHARD 1:39.235 **17** | N. PIQUET 1:38.744 **15** | T. GLOCK 1:38.499 **13** | K. NAKAJIMA 1:38.428 **11** | N. ROSBERG 1:40.721 **9** | J. TRULLI 1:40.309 **7** | H. KOVALAINEN 1:39.937 **5** | R. KUBICA 1:39.392 **3** | F. MASSA 1:38.989 **1** (197.076 km/h) |

Felipe laughs, Kimi cries, Ferraris is worried…

The Ferrari garage was bubbling over with excitement at the end of the Valencia Grand Prix. On one side, the mechanics were clapping one another on the back, congratulating themselves over Felipe Massa's faultless performance.

On the other side, Kimi Raikkonen's race engineer and the engine specialists were asking themselves about the mysterious ills that reduced the Finn's efforts to nothing.

And in another corner, the photographers were falling over themselves, trying to organise a souvenir photo of the Brazilian's one hundredth Grand Prix (see above.) The tableau was a fair representation of the levels of performance within the Italian team at the European Grand Prix. No one could argue with Massa's win, but two refuelling errors nearly cost them dear, while Kimi Raikkonen's engine went up in smoke on lap 45.

For Ferrari, the explosion of the Finn's V8 was nevertheless a less bitter pill to swallow than the failure suffered by Massa in Budapest. Because, while it happened to the Brazilian just 3 laps from certain victory, Raikkonen was only sixth, having dropped two places at his second pit stop, after ignoring the red lights holding him in the pits. "*It was my fault,*" he admitted later.

In the constructors' classification, Ferrari's lead over McLaren was now down to 8 points. With six Grand Prix to go, the fight between the two teams looked like being a titanic struggle. "*Today, we have to salute an amazing performance from Felipe Massa, who delivered us a photocopy of his Budapest performance and brought home the win,*" analysed Scuderia Ferrari team manager, Luca Baldisserri. "*It's very encouraging, although on the other hand, we were not reliable enough, both technically and operationally. Initial investigation suggests that Kimi's engine failure is down to the same fault that caused Felipe's to break in Hungary. Today, we have stupidly thrown away some points and we will have to sort out our problems in the next few days.*"

The very next day, the Scuderia was at Monza for four days of testing. Engine reliability was a major feature on the job list.

Sleepless nights at Ferrari

After Felipe Massa's engine failed in Hungary, here, it was Kimi Raikkonen's power plant that let go and the team did not know why. "*We will investigate the causes of these engine problems and we will find them,*" insisted Stefano Domenicali. "*It's a painful situation, because the championship is very close. It weighs heavily on us and we're not sleeping well. The end of the season will be very tough. But you can expect to see a more aggressive Scuderia Ferrari. We will work flat out right up to the final kilometre of the season, just as we did in 2007 to take the title.*"

The Scuderia had suffered an additional problem: Kimi Raikkonen drove away too early from his pit stop. Ferrari was the only team to use a traffic light system to release its drivers, and some people criticised its complexity. "*To be honest, I don't think it's that complicated,*" continued Domenicali. "*When the fuel line is locked onto the car, it's red. When the refuelling is almost complete, it flashes orange to warn the driver to get ready to go and when the line is disconnected it turns green, unless the chief mechanic wants to hold the driver, because another car is coming past in pit lane. In this instance, Kimi left when it was on red.*"

The same Kimi that some pundits reckoned had lost his motivation. "*That's absolutely not the case! It's too easy to pat a driver on the back when everything's going well and to accuse him of being demotivated when the results don't* come. *That's not how we operate at Ferrari. We are a team and we have total confidence in Kimi. We have no doubts about his motivation or his performance. Believe me, he will fight back!*"

<
Lap 45: having been sixth, Kimi Raikkonen retires and has one last lock at his car after his engine broke. Sombre times for the Scuderia.

CRAZY CLOSING LAPS

Lewis Hamilton had spent the entire race behind Kimi Raikkonen. With a few minutes to go before the finish, the rain began to fall and the Englishman tried to make the most of the conditions to pass the Finn.

It was an epic duel that finished with a penalty for the McLaren man and a crash into the barriers for the Ferrari driver.

Just behind them, Felipe Massa salvaged something, while Sebastien Bourdais, who had been running third with one lap to go, missed the chance of a lifetime and finished seventh. It was a chaotic, crazy, unbelievable and memorable end to the race. Who had won the race was only decided several days after it was over and the championship fight was now even closer than ever.

> Felipe Massa put up a good fight, but he could not beat Lewis Hamilton to pole position, even if the Spa-Francorchamps rollercoaster seemed well suited to the Ferrari chassis.

Lewis Hamilton and Felipe Massa recreate the battle of the Ardennes

The Spa-Francorchamps rollercoaster is the longest track on the calendar, at 7.004 kilometres. This made the fact that Saturday's qualifying times were so close, even more impressive. In order to get into Q3, the highpoint of qualifying for the top ten drivers, one had to do a time within just eight tenths of the best time.

At the end of the session, Lewis Hamilton found himself back in pole position, confirming the optimism he displayed when he arrived in Spa. "It's fantastic," he confirmed later. "It was a

wonderful day and the four laps I did this afternoon were perfect. This circuit is super when you manage to string together all the corners absolutely on the limit, just like you see it in your head before going out. I am so happy to be in front. I can't stop smiling."

In second place, Felipe Massa was despondent at not having been able to beat his rival, as he had done in Valencia. "*My last lap was almost perfect, but it wasn't enough,*" said the Brazilian, regretfully. "*Sometimes you pull off a fantastic lap and it's still not enough. Having said that,*

these guys (the McLaren drivers. Ed.) did a better job than us today and we must try and work out why, especially as our car is working fine and is well balanced."

The forecast predicted rain for the race, which risked affecting the outcome. "*I'll adapt to any circumstances,*" insisted Hamilton. "*But driving in the rain here is very difficult. Without traction control, it will be a real challenge, especially with the white lines along the side of the track, which are very slippery. I'll do my best.*"

> They know how to put on a leaving do at Sauber: having been part of the team since its Formula 1 debut in 1993, one of the mechanics was leaving.

IN BRIEF

+ Nick Heidfeld was in danger of losing his seat for 2009 if he didn't produce some good results and here, the German equalled his best qualifying results of the year, with those in Melbourne and Silverstone. Fifth on the grid, it was only the second time the German had out-qualified his team-mate, Robert Kubica. Which only goes to show that threats can sometimes work wonders. "*We will struggle to be on the pace tomorrow,*" he commented. "*But all the same, I think we are a bit closer to the McLarens and Ferraris here.*"

+ Also under pressure, for the first time in his F1 career, Sebastien Bourdais set the fastest time in the first qualifying session.

"*I ought to take a photo of the timing screen with my name on top,*" joked the Frenchman, who finally ended up ninth on the grid. It was a timely showing, given it was rumoured that the Toro Rosso management might replace him for the rest of the season.

+ Although the Japanese team seemed ever more competitive this season, neither Toyota driver managed to get into Q3. Jarno Trulli started from eleventh place, one row ahead of team-mate, Timo Glock. "*We are very disappointed,*" confirmed technical director, Pascal Vasselon. "*We are really struggling to get our tyres up to temperature in this cold weather.*"

STARTING GRID

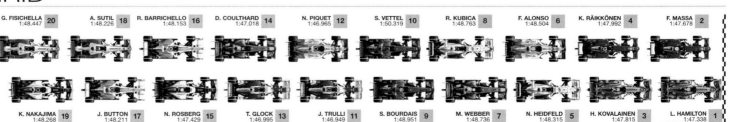

G. FISICHELLA 1:48.447 **20**	A. SUTIL 1:48.226 **18**	R. BARRICHELLO 1:48.153 **16**	D. COULTHARD 1:47.018 **14**	N. PIQUET 1:46.965 **12**	S. VETTEL 1:50.319 **10**	R. KUBICA 1:48.763 **8**	F. ALONSO 1:48.504 **6**	K. RÄIKKÖNEN 1:47.992 **4**	F. MASSA 1:47.678 **2**
K. NAKAJIMA 1:48.268 **19**	J. BUTTON 1:48.211 **17**	N. ROSBERG 1:47.429 **15**	T. GLOCK 1:46.995 **13**	J. TRULLI 1:46.949 **11**	S. BOURDAIS 1:48.951 **9**	M. WEBBER 1:48.736 **7**	N. HEIDFELD 1:48.315 **5**	H. KOVALAINEN 1:47.815 **3**	L. HAMILTON 1:47.338 (234.906 km/h) **1**

Two chaotic laps bring a fantastic Belgian Grand Prix to an end

It had rained an hour before the race and the track was still very damp when the drivers set off to start the Belgian Grand Prix.

When Lewis Hamilton, who had got away in the lead, slid wide, Kimi Raikkonen helped himself to the lead on lap 2 and kept it until the 43rd and penultimate lap. That's when the rain returned to the Francorchamps region and confusion reigned for the last two laps. A summary:

- At the head of the field, Lewis Hamilton charges up behind Kimi Raikkonen. A first attack at the last chicane fails, with the Finn keeping his line, as the Englishman ends up cutting the chicane to go ahead. As one is not allowed to overtake in this fashion, Hamilton lifts off and allows the Ferrari to re-pass him.

- A few hundred metres further on, braking for the "La Source" hairpin, Hamilton finally manages to move into the lead. Caught out by the rain, both he and Raikkonen go off the track at Pouhon, but get back on track.

- At the next corner, a Williams in trouble forces Hamilton to pass going on the grass and Raikkonen is back in front.

- Not long after, the Finn gets into a slide and Hamilton now leads. In his haste, the Finn finally crashes his Ferrari into the barriers, just before the start of the last lap.

- Hamilton crosses the finish line as the winner, while Felipe Massa is second, having given away nine seconds in the final lap to the McLaren man. "*I had no reason to take any risks,*" explained the Brazilian. "*I preferred to make sure of a good finish.*"

- At 18h00, the Stewards announced that Lewis Hamilton had been given a drive-through penalty for having cut the final corner and benefited from so doing, thus contravening article 30.3 (a) of the Formula 1 Sporting Regulations. 25 seconds were therefore added to his finish time, which relegated the Englishman to third place.

- One week before the Italian Grand Prix, the Steward's decision opened up the championship fight once again, as it meant that Felipe Massa was now just two points behind Lewis Hamilton, having actually been eight adrift as they took the chequered flag in Spa.

- On Sunday night, the McLaren team said it planned to appeal against the race result, explaining that its telemetry data showed that its driver was travelling 6 km/h slower than Raikkonen as he crossed the line after the incident. The appeal had little chance of succeeding. The FIA sporting code, article 1.5.2, states that drive through penalties cannot be the subject of an appeal.

Bourdais, one lap from happiness

^
Sebastien Bourdais charges through the rain. The Frenchman lost 4 places on the final lap, dropping from third to seventh place.

Sebastien Bourdais was close to tears at the finish and with good reason. One lap from the chequered flag, the Frenchman was lying a miraculous third and hoped to make it to the podium.

However, seven kilometres later, he crossed the line in seventh place, overtaken by Heidfeld, Alonso, Vettel and Kubica! Nick Heidfeld completed that last lap 19 seconds quicker than the Frenchman and Bourdais

had missed a great opportunity to impress his bosses at a time when he was fighting for his 2009 race seat. *"The good result was so close, I could almost touch it. How frustrating,"* he moaned. *"That last lap was a real lottery, with the car sliding with every movement on the steering wheel. It was horrible because everything had been under total control up until then. Having said that, I wasn't in a position to*

risk losing everything at the end of a race. As I took the chequered flag, I didn't even know where I'd finished."
Sebastian Vettel had passed his team-mate on the last lap, before being passed in turn by Nick Heidfeld and Fernando Alonso in the final metres of the race. *"They were on intermediates and they came past me like lightning,"* lamented the German.

Lewis Hamilton penalised two hours after the race

After an epic struggle with the elements, it was Lewis Hamilton who stood on the top step of the podium. Two hours later he was moved back to third. In the rain, the Englishman had proved he was the strongest and this fifth win of the season seemed more than well deserved.
The Spa Stewards decided otherwise. Judging that the McLaren driver had gained an advantage when went across the grass - and truth be told, he did gain a small advantage, coming out of the chicane glued to Kimi Raikkonen's rear wing, which would not have

been the case if he'd taken the corner conventionally - they penalised him. It seemed rather harsh, given that Hamilton finally got past Raikkonen at the corner after the one where he went off the track and that the Englishman was so much quicker than the Finn, that he would in any case have passed him a bit further on.
Lewis Hamilton was gutted when he heard the news. *"Kimi pushed me off the track! He could have shown a bit more fair play, because I had nowhere to go and had to go off the track so as*

not to crash into him. He braked very early at that point, I found myself ahead and so I gained no advantage from this. Honestly, penalising me for this shows something's not quite right. It's totally unjust."
An injustice against which McLaren announced it would appeal. The legal case was not looking favourable for the English team.
Lewis Hamilton would have to find it in him and fight against Felipe Massa with a lead now reduced to just two little points, with five Grands Prix remaining.

Lewis is sure of himself

>
He led 37 of the 44 laps, but it was not enough: Kimi Raikkonen finished the Belgian Grand Prix in the barriers.
"On the soft tyres, the car worked very well, but when the rain came it didn't help me. When you are in front, you never know what the grip level will be, which is why Lewis caught me in a few kilometres. After that, everyone saw what happened."

Lewis Hamilton missed out on the 2007 title by two little points in his very first season in Formula 1.
This year, the youngster was determined not to let the crown be whisked away from him a second time. Going into the Belgian Grand Prix, with six races remaining, he had a six point lead over Felipe Massa and thirteen over Kimi Raikkonen. It was a small advantage, but it still made him favourite, bolstered by the fact he felt his McLaren would have the edge over the Ferraris in the final part of the season. *"I think we have the advantage,"* confided Hamilton. *The Ferraris might be slightly quicker at circuits with long straights, like Monza, but overall, we should be better."*
Spa is the archetypal long corner circuit, where a well balanced chassis is vital. In 2007, the Scuderia's cars had finished an undisputed first and second. *"Last year, we couldn't do anything about the Ferraris, but this year, we have made a big step forward."* Elsewhere, if Hamilton was to be believed, everything should go well. *"The Ferraris might be quick in Singapore, as it's a bit similar to Valencia. But, at other tracks, Mount Fuji and Shanghai, we should have the upper hand."*

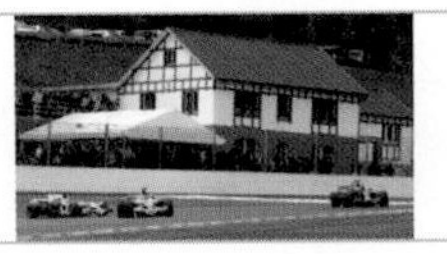

PRACTICE

Date	Weather (AM)	Air temperature	Track temperature	Weather (PM)	Air temperature	Track temperature
Friday September 5, 2008	Cloudy	14-16°c	15-16°c	Cloudy, drizzle	16-18°c	17-18°c
Saturday September 6, 2008	Rainy	16-17°c	16-17°c	Cloudy	17°c	18-19°c

All the time trials

N° Driver	Nat.	N° Chassis- Engine [Nbr. GP]	Pos. Free 1 Friday 10:00-11:30	Laps	Pos. Free 2 Friday 14:00-15:30	Laps	Pos. Free 3 Saturday 11:00-12:00	Laps	Pos. Q1 Saturday 14:00-14:20	Laps	Pos. Q2 Saturday 14:27-14:42	Laps	Pos. Q3 Saturday 14:50-15:00	Laps
1. Kimi Räikkönen	FIN	Ferrari F2008 271 [1]	2. 1:47.284	26	5. 1:49.328	10	7. 1:48.815	10	5. 1:46.960	5	3. 1:46.298	3	4. **1:47.992**	6
2. Felipe Massa	BR	Ferrari F2008 269 [2]	1. 1:47.623	26	2. 1:48.504	16	5. 1:48.692	6	3. 1:46.873	3	5. 1:46.391	3	2. **1:47.678**	6
3. Nick Heidfeld	D	BMW Sauber F1.08-07 [1]	12. 1:49.185	26	10. 1:49.725	22	1. 1:47.876	19	14. 1:47.419	5	4. 1:46.311	7	5. **1:48.315**	6
4. Robert Kubica	PL	BMW Sauber F1.08-05 [2]	11. 1:49.139	25	11. 1:49.875	22	13. 1:49.250	12	7. 1:47.093	8	7. 1:46.494	6	8. **1:48.763**	6
5. Fernando Alonso	E	Renault R28-02 [2]	5. 1:48.104	26	1. 1:48.454	21	3. 1:48.307	19	9. 1:47.154	6	6. 1:46.491	6	6. **1:48.504**	6
6. Nelson Piquet	BR	Renault R28-01 [2]	10. 1:49.068	25	19. 1:51.334	19	9. 1:18.946	17	6. 1:47.052	9	12. **1:46.965**	6		
7. Nico Rosberg	D	Williams FW30-05 - Toyota [1]	13. 1:49.611	30	6. 1:49.405	17	8. 1:48.836	13	15. 1:47.503	6	15. **1:47.429**	6		
8. Kazuki Nakajima	J	Williams FW30-04 - Toyota [1]	18. 1:50.125	30	15. 1:50.364	20	16. 1:49.830	12	19. **1:48.268**	9				
9. David Coulthard	GB	Red Bull RB4 4 - Renault [1]	15. 1:49.849	18	12. 1:49.922	20	12. 1:49.125	11	8. 1:47.132	9	14. **1:47.018**	6		
10. Mark Webber	AUS	Red Bull RB4 5 - Renault [1]	6. 1:48.428	29	20. 1:51.540	7	10. 1:49.054	14	11. 1:47.270	7	10. 1:46.814	6	7. **1:48.736**	6
11. Jarno Trulli	I	Toyota TF108-05 [2]	14. 1:49.625	14	9. 1:49.715	23	11. 1:49.057	16	13. 1:47.400	7	11. **1:46.949**	6		
12. Timo Glock	D	Toyota TF108-06 [1]	9. 1:48.997	26	14. 1:50.281	24	15. 1:49.535	18	12. 1:47.359	7	13. **1:46.995**	6		
14. Sébastien Bourdais	F	Toro Rosso STR3-04 - Ferrari [2]	7. 1:48.557	31	13. 1:49.948	20	14. 1:49.256	19	1. 1:46.777	7	8. 1:46.544	6	9. **1:48.951**	6
15. Sebastian Vettel	D	Toro Rosso STR3-03 - Ferrari [2]	8. 1:48.958	24	7. 1:49.427	29	6. 1:48.768	16	10. 1:47.152	7	9. 1:46.804	6	10. **1:50.319**	3
16. Jenson Button	GB	Honda RA108-05 [2]	19. 1:50.464	25	17. 1:50.925	19	20.	1	17. **1:48.211**	9				
17. Rubens Barrichello	BR	Honda RA108-03 [1]	20. 1:50.905	25	18. 1:51.238	22	19. 1:50.061	17	16. **1:48.153**	9				
20. Adrian Sutil	D	Force India VJM01/06 - Ferrari [1]	17. 1:50.117	19	8. 1:49.585	22	18. 1:50.034	16	18. **1:48.226**	9				
21. Giancarlo Fisichella	I	Force India VJM01/05 - Ferrari [2]	16. 1:49.986	27	16. 1:50.740	11	17. 1:49.949	16	20. **1:48.447**	9				
22. Lewis Hamilton	GB	McLaren MP4-23 07 - Mercedes [1]	3. 1:47.878	27	4. 1:48.805	17	4. 1:48.356	10	4. 1:46.887	3	2. 1:46.088	3	1. **1:47.338**	6
23. Heikki Kovalainen	FIN	McLaren MP4-23 05 - Mercedes [1]	4. 1:47.932	24	3. 1:48.740	19	2. 1:48.165	10	2. 1:46.812	7	1. 1:46.037	3	3. **1:47.815**	6

Fastest lap overall

H. Kovalainen 1:46.037 (237,788 km/h)

Maximum speed

N° Driver	S1 Qualifs	Pos.	S1 Race	Pos.	S2 Qualifs	Pos.	S2 Race	Pos.	Finish Qualifs	Pos.	Finish Race	Pos.	Radar Qualifs	Pos.	Radar Race	Pos.
1. K. Räikkönen	318,7	7	320,0	11	206,5	2	205,3	1	224,8	4	220,4	4	307,7	7	308,3	8
2. F. Massa	319,8	2	323,6	4	297,9	1	204,0	3	224,2	6	221,7	2	308,3	6	311,5	3
3. N. Heidfeld	320,0	1	324,5	2	206,2	3	202,2	5	222,7	11	218,7	6	308,7	4	310,7	5
4. R. Kubica	318,3	8	320,0	10	206,1	4	203,1	4	222,9	9	220,7	3	307,4	9	308,0	10
5. F. Alonso	317,5	9	317,9	14	203,6	10	201,0	7	224,5	5	217,0	10	307,7	8	306,2	14
6. N. Piquet	317,2	10	316,3	16	205,9	5	197,5	15	223,0	8	213,5	20	306,7	10	303,2	19
7. N. Rosberg	316,6	12	320,0	9	205,2	7	199,6	10	225,0	3	215,0	17	305,2	15	304,0	17
8. K. Nakajima	316,8	11	323,2	5	201,3	15	195,6	19	220,6	17	214,2	19	304,8	17	305,3	15
9. D. Coulthard	314,5	17	314,6	17	202,7	12	198,0	13	223,3	7	217,2	9	308,8	2	308,5	7
10. M. Webber	314,5	18	314,4	19	201,9	14	198,1	12	222,6	12	216,4	11	308,5	5	308,8	6
11. J. Trulli	312,7	20	313,4	20	200,7	16	195,1	20	221,9	13	216,1	12	302,1	20	300,4	20
12. T. Glock	313,9	19	314,6	18	205,1	8	199,2	11	221,6	14	218,0	7	305,3	14	303,9	18
14. S. Bourdais	319,1	4	320,7	7	203,8	9	200,8	8	222,7	10	217,5	8	305,8	12	307,0	11
15. S. Vettel	315.7	13	321,7	6	203,1	11	200,0	9	219,8	18	215,9	13	304,3	18	308,1	9
16. J. Button	314,6	16	318,5	12	199,7	18	195,9	17	218 7	20	215,3	15	305,6	13	306,8	13
17. R. Barrichello	315,1	14	318,3	13	199,7	17	197,1	16	221,2	15	214,7	18	304,9	16	306,9	12
20. A. Sutil	318,9	5	325,2	1	197,2	20	195,9	18	220,9	16	215,3	16	306,2	11	312,2	2
21. G. Fisichella	314,7	15	317,7	15	199,1	19	197,9	14	219,2	19	215,8	14	303,2	19	304,5	16
22. L. Hamilton	318,8	6	320,5	8	202,6	13	204,2	2	226,7	2	220,2	5	309,0	1	310,8	4
23. H. Kovalainen	319,5	3	324,2	3	205,8	6	202,2	6	227,2	1	222,2	1	308,7	3	315.4	1

Best sector times

	S1		S2		S3		
Qualifs	**S1** L. Hamilton	31.014	**S2** K. Räikkönen	46.178	**S3** H. Kovalainen	28.612	= 1:45.804
Race	**S1** F. Massa	31.335	**S2** K. Räikkönen	47.024	**S3** K. Räikkönen	28.820	= 1:47.179

RACE

Date	Weather	Air temperature	Track temperature	Humidity	Wind speed
Sunday September 7, 2008 (14:00)	Cloudy then rain	15°c	16°c	72%	4.3 m/s

Classification & retirements

Pos.	Driver	Constructor	Tyres	Laps	Time	Km/h	
1.	F. Massa	Ferrari	MMH	44	1:22:59.394	222,715	
2.	N. Heidfeld	BMW	MMHW	44	+ 9.383	222,296	
3.	L. Hamilton	McLaren Mercedes	MMH	44	+ *10.539	222,244	1:22:44.933 + penalty of 25 sec.
4.	F. Alonso	Renault	MMHW	44	+ 14.478	222,069	
5.	S. Vettel	STR Ferrari	MMH	44	+ 14.576	222,065	
6.	R. Kubica	BMW	MMH	44	+ 15.037	222,044	
7.	S. Bourdais	STR Ferrari	MMH	44	+ 16.735	221,969	
8.	M. Webber	Red Bull Renault	MMH	44	+ 42.776	220,818	
9.	T. Glock	Toyota	MHW	44	+ *1:07.045	219,756	56.506 + penalty of 25 sec
10.	H. Kovalainen	McLaren Mercedes	MMMH	43	1 lap	223,057	Gearbox
11.	D. Coulthard	Red Bull Renault	MHW	43	1 lap	218,278	
12.	N. Rosberg	Williams Toyota	MHE	43	1 lap	218,192	
13.	A. Sutil	Force India	MMH	43	1 lap	218,104	
14.	K. Nakajima	Williams Toyota	MHE	43	1 lap	217,697	
15.	J. Button	Honda	MHW	43	1 lap	217,630	
16.	J. Trulli	Toyota	MHM	43	1 lap	215,864	
17.	G. Fisichella	Force India	MMHW	43	1 lap	212,960	
18.	K. Räikkönen	Ferrari	MMH	42	2 laps	227,020	Went off, hits the wall

Driver	Constructor	Tyres	Laps	Reason
R. Barrichello	Honda	MM	19	Gearbox
N. Piquet	Renault	H	13	Spin… hits the tyre wall

Tyres M: Medium & H: Hard // E: Extreme Wet & W: Wet

Fastest laps

	Driver	Time	Lap	Km/h
1.	K. Räikkönen	1:47.930	24	233,618
2.	L. Hamilton	1:48.136	20	233,175
3.	F. Massa	1:48.222	26	232,987
4.	H. Kovalainen	1:48.223	35	232,985
5.	R. Kubica	1:48.965	36	231,399
6.	S. Bourdais	1:49.002	31	231,320
7.	N. Heidfeld	1:49.067	36	231,182
8.	S. Vettel	1:49.086	16	231,142
9.	F. Alonso	1:49.238	25	230,820
10.	M. Webber	1:49.516	34	230,236
11.	D. Coulthard	1:50.177	19	228,853
12.	T. Glock	1:50.255	37	228,691
13.	A. Sutil	1:50.487	27	228,211
14.	J. Trulli	1:50.543	32	228,095
15.	N. Rosberg	1:50.656	32	227,862
16.	J. Button	1:50.671	19	227,832
17.	K. Nakajima	1:50.970	35	227,218
18.	N. Piquet	1:51.118	12	226,915
19.	G. Fisichella	1:51.701	17	225,731
20.	R. Barrichello	1:52.072	10	224,983

*Penalty of 25 seconds for Hamilton for missing the chicane and gaining an advantage.
*Penalty of 25 seconds for Glock for having passed Webber under yellow flags.

Pit stops

	Driver	Lap	Duration	Stop	Total
1.	G. Fisichella	1	38.763	1	38.763
2.	L. Hamilton	11	27.412	1	27.412
3.	K. Räikkönen	12	27.586	1	27.586
4.	M. Webber	12	30.492	1	30.492
5.	F. Massa	13	28.335	1	28.335
6.	F. Alonso	13	28.880	1	28.880
7.	H. Kovalainen	13	29.413	1	29.413
8.	N. Heidfeld	14	28.952	1	28.952
9.	H. Kovalainen	•14•	17.517	2	46.930
10.	J. Trulli	14	29.175	1	29.175
11.	S. Bourdais	15	28.972	1	28.972
12.	R. Kubica	15	28.566	1	28.566
13.	A. Sutil	16	29.723	1	29.723
14.	S. Vettel	17	28.171	1	28.171
15.	R. Barrichello	17	28.790	1	28.790
16.	D. Coulthard	22	32.573	1	32.573
17.	J. Button	22	29.988	1	29.988
18.	G. Fisichella	22	31.347	2	1:10.110
19.	K. Räikkönen	25	29.127	2	56.713
20.	L. Hamilton	25	28.807	2	56.219
21.	N. Rosberg	25	29.172	1	29.172
22.	T. Glock	26	28.725	1	28.725
23.	F. Alonso	27	28.195	2	57.075
24.	K. Nakajima	27	28.672	1	28.672
25.	F. Massa	28	28.193	2	56.528
26.	A. Sutil	28	27.523	2	56.976
27.	N. Heidfeld	31	26.710	2	55.662
28.	S. Bourdais	32	26.868	2	55.840
29.	M. Webber	32	27.645	2	58.137
30.	R. Kubica	33	32.437	2	1:01.003
31.	S. Vettel	33	26.000	2	54.171
32.	H. Kovalainen	33	26.475	3	1:13.405
33.	J. Trulli	35	26.395	2	55.570
34.	G. Fisichella	40	27.741	3	1:37.851
35.	N. Heidfeld	42	26.115	3	1:21.777
36.	T. Glock	42	25.920	2	54.645
37.	N. Rosberg	42	30.032	2	59.204
38.	D. Coulthard	42	27.804	2	1:00.377
39.	K. Nakajima	42	36.578	2	1:05.250
40.	J. Button	42	28.341	2	58.329
41.	F. Alonso	43	29.612	3	1:26.687

•• Drive-through penalty: Kovalainen
For causing a collision with Webber.

Race leader

Driver	Laps in the lead	Nbr of laps
L. Hamilton	1	1
K. Räikkönen	2 > 12	11
F. Massa	13	1
K. Räikkönen	14 > 25	12
F. Massa	26 > 28	3
K. Räikkönen	29 > 42	14
I. Hamilton	43 > 44	2

Driver	Nbr of laps	Kilometers
K. Räikkönen	37	259,148 km
F. Massa	4	28,016 km
L. Hamilton	3	20,888 km

Gaps on the lead board

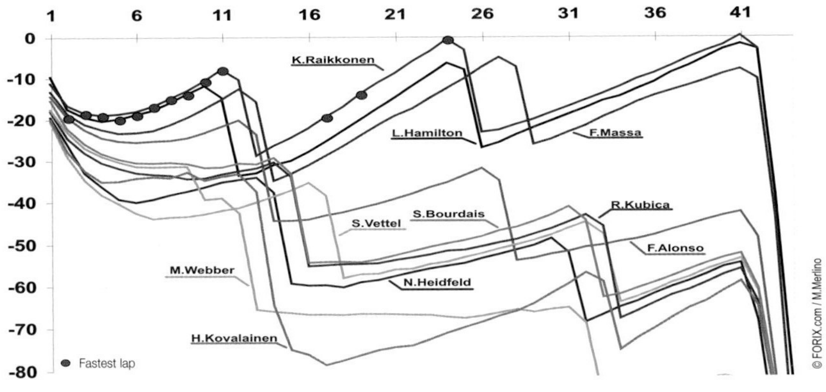
1
6
11
16
21
26
31
36
41
0
-10
-20
-30
-40
-50
-60
-70
-80
K.Raikkonen
L.Hamilton
F.Massa
R.Kubica
S.Vettel
S.Bourdais
F.Alonso
M.Webber
N.Heidfeld
H.Kovalainen
Fastest lap
© FORIX.com / M.Merlino

Lap chart

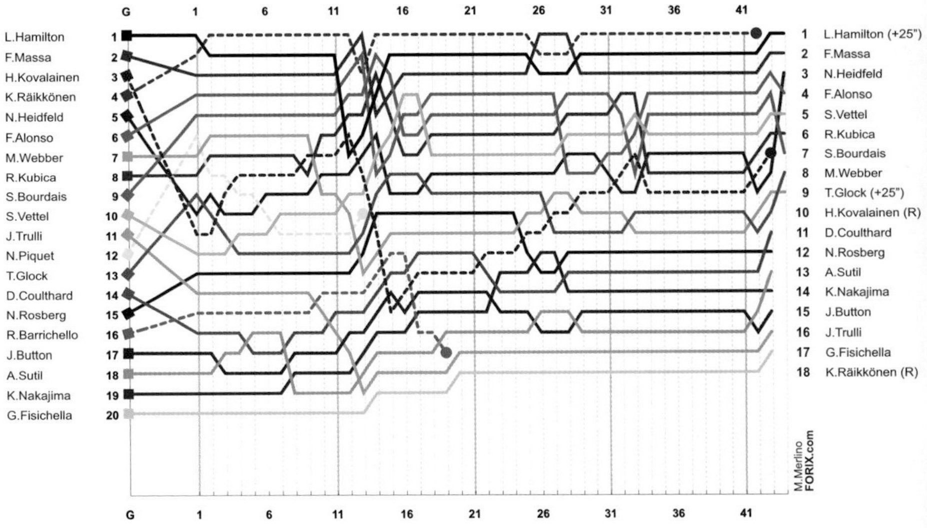
G
1
6
11
16
21
26
31
36
41
L.Hamilton
F.Massa
H.Kovalainen
K.Räikkönen
N.Heidfeld
F.Alonso
M.Webber
R.Kubica
S.Bourdais
S.Vettel
J.Trulli
N.Piquet
T.Glock
D.Coulthard
N.Rosberg
R.Barrichello
J.Button
A.Sutil
K.Nakajima
G.Fisichella
1 L.Hamilton (+25")
2 F.Massa
3 N.Heidfeld
4 F.Alonso
5 S.Vettel
6 R.Kubica
7 S.Bourdais
8 M.Webber
9 T.Glock (+25")
10 H.Kovalainen (R)
11 D.Coulthard
12 N.Rosberg
13 A.Sutil
14 K.Nakajima
15 J.Button
16 J.Trulli
17 G.Fisichella
18 K.Räikkönen (R)
M.Merlino
FORIX.com

CHAMPIONSHIPS 13/18

Drivers

	Driver	Constructor	Wins	Points
1.	L. Hamilton	McLaren Mercedes	4	76
2.	F. Massa	Ferrari	5	74
3.	R. Kubica	BMW	1	58
4.	K. Räikkönen	Ferrari	2	57
5.	N. Heidfeld	BMW		49
6.	H. Kovalainen	McLaren Mercedes	1	43
7.	J. Trulli	Toyota		26
8.	F. Alonso	Renault		23
9.	M. Webber	Red Bull Renault		19
10.	T. Glock	Toyota		15
11.	N. Piquet	Renault		13
12.	S. Vettel	STR Ferrari		13
13.	R. Barrichello	Honda		11
14.	N. Rosberg	Williams Toyota		9
15.	K. Nakajima	Williams Toyota		8
16.	D. Coulthard	Red Bull Renault		6
17.	S. Bourdais	STR Ferrari		4
18.	J. Button	Honda		3
19.	G. Fisichella	Force India		0
20.	T. Sato	Super Aguri Honda		0
21.	A. Davidson	Super Aguri Honda		0
22.	A. Sutil	Force India		0

Constructors

	Constructor	Wins	Points
1.	Scuderia Ferrari Marlboro	7	131
2.	Vodafone McLaren Mercedes	4	119
3.	BMW Sauber F1 Team	2	107
4.	Panasonic Toyota Racing		41
5.	ING Renault F1 Team		36
6.	Red Bull Racing		25
7.	AT&T Williams		17
8.	Scuderia Torro Rosso		17
9.	Honda Racing F1 Team		14
10.	Force India F1 Team		0
11.	Super Aguri F1 Team		0

THE CIRCUIT

Name Circuit de Spa-Francorchamps; Spa
Lenght 7004 m
Distance 44 laps, 308,052 km
Latitude 50°26'40.00"N
Longitude 5°57'53.00"E

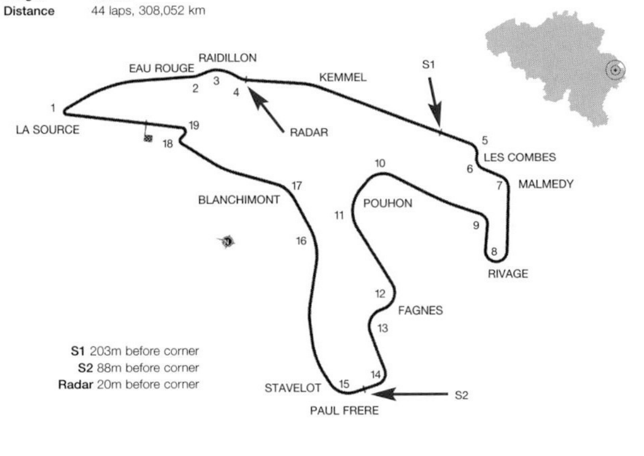
EAU ROUGE
RAIDILLON
KEMMEL
S1
LA SOURCE
RADAR
LES COMBES
MALMEDY
BLANCHIMONT
POUHON
RIVAGE
FAGNES
STAVELOT
PAUL FRERE
S2
1
2
3
4
5
6
7
8
9
10
11
12
13
14
15
16
17
18
19

S1 203m before corner
S2 88m before corner
Radar 20m before corner

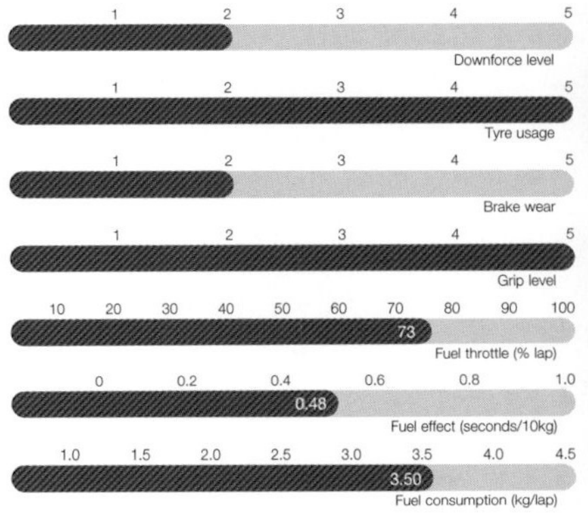
1 2 3 4 5
Downforce level
1 2 3 4 5
Tyre usage
1 2 3 4 5
Brake wear
1 2 3 4 5
Grip level
10 20 30 40 50 60 70 80 90 100
73
Fuel throttle (% lap)
0 0.2 0.4 0.6 0.8 1.0
0.48
Fuel effect (seconds/10kg)
1.0 1.5 2.0 2.5 3.0 3.5 4.0 4.5
3.50
Fuel consumption (kg/lap)

VIVA TORO ROSSO !
VIVA SEBASTIAN !

It was one of those season-defining races, a Grand Prix where it seemed anything could happen -the impossible included.

In normal conditions Monza, a circuit made for mighty engines, epitomises the power struggle between the haves and the have-nots. But in the rain, F1's temple of speed became the backdrop to a motor racing miracle as Sebastian Vettel took full advantage, disappearing into the distance, no-one able to challenge him on this day of days.

The young German took his chance with both hands and turned it into a magnificent win - the first of his career, the first for Toro Rosso. It was some performance.

> Lewis Hamilton got caught out in the rain in qualifying. Knocked out in Q2, he started from 15th on the grid - his worst qualifying result of the season.

Pole for Sebastian Vettel on a funny old grid

The good people of Milan couldn't recall a downpour like it. On Friday morning enough water had already fallen on Monza's royal park to cause short-circuits and flooding in several teams' garages.

On Saturday the deluge started in late morning and simply intensified as qualifying went on.

That meant you had to be among the first out if you were to have any hope of a decent time - but that thinking was the trap some of F1's biggest names fell into, Lewis Hamilton among them down in 15th and Kimi Räikkönen one place in front.

Right at the front young Sebastian Vettel was making the most of things. He showed rare control in the wet, enjoying the Toro Rosso's handling in these conditions - as confirmed by

Sébastien Bourdais' fourth-fastest time. Such was the unbridled joy in the Toro Rosso camp after the session you'd have thought they'd just taken the world title.

"*I do like driving in the wet,*" beamed Vettel between sips of champagne. "*Two weeks ago, before the Belgian Grand Prix, I went karting on Michael Schumacher's track at Kerpen in the rain. I asked them to put me on slicks, just to get a feel for the extreme conditions. My mechanics thought I was crazy, but I think it was a pretty good idea! Qualifying on pole is a dream come true.*"

Mind you, the big winner in qualifying looked like being Heikki Kovalainen. Second behind Vettel, he was the only driver from a front-running team to qualify in the top five. The big

loser, meanwhile, was one Lewis Hamilton, the World Championship leader finding himself down in 15th spot on the grid.

"*At the start of Q2 we thought the track had dried enough for us to try intermediates,*" the British driver explained, "*but that's when the rain started again. And it was hard to work out the braking-points. But anyway it's the first time this has happened to me in F1 so I can't really compain.*"

Kimi Räikkönen, 14th on the grid, wasn't much better off than the McLaren man. "*Not much to say,*" commented the Finn, "*I just couldn't put in a time in Q2. I went off at the Ascari chicane, where there was a lot of water on the track. We just have to make the best of it, but it's definitely not the ideal situation to be in.*"

No, it's not a dress rehearsal for the night race in Singapore: it's Friday morning and a violent thunderstorm has just hit Monza.

SNAPSHOTS OF THE WEEKEND

+ The F1 drivers seemed unanimous in welcoming the penalty handed out to Lewis Hamilton at the Belgian Grand Prix. "Lewis gained from the chicane," asserted Felipe Massa, who benefited most from the whole business when he won the Spa race in the stewards' room. "The straight is too short to be able to overtake someone in the first corner. Nobody can pass at that point, which shows Lewis gained an advantage by straight-lining the chicane and the penalty is justified." Among the drivers we asked, Sébastien Bourdais and Nico Rosberg were the only ones to find the 25-second penalty a bit harsh, although they supported it in principle.

+ The brand-new FOTA (Formula One Teams' Association) met to work out exactly what they were

supposed to be trying to achieve. Set up as a counter-balance to the omnipotent Bernie Ecclestone, they seemed to have rounded their ambitions down a bit. On Friday evening the leading figures issued a statement to the effect that their aim was 'to improve the spectacle while reducing costs'. Among the so-called detailed objectives was 'to represent and protect the interests of our members'.

+ Thursday, as always, was party night at Red Bull. This time the pretext was 'David Coulthard's final Grand Prix in Europe'. The team distributed a leaflet called 'Re Bull Ra ing'. i.e. Red Bull Racing with no 'DC'. Red Bull, they expained, wouldn't be the same without David Coulthard…

STARTING GRID

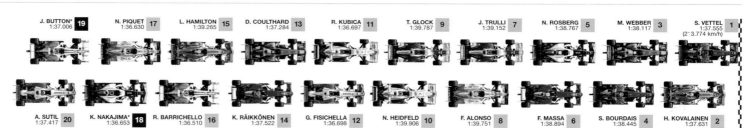

| J. BUTTON* 19 | N. PIQUET 17 | L. HAMILTON 15 | D. COULTHARD 13 | R. KUBICA 11 | T. GLOCK 9 | J. TRULLI 7 | N. ROSBERG 5 | M. WEBBER 3 | S. VETTEL 1 |
| 1:37.006 | 1:36.630 | 1:39.265 | 1:37.284 | 1:36.697 | 1:39.787 | 1:39.152 | 1:38.767 | 1:38.117 | 1:37.555 (2^3.774 km/h) |

| A. SUTIL 20 | K. NAKAJIMA* 18 | R. BARRICHELLO 16 | K. RÄIKKÖNEN 14 | G. FISICHELLA 12 | N. HEIDFELD 10 | F. ALONSO 8 | F. MASSA 6 | S. BOURDAIS 4 | H. KOVALAINEN 2 |
| 1:37.417 | 1:36.653 | 1:36.510 | 1:37.522 | 1:36.698 | 1:39.906 | 1:39.751 | 1:38.894 | 1:38.445 | 1:37.631 |

<
A few weeks earlier Red Bull had announced that Sebastian Vettel would replace David Coulthard in 2009, news that had some German fans seeing the youngster as heir apparent to Michael Schumacher. *"It's a ridiculous comparison to make,"* said our race-winner. *"I'm still far too young for people to start comparing me with Michael, whom I know well and who is a fantastic person."* Winning the Italian Grand Prix at just 21, Vettel became the youngest F1 race-winner in history. He was already the youngest driver to score a point, in his very first Grand Prix at Indianapolis in 2007, where he stood in at short notice for Robert Kubica when the BMW Sauber driver had his accident in Canada.

Heart-warming stuff as Sebastian Vettel wins for Toro Rosso

Just 160 people work in F1's smallest team, the Toro Rosso HQ at Faenza, about 160 kilometres from the Imola circuit. They don't, of course, build their own cars, which are Red Bulls, nor their own engines, buying those from Ferrari just a few kilometres down the road.

So Toro Rosso can afford to run very lean in comparison to the major teams and their thousand or so employees.

All of which made their Monza exploit all the more remarkable. After taking pole on Saturday, Sebastian Vettel skipped away in the lead for almost the entire race, relinquishing it only through the pit stops.

Of course, the young German was helped by the rain, which meant a rolling start behind the Safety Car and gave him the chance to streak into the lead with visibility unimpaired.

As the other cars threw up a wall of spray behind him, there was no-one who could match his pace.

After three laps Vettel was already two seconds ahead of Kovalainen; by lap 15 his lead had gone out to 10 seconds. The die was cast, and the improbable story of a Toro Rosso win was about to become a reality.

In the constructors' standings the little Faenza outfit now led sister team Red Bull, yet to record a Grand Prix victory of their own.

Jubilation as the race finishes and Toro Rosso (formerly Minardi) claim their first victory.
V

A tale of two Sebs: Vettel first, Bourdais last!

Sebastian Vettel was having trouble putting his emotions into words after winning the race. *"It was just crazy, unbelievable. It's just so hard to describe my feelings. It was only when I crossed the line that I realised I had won. I slowed down, the marshals were clapping and waving their flags... Then there was the podium, an unbelievable crowd and a feeling I will never forget. It's the greatest day of my life."*

The rolling start behind the Safety Car was crucial to the young German's win: *"I think the rolling start really helped me,"* he agreed. *"Being able to see was the key today and I was able to get into a good lead right from the start. We thought the race would be on a dry track so we didn't have much wing on and I was very quick in a straight line. But the track was very tricky - I nearly spun a*

few times. I had to keep my concentration right to the end, and that wasn't easy because the track was still very wet and you couldn't afford to put a wheel off line."

But Vettel's feet were still firmly on the ground. *"I won't be going to Singapore next week thinking I can win the race. I'm sensible enough to know I still have a long way to go before I'm a regular race-winner."*

While Vettel was heading off into the distance, team-mate Sébastien Bourdais was trailing along in last place in the Italian Grand Prix. Though he qualified fourth, the Frenchman stalled on the grid and started from pit lane a lap down.

He couldn't overtake a single car - the one place he made up late in the race came when Germany's Adrian Sutil made a final visit to the pits.

YOUNGEST EVER

Sebastian Vettel en route to his maiden win. Starting from
pole, the German enjoyed a clear line of sight as the rest of
the field made their way through the wall of spray, but that
doesn't detract from his victory.

^
Fernando Alonso gets it sideways as only he knows how. The way these guys control an F1 car in the rain leaves you lost for words.

Alonso saga goes on

There is little doubt that leaving McLaren at the end of the 2007 season was the biggest blunder of Fernando Alonso's career. If he had stayed with the British team, by the Italian Grand Prix he would probably have been streaking away towards the 2008 title instead of down behind Jarno Trulli in eighth place overall.

When he signed for Renault Alonso knew 2008 would be no easy year - but he wasn't expecting it to be this bad. The Renault R26 was reliable enough but making no headway; even the double World Champion's skills were not enough to recreate the magic formula that took him to the title in 2005 and 2006.

Early in the season the French team and their prodigal son were respectful enough in anything they said about each other, but as one dismal showing followed another, the tone gradually grew more bitter until things reached the point of no return the weekend before Italy. "*We work together, and we should take responsibiity for failure together,*" thundered Flavio Briatore. "*I know the car has let us down sometimes, but the drivers also have to take their share of the blame,*" he continued, a reference to mistakes by Alonso when he went off in Canada and had a collision in Valencia.

Sources close to the Spaniard said he couldn't put up with Briatore's simplistic view of things any more and would do whatever it took to switch teams. Of the options open to him, he seemed to be leaning towards BMW Sauber, where he might replace Nick Heidfeld and team up with his best friend Robert Kubica. In Monza Mario Theissen confirmed that he would wait till the following Monday to decide on his driver line-up for 2009, and if Alonso decided that was what he wanted, he would be welcome at Hinwil.

Otherwise, the Spanish dual champion might choose Honda, who would welcome him with open arms, or stay another year with Renault before moving to Ferrari in 2010.

His decision was the key to several other driver transfers. Romain Grosjean was having to wait and see at Renault: if Alonso stayed, there was no guarantee the Geneva driver would be in F1 the following year. If, on the other hand, the Spaniard left, then there would be a place for him in the Renault F1 Team.

Hamilton caught out by the elements

Qualifying outside the top 10, Lewis Hamilton was able to start with a fully fuelled car, meaning he could run to the finish on a single stop.

It was a bold strategy backed up by his brilliance as he fought through to second place by lap 35. The win was there for the taking if the track hadn't started to dry, forcing the Briton to make a second stop that wiped out the advantage those tactics had given him. He finished seventh, behind Felipe Massa, losing a point to him in the Championship. On 78, the McLaren man was now just one ahead of the Brazilian.

Two more years for Räikkönen and Massa

Scuderia Ferrari used their home Grand Prix to announce contract extensions through to the end of 2010 for current drivers Kimi Räikkönen and Felipe Massa, ending speculation that the Finnish driver, detuned after winning his world title, might take early retirement.

For Massa it couldn't have come at a better time, even though it was simply confirmation of contract terms put in place in the Todt era.

The Brazilian was just two points behind Hamilton in the World Championship, and this display of confidence from Ferrari would be a reassurance heading into the final five races of the season.

And he could surely count on Räikkönen's support now that Kimi knew he could go for another title with Ferrari in 2009 or 2010.

The news had other consequences. Fernando Alonso now knew the Ferrari drive he was after wouldn't be available until at least 2011. The Spaniard clearly hadn't the patience to wait it out with Renault, which meant he would most likely accept a two-year deal with BMW-Sauber (see above), keen to welcome him as replacement for Nick Heidfeld.

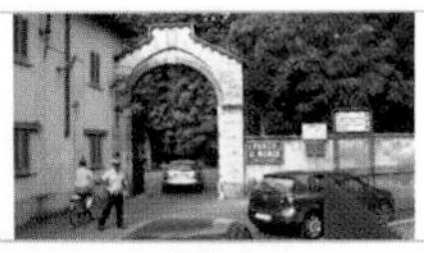

PRACTICE

Date	Weather (AM)	Air temperature	Track temperature	Weather (PM)	Air temperature	Track temperature
Friday September 12, 2008	Cloudy, rain	23-21°c	23-20°c	Sunny	24-27°c	26-31°c
Saturday September 13, 2008	Rain	21-20°c	21-20°c	Rain	19-20°c	18-19°c

All the time trials

N° Driver	Nat.	N° Chassis- Engine [Nbr. GP]	Pos. Free 1 Friday 10:00-11:30	Laps	Pos. Free 2 Friday 14:00-15:30	Laps	Pos. Free 3 Saturday 11:00-12:00	Laps	Pos. Q1 Saturday 14:00-14:20	Laps	Pos. Q2 Saturday 14:27-14:42	Laps	Pos. Q3 Saturday 14:50-15:00	Laps
1. Kimi Räikkönen	FIN	Ferrari F2008 271 [1]	9. 1:37.392	5	1. 1:23.861	31	18. 1:41.164	3	11. 1:35.965	13	14. **1:37.522**	8		
2. Felipe Massa	BR	Ferrari F2008 269 [1] -> [1]	14. 1:40.233	5	6. 1:24.247	34	3. 1:37.263	6	5. 1:35.536	13	10. 1:36.676	9	6. **1:38.894**	7
3. Nick Heidfeld	D	BMW Sauber F1.08-07 [2]	15.	1	3. 1:23.947	29	6. 1:36.972	12	8. 1:35.709	12	9. 1:36.626	7	10. **1:39.906**	7
4. Robert Kubica	PL	BMW Sauber F1.08-05 [1]	17.	1	2. 1:23.931	26	12. 1:37.671	7	7. 1:35.553	12	11. **1:36.697**	9		
5. Fernando Alonso	E	Renault R28-02 [1]	6. 1:36.965	10	18. 1:25.481	22	9. 1:37.270	10	14. 1:36.297	12	7. 1:36.518	9	8. **1:39751**	7
6. Nelson Piquet	BR	Renault R28-01 [1]	11. 1:38.057	11	20. 1:26.195	23	14. 1:37.833	9	17. **1:36.630**	13				
7. Nico Rosberg	D	Williams FW30-05 - Toyota [2]	5. 1:36.900	9	5. 1:24.110	33	3. 1:36.347	13	4. 1:35.485	12	3. 1:35.898	9	5. **1:38.767**	7
8. Kazuki Nakajima	J	Williams FW30-04 - Toyota [2]	16.	2	16. 1:25.330	28	5. 1:36.706	10	18. **1:36.653**	13				
9. David Coulthard	GB	Red Bull RB4 4 - Renault [2]	12. 1:38.303	7	11. 1:25.100	25	7. 1:37.015	7	15. 1:36.485	12	13. **1:37.284**	9		
10. Mark Webber	AUS	Red Bull RB4 5 - Renault [1]	19.	1	8. 1:24.521	35	13. 1:37.778	8	12. 1:36.001	11	6. 1:36.306	5	3. **1:38.117**	7
11. Jarno Trulli	I	Toyota TF108-05 [1]	8. 1:37.214	13	19. 1:25.753	29	4 1:36.686	9	10. 1:35.906	12	4. 1:36.008	8	7. **1:39.152**	6
12. Timo Glock	D	Toyota TF108-06 [2]	4. 1:36.800	13	17. 1:25.397	28	1. 1:35.464	16	9. 1:35.737	13	8. 1:36.525	8	9. **1:39.787**	7
14. Sébastien Bourdais	F	Toro Rosso STR3-04 - Ferrari [1]	7. 1:37.142	20	12. 1:25.192	39	17. 1:39.319	8	6. 1:35.543	12	5. 1:36.175	9	4. **1:38.445**	7
15. Sebastian Vettel	D	Toro Rosso STR3-03 - Ferrari [1]	10. 1:37.754	13	10. 1:24.773	35	2. 1:36.129	11	3. 1:35.464	12	1. 1:35.837	9	1. **1:37.555**	7
16. Jenson Button	GB	Honda RA108-02 [1]	13. 1:39.062	12	15. 1:25.309	34	15. 1:37.882	11	19. **1:37.006**	13				
17. Rubens Barrichello	BR	Honda RA108-04 [1]	2. 1:33.428	18	14. 1:25.296	25	16. 1:38.689	8	16. **1:36.510**	12				
20. Adrian Sutil	D	Force India VJM01/06 - Ferrari [2]	1. 1:32.842	18	9. 1:24.669	22	11. 1:37.504	11	20. **1:37.417**	12				
21. Giancarlo Fisichella	I	Force India VJM01/05 - Ferrari [1]	3. 1:33.695	19	13. 1:25.204	24	10. 1:37.285	9	13. 1:36.280	11	12. **1:36.698**	8		
22. Lewis Hamilton	GB	McLaren MP4-23 07 - Mercedes [2]	20.	1	4. 1:23.983	25	20. 1:46.325	8	2. 1:35.394	11	15. **1:39.265**	8		
23. Heikki Kovalainen	FIN	McLaren MP4-23 05 - Mercedes [1]	18.	1	7. 1:24.365	29	19. 1:42.683	6	1. 1:35.214	10	2. 1:35.843	7	2. **1:37.631**	7

Fastest lap overall
H. Kovalainen 1:35.214 (219,030 km/h)

Maximum speed

N° Driver	S1 Qualifs	Pos.	S1 Race	Pos.	S2 Qualifs	Pos.	S2 Race	Pos.	Finish Qualifs	Pos.	Finish Race	Pos.	Radar Qualifs	Pos.	Radar Race	Pos.
1. K. Räikkönen	310,9	11	325,3	5	318,3	8	330,9	2	301,8	4	311,0	2	317,6	11	338,3	3
2. F. Massa	313,1	8	326,0	2	318,3	7	330,8	3	299,6	11	311,6	1	295,4	20	331,7	12
3. N. Heidfeld	314,4	6	325,7	3	318,3	9	327,8	6	300,6	9	308,1	11	324,3	4	337,0	4
4. R. Kubica	314,4	5	322,0	11	319,3	4	325,9	11	300,9	7	308,3	10	319,6	9	336,9	4
5. F. Alonso	310,5	13	320,2	13	312,7	19	322,9	14	299,7	10	304,9	14	309,1	15	329,7	13
6. N. Piquet	308,6	18	319,0	15	312,5	20	318,7	20	298,2	17	303,4	17	315,1	14	328.4	16
7. N. Rosberg	308,4	20	316,8	18	313,2	17	320,2	18	297.4	18	303,7	15	316,8	12	327,7	18
8. K. Nakajima	309,6	17	318,9	16	312,8	18	320,6	17	298,3	16	303,5	16	316,1	13	328,3	17
9. D. Coulthard	314,0	7	325,2	6	317,8	10	327,3	8	301.4	6	307,6	12	326.0	3	335,8	8
10. M. Webber	312,1	9	323,9	9	319,0	6	331,0	1	300,7	8	308,5	9	327,4	1	335,5	9
11. J. Trulli	310,7	12	317,5	17	316,5	12	321,7	15	299,0	12	302,6	19	307,2	17	328.5	15
12. T. Glock	309,7	15	320,1	14	315,1	13	324,0	13	298,5	15	306,8	13	318,2	10	334,6	10
14. S. Bourdais	314,5	4	325,4	4	319,0	5	330,6	4	301,6	5	309,7	5	324,2	5	338,9	2
15. S. Vettel	316,6	1	323,9	8	322,9	1	327,5	7	304,3	1	308,9	8	327,1	2	336,6	6
16. J. Button	309,8	14	315,8	19	314,5	15	320,6	16	298,6	13	303,2	18	319,7	8	326,5	19
17. R. Barrichello	311,9	10	320,6	12	316,5	11	327,0	9	298,5	14	309,0	6	320,7	6	336,2	7
20. A. Sutil	309,6	16	324,0	7	315,0	14	325,9	10	295,4	20	309,0	7	320,3	7	333,5	11
21. G. Fisichella	308,5	19	313,4	20	314,2	16	318,9	19	296,5	19	298,7	20	305,2	18	296,5	20
22. L. Hamilton	315,8	2	326,3	1	320,9	3	329,7	5	303,2	2	310,1	3	303,0	19	339,7	1
23. H. Kovalainen	314,8	3	323,7	10	322,4	2	325,3	12	302,5	3	309,7	4	307,9	16	329,5	14

Best sector times

Qualifs	**S1** H. Kovalainen	30.148	**S2** H. Kovalainen	32.781	**S3** J. Trulli	31.789	= 1:34.718
Race	**S1** K. Räikkönen	28.681	**S2** K. Räikkönen	29.675	**S3** K. Räikkönen	29.496	= 1:27.852

RACE

Date	Weather	Air temperature	Track temperature	Humidity	Wind speed
Sunday September 14, 2008 (14:00)	Rain	15-17°c	16-18°c	82%	1.5 m/s

Classification & retirements

Pos.	Driver	Constructor	Tyres	Laps	Time	Km/h
1.	S. Vettel	STR Ferrari	EEW	53	1:26:47.494	212,039
2.	H. Kovalainen	McLaren Mercedes	EEW	53	+ 12.512	211,530
3.	R. Kubica	BMW	EW	53	+ 20.471	211,208
4.	F. Alonso	Renault	EW	53	+ 23.903	211,070
5.	N. Heidfeld	BMW	EW	53	+ 27.748	210,915
6.	F. Massa	Ferrari	EEW	53	+ 28.816	210,872
7.	L. Hamilton	McLaren Mercedes	EEW	53	+ 29.912	210,828
8.	M. Webber	Red Bull Renault	EEW	53	+ 32.048	210,742
9.	K. Räikkönen	Ferrari	EEW	53	+ 39.468	210,444
10.	N. Piquet	Renault	EW	53	+ 54.445	209,845
11.	T. Glock	Toyota	EEW	53	+ 58.888	209,668
12.	K. Nakajima	Williams Toyota	EW	53	+ 1:02.015	209,543
13.	J. Trulli	Toyota	EEW	53	+ 1:05.954	209,387
14.	N. Rosberg	Williams Toyota	EEW	53	+ 1:08.635	209,280
15.	J. Button	Honda	EWW	53	+ 1:13.370	209,093
16.	D. Coulthard	Red Bull Renault	EWW	52	1 lap	207,162
17.	R. Barrichello	Honda	EWM	52	1 lap	206,057
18.	S. Bourdais	STR Ferrari	EEW	52	1 lap	205,823
19.	A. Sutil	Force India		51	2 laps	201,800

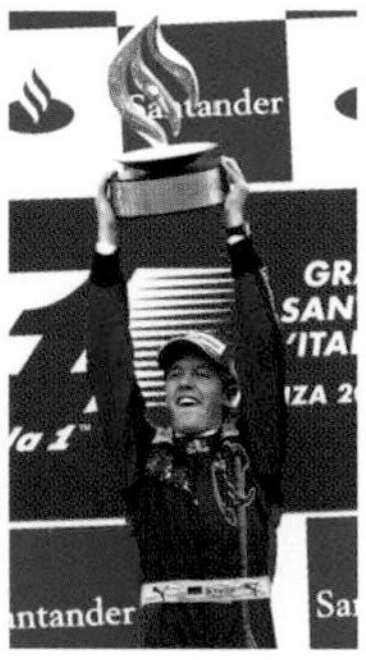
Santander
GR
SAN
'ITA
ZA 2
ntander
Sa

Driver	Constructor	Tyres	Laps	Reason
G. Fisichella	Force India	E	11	Contact with Coulthard… car goes straight on in Parabolica corner

Tyres H: Hard & M: Medium // E: Extreme Wet & W: Wet

Fastest laps

	Driver	Time	Lap	Km/h
1.	K. Räikkönen	1:28.047	53	236,859
2.	S. Bourdais	1:29.258	22	233,646
3.	M. Webber	1:29.681	52	232,544
4.	F. Massa	1:29.696	52	232,505
5.	L. Hamilton	1:29.721	52	232,440
6.	N. Heidfeld	1:29.807	53	232,217
7.	J. Button	1:29.827	52	232,166
8.	T. Glock	1:29.948	53	231,853
9.	F. Alonso	1:29.948	53	231,820
10.	N. Rosberg	1:30.019	53	231,671
11.	K. Nakajima	1:30.215	53	231,167
12.	R. Kubica	1:30.298	52	230,955
13.	H. Kovalainen	1:30.300	53	230,950
14.	S. Vettel	1:30.510	53	230,414
15.	J. Trulli	1:30.853	52	229,544
16.	N. Piquet	1:30.918	53	229,380
17.	D. Coulthard	1:30.459	49	225,557
18.	A. Sutil	1:33.458	51	223,146
19.	R. Barrichello	1:33.918	42	222,053
20.	G. Fisichella	1:37.304	6	214,326

Pit stops

	Driver	Lap	Duration	Stop	Total
1.	R. Barrichello	16	31.829	1	31.829
2.	S. Vettel	18	30.842	1	30.842
3.	H. Kovalainen	22	31.709	1	31.709
4.	M. Webber	22	30.699	1	30.699
5.	F. Massa	22	30.773	1	30.773
6.	S. Bourdais	21	32.465	1	32.465
7.	J. Button	22	30.664	1	30.664
8.	T. Glock	25	33.643	1	33.643
9.	J. Trulli	26	33.113	1	33.113
10.	K. Räikkönen	26	28.777	1	28.777
11.	A. Sutil	26	36.735	1	36.735
12.	L. Hamilton	27	32.744	1	32.744
13.	N. Rosberg	28	36.204	1	36.204
14.	D. Coulthard	28	36.543	1	36.543
15.	N. Heidfeld	29	33.606	1	33.606
16.	S. Bourdais	28	29.045	2	1:01.510
17.	F. Alonso	30	33.806	1	33.806
18.	K. Nakajima	31	32.090	1	32.090
19.	F. Massa	33	29.120	2	59.893
20.	T. Glock	33	29.142	2	1:02.785
21.	N. Rosberg	33	29.627	2	1:05.831
22.	H. Kovalainen	34	29.820	2	1:01.529
23.	R. Kubica	34	30.645	1	30.645
24.	M. Webber	34	30.187	2	1:00.886
25.	K. Räikkönen	35	28.980	2	57.757
26.	J. Trulli	35	28.961	2	1:02.074
27.	S. Vettel	36	29.189	2	1:00.31
28.	L. Hamilton	36	28.460	2	1:01.204
29.	N. Piquet	36	31.314	1	31.314
30.	A. Sutil	37	30.703	2	1:07.438
31.	R. Barrichello	43	31.296	2	1:03.125
32.	A. Sutil	43	45.326	3	1:52.764
33.	J. Button	45	27.666	2	58.330
34.	D. Coulthard	50	47.043	2	1:23.586

Race leader

Driver	Laps in the lead	Nbr of laps
S. Vettel	1 > 18	18
H. Kovalainen	19 > 22	4
S. Vettel	23 > 53	31

Driver	Nbr of laps	Kilometers
S. Vettel	49	283,548 km
H. Kovalainen	4	23,172 km

Lap chart

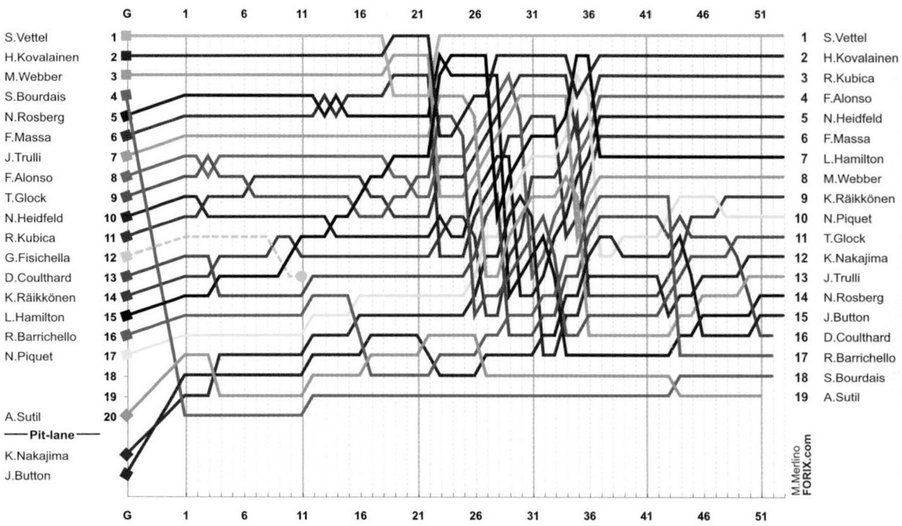
G 1 6 11 16 21 26 31 36 41 46 51
S.Vettel 1
H.Kovalainen 2
M.Webber 3
S.Bourdais 4
N.Rosberg 5
F.Massa 6
J.Trulli 7
F.Alonso 8
T.Glock 9
N.Heidfeld 10
R.Kubica 11
G.Fisichella 12
D.Coulthard 13
K.Räikkönen 14
L.Hamilton 15
R.Barrichello 16
N.Piquet 17
18
19
A.Sutil 20
Pit-lane
K.Nakajima
J.Button
1 S.Vettel
2 H.Kovalainen
3 R.Kubica
4 F.Alonso
5 N.Heidfeld
6 F.Massa
7 L.Hamilton
8 M.Webber
9 K.Räikkönen
10 N.Piquet
11 T.Glock
12 K.Nakajima
13 J.Trulli
14 N.Rosberg
15 J.Button
16 D.Coulthard
17 R.Barrichello
18 S.Bourdais
19 A.Sutil
M.Merlino
FORIX.com

Gaps on the lead board

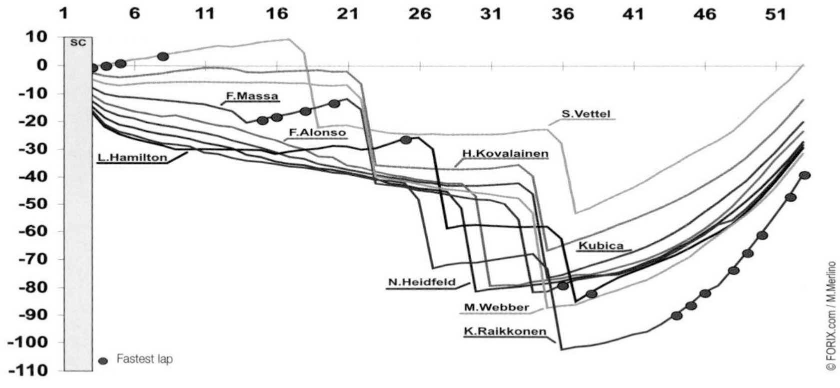
1 6 11 16 21 26 31 36 41 46 51
10
0
-10
-20
-30
-40
-50
-60
-70
-80
-90
-100
-110
SC
F.Massa
F.Alonso
L.Hamilton
S.Vettel
H.Kovalainen
Kubica
N.Heidfeld
M.Webber
K.Raikkonen
Fastest lap
© FORIX.com / M.Merlino

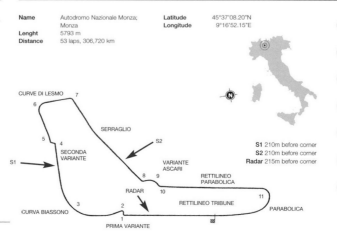

CHAMPIONSHIPS 14/18

Drivers

1.	L. Hamilton	McLaren Mercedes	4🏆	78
2.	F. Massa	Ferrari	5🏆	77
3.	R. Kubica	BMW	1🏆	64
4.	K. Räikkönen	Ferrari	2🏆	57
5.	N. Heidfeld	BMW		53
6.	H. Kovalainen	McLaren Mercedes	1🏆	51
7.	F. Alonso	Renault		28
8.	J. Trulli	Toyota		26
9.	S. Vettel	STR Ferrari	1🏆	23
10.	M. Webber	Red Bull Renault		20
11.	T. Glock	Toyota		15
12.	N. Piquet	Renault		13
13.	R. Barrichello	Honda		11
14.	N. Rosberg	Williams Toyota		9
15.	K. Nakajima	Williams Toyota		8
16.	D. Coulthard	Red Bull Renault		6
17.	S. Bourdais	STR Ferrari		4
18.	J. Button	Honda		3
19.	G. Fisichella	Force India		0
20.	T. Sato	Super Aguri Honda		0
21.	A. Davidson	Super Aguri Honda		0
22.	A. Sutil	Force India		0

Constructors

1.	Scuderia Ferrari Marlboro	7🏆	134
2.	Vodafone McLaren Mercedes	4🏆	129
3.	BMW Sauber F1 Team	2🏆	117
4.	Panasonic Toyota Racing		41
5.	ING Renault F1 Team		41
6.	Scuderia Torro Rosso	1🏆	27
7.	Red Bull Racing		26
7.	AT&T Williams		17
9.	Honda Racing F1 Team		14
10.	Force India F1 Team		0
11.	Super Aguri F1 Team		0

THE CIRCUIT

Name Autodromo Nazionale Monza; Monza
Lenght 5793 m
Distance 53 laps, 306,720 km
Latitude 45°37'08.20"N
Longitude 9°16'52.15"E

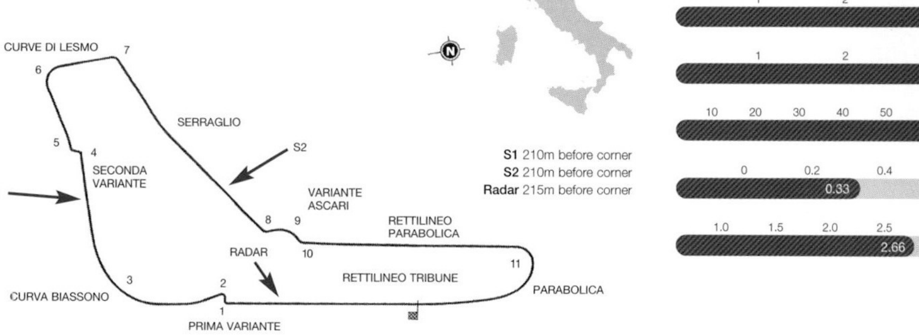
CURVE DI LESMO
SERRAGLIO
S2
S1
SECONDA VARIANTE
VARIANTE ASCARI
RETTILINEO PARABOLICA
RADAR
RETTILINEO TRIBUNE
PARABOLICA
CURVA BIASSONO
PRIMA VARIANTE
1 2 3 4 5 6 7 8 9 10 11
N

S1 210m before corner
S2 210m before corner
Radar 215m before corner

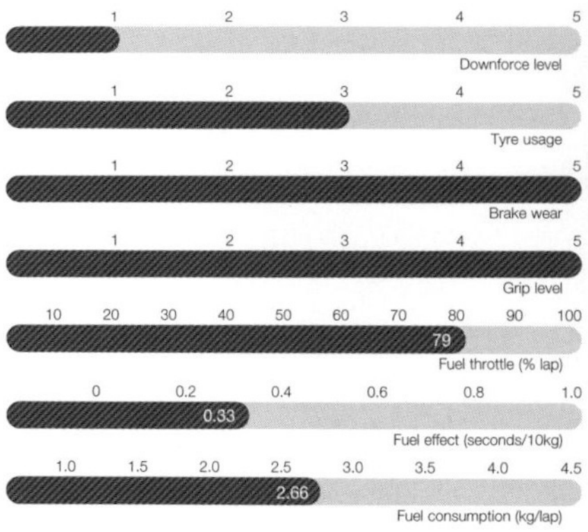
1 2 3 4 5
Downforce level
1 2 3 4 5
Tyre usage
1 2 3 4 5
Brake wear
1 2 3 4 5
Grip level
10 20 30 40 50 60 70 80 90 100
79
Fuel throttle (% lap)
0 0.2 0.4 0.6 0.8 1.0
0.33
Fuel effect (seconds/10kg)
1.0 1.5 2.0 2.5 3.0 3.5 4.0 4.5
2.66
Fuel consumption (kg/lap)

FERNANDO, AN INCREDIBLE SCENARIO

He was 15th on the starting grid and had no chance of finishing on the podium, especially as he was due to be the very first driver to refuel as early as lap 12. On a street circuit, such a strategy could only lead to disaster. Indeed, the Spaniard rejoined the track plum last after his stop and would have finished way down the order, but for an accident bringing out the safety car on lap 14.

It was a minor miracle, combined with some other lucky breaks: Robert Kubica and Nico Rosberg were about to run out of fuel and had to pit when it was forbidden, thus incurring penalties, without which the Williams driver would have won. Fernando Alonso also profited from the fact that Giancarlo Fisichella, who did not refuel at this point, found himself leading the pack and conveniently held up everyone, while the Spaniard pulled away in front.

All these factors led to Fernando Alonso taking a fantastic Singapore Grand Prix victory, in the first night race in history.

> Giancarlo Fisichella climbing the kerbs. In Singapore, the Italian qualified 20th and last.

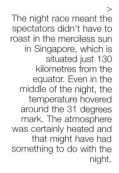

Felipe Massa, king of the streets, on pole again

With just one little point separating them in the championship table and four Grands Prix remaining, the end of season tussle between Lewis Hamilton (78 points) and Felipe Massa (77 points,) looked like being a nail biter. 21 points down, it seemed that Kimi Raikkonen was no longer a contender.

Felipe Massa struck the first blow on Saturday, taking pole position for the Singapore Grand Prix. He was so much quicker than Hamilton, that the Brazilian wished he'd run with a heavier fuel load: "*I think I did an absolutely perfect lap, getting every corner right,*" reckoned Massa. "*Getting the most out of your car is the most incredible feeling a driver can experience. So of course, I did feel I could have had more fuel on board, but let's just say our strategy is still the right one.*"

The artificial lighting was apparently no problem for the drivers. "*To be honest, it's just like driving in full daylight,*" admitted Lewis Hamilton, second on the starting grid. "*It's even better, because the light is more consistent. If you look up, you can see it's black all around, but in any case, you concentrate on the track and don't have time to look at the sky.*"

The main difficulty in the race would seem to come from the track itself, which was bumpy and tricky as you like. "*It will be almost impossible for the driver to go 61 laps without making the slightest error,*" suggested Denis Chevrier, Renault's operations director. "*If you go down an escape road, as we've seen happen a lot in practice, then you lose 30 seconds and it's race over.*"

For Felipe Massa therefore, the main concern would be to maintain concentration. "*There are a lot of bumps here, between turns 5 and 7. Staying focussed for the whole race will be very, very tough.*"

In any case, the threat would not come from behind, as overtaking did not look very likely. "*Overtaking? I wouldn't count on it,*" regretted Hamilton. "*This afternoon, I was following David Coulthard's Red Bull and, although I was definitely quicker than him, I wasn't able to keep up through the corners. The only way to overtake will be through our strategies.*"

IN BRIEF

+ The paddock regulars decided to stay on European time to fit in with the night timetable, rather than switching to Singapore time. "I've decided to go to bed every "night" at five in the morning," explained David Coulthard. "The problem is that the locals haven't planned for that and all the restaurants close around midnight, so I've had to make do with room service."

+ Fernando Alonso doesn't seem ready to put his rivalry with Lewis Hamilton behind him. He told a Spanish daily paper that he'd rather see Felipe Massa take the title. "Because if he doesn't manage to win, it will go to Hamilton. Having said that, if I had to bet on it, I'd put my money on Lewis. He is more consistent."

+ Jarno Trulli was the first man to be fined at night in F1: after spinning on the pit straight in Friday's first session, the Italian drove the wrong way down the track to come into the pits. A "crime" for which he was "reprimanded" by the Stewards and fined 10,000 Euros.

+ Martin Whitmarsh, McLaren's managing director, is not known for his sense of humour. However, for this

Grand Prix, the team ran a film clip that took a funny view of night racing. To have a look go to www.YouTube.com and type in "McLaren Singapore."

+ Coming into the pits, Nick Heidfeld impeded Rubens Barrichello in the first qualifying session. The German was moved back three places on the grid, to ninth spot.

+ Blocked by Nick Heidfeld (see above,) Rubens Barrichello decided to abort his quick lap to suddenly dive into the pits. Bad idea: he cut the entry to pit lane and was fined 10,000 Euros!

+ While Sebastian Vettel displayed his usual virtuosity to qualify sixth, Sebastien Bourdais could only manage 17th place. The Frenchman complained his car was sliding every time he braked. "There was no way I could attack, because I had no stability or traction."

+ Apart from the final corner, where there was a patch of shadow, overall the lighting seemed spot on. "You can see as though it was daylight, even better than at some circuits where the light varies from corner to corner," said Bourdais.

> The night race meant the spectators didn't have to roast in the merciless sun in Singapore, which is situated just 130 kilometres from the equator. Even in the middle of the night, the temperature hovered around the 31 degrees mark. The atmosphere was certainly heated and that might have had something to do with the night.

STARTING GRID

* N. HEIDFELD relegated of 3 positions for having blocking BARRICHELLO in his fast lap in Q1.

G. FISICHELLA starts from the pit lane.

G. FISICHELLA* 20	R. BARRICHELLO 18	N. PIQUET 16	D. COULTHARD 14	J. BUTTON 12	K. NAKAJIMA 10	N. ROSBERG 8	S. VETTEL 6	R. KUBICA 4	L. HAMILTON 2
	1:46.583	1:46.037	1:45.298	1:45.133	1:47.547	1:46.611	1:46.244	1:45.779	1:45.465

A. SUTIL 19	S. BOURDAIS 17	F. ALONSO 15	M. WEBBER 13	J. TRULLI 11	N. HEIDFELD* 9	T. GLOCK 7	H. KOVALAINEN 5	K. RÄIKKÖNEN 3	F. MASSA 1
1:47.940	1:46.389		1:45.212	1:45.038	1:45.964	1:46.328	1:45.873	1:45.617	1:44.801 (174.055 km/h)

<
It got off to a good start for Felipe Massa and the Brazilian would no doubt have won, but for his refueling problem.

The shiny Ferrari train is derailed again

Ferrari lost the Singapore Grand Prix at the first refuelling stop. The Scuderia was the only team using a system of red, orange and green lights to indicate to its drivers when they could leave the pits after a stop.

In Valencia, Kimi Raikkonen left too early, knocking over one of his mechanics. Then, in Singapore, when the team decided to call in both its cars at the same time, on lap 17, it switched the light system from automatic to manual control. Unfortunately, the mechanic in charge of operating the lights made a mistake, showing Felipe Massa the green light when the refuelling hose was still attached to the car. Storming away from the pit, the Brazilian pulled the line with him, also knocking over a mechanic, who fortunately escaped with just a few bruises. In the time it took the crew to refuel Kimi Raikkonen, who was queuing behind his team-mate, then sprint to the end of pit lane to sort out the stricken Massa, his race was effectively over.

Rejoining last, the Brazilian was then also given a penalty for a dangerous release from the pit stop, before hitting a wall and cutting several chicanes. He finished 13th. "*It was a human error*," insisted Ferrari team principal, Stefano Domenicali. "*But we are not looking to find someone to blame. We are a team: we win together and we lose together.*"

For his part, Kimi Raikkonen could have finished third, if he hadn't finally crashed off the track, trying to keep up with Nico Rosberg. Ferrari left the Singapore Grand Prix grumbling about what might have been. Sometimes there are days like that.

Robert Kubica could have won. At the precise moment that Nelsinho Piquet had his huge crash, prompting the appearance of the safety car, Robert Kubica had just driven past the pits. "*If Robert had come along 20 seconds later, we would have brought him in and he would have won. We were ready for him*," sighed one of the BMW Sauber engineers. As was the case with Nico Rosberg, the Pole finally had to refuel when coming into pit lane was forbidden, otherwise he would have run out of fuel. He incurred a penalty for this and came home eleventh.

Fernando Alonso, talent and luck

It was Nelsinho Piquet's accident which kicked it all off. Up until then, Felipe Massa was leading the race as he pleased, followed by Lewis Hamilton and Kimi Raikkonen. Nothing, it seemed, could halt the triumphal march to victory of the Brazilian Ferrari driver. That didn't take into account the imponderable nature of F1. On lap 14, Nelsinho Piquet piled his Renault really heavily into a concrete wall, forcing the race director to call out the safety car.

It happened at around the time the first run of pit stops was about to start and, as soon as it was permitted, all the drivers rushed for the pits.

All of them except Fernando Alonso that is, who had been the first to stop, two laps before his team-mate's accident. Up to that point, he'd been running last, but the Spaniard made the most of it to get ahead of all those in the pits, to find himself fifth, behind Nico Rosberg and Robert Kubica, who were going to be penalised and behind Jarno Trulli and Giancarlo Fisichella, who had yet to refuel.

The Spaniard had the win in his pocket. The hand of fate had picked him up from the back of the pack and installed him at the head of the field. "*It's true, we were lucky,*" admitted the double world champion after the race. "*But it was well deserved. The team has worked very hard this season and we had started so far back.*"

He needed that luck on several levels: it was because of brake problems and his poor qualifying (15th on the grid) that he had decided to refuel so early. "*We still don't know why I stopped on Saturday,*" he added. "*Maybe the bumps had cut the fuel supply. So you can imagine how nervous I was during the final laps.*"

Inheriting third place, Lewis Hamilton did well out of the night: thanks to his 6 points here, he now led Felipe Massa by 7, with three races to go.

The first ever night race in the history of F1 had been a total success. For the drivers, it was just like a normal race. "*I couldn't tell the difference,*" admitted Lewis Hamilton. "*I even completely forgot we were racing at night.*"

Fernando Alonso and Nico Rosberg on the podium: an original result for an original race.

∨

SUPER SINGAPORE

A unique décor, a unique timetable, faultless organization and a splendid race: the Singapore Grand Prix kept to all its promises. Seen from the big wheel, the biggest in the world, the track lighting is very impressive.

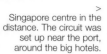

> Singapore centre in the distance. The circuit was set up near the port, around the big hotels.

The biggest port in the world, Singapore gambles on tourism

When Thomas Raffles first set up shop in these parts, in 1819, he had no doubt that one day, Singapore would become the most important commercial port in the world. Having gained independence, almost 50 years ago, the city-state soon developed into a hub for international trade. Seeing itself as the Switzerland of Asia, Singapore and its 4.5 million inhabitants, cultivates a difference between itself and neighbouring Malaysia and Indonesia. Here, there is no corruption, violence or litter in the streets. In Singapore, it is forbidden to sell chewing gum, so that it doesn't end up stuck on the pavement! It is a crime not to flush the cistern in a public toilet, a crime monitored by a special squad who issue salty on the spot fines. If one is caught littering three times, one has to clean the streets on Sunday morning, wearing a T shirt with the inscription, "I'm a litter lout." Now, Singapore does not want to rest on its laurels as Asia's commercial centre. The town wants to attract tourists too, who have never really considered it a destination, save as a stop over on the way to Australia.

The Singapore Tourist Board therefore embarked on a huge development programme, which got underway this weekend with the first ever nighttime Grand Prix. *"From an international point of view, we hope to transform Singapore into the destination of choice for both business and tourism. We hope to attract 10.8 million visitors this year,"* explained Simon Israel, the director of the STB. *"That's a 5% increase on last year."*

So far, the gamble had not paid off, as figures for the first quarter actually showed a slight drop in numbers compared to 2007. Therefore, all hopes rested with the Grand Prix and the city had aligned itself in this endeavor with a major business player, Ong Beng Seng. *"Personally, I like F1,"* explained the multi-millionaire. *"And I think this Grand Prix is a very good thing for Singapore. F1 isn't just an event, it's iconic."*

Ong Beng Seng was key in convincing his old friend and Formula 1 commercial rights holder Bernie Ecclestone to bring the race here. *"I have several projects that are already well advanced,"* revealed the Englishman, during a lightning visit to the media centre. *"Ong used all his powers of persuasion to convince me to come here. Seeing what they have done here in Singapore, I don't regret it!"*

And with good cause, because the organizers used incredibly inventive solutions to create the circuit, running around its historic centre, alongside the sea. The facility cost a total of 150 million Singapore dollars, with 60% financed by the city, which it hopes to recover thanks to the influx of visitors coming to the race. *"We are expecting 100,000 spectators for the Grand Prix,"* reckoned Michael Roche, the event's commercial director. *"We hope that at least 40% of them come from abroad, which will have a major impact on hotels, restaurants, taxis and nightlife."*

The government had actually imposed a 30% tax on the hotels surrounding the track, with a tariff of 15% for those further away. It was the first time in the history of F1 that a tax has been imposed, specifically relating to the event.

Along with the 7% sales tax applied to all other activities, the revenue should be enough to cover a large part of the money invested in the circuit. A five year contract with Bernie Ecclestone should see the Grand Prix turning a profit.

The increase in popularity of Singapore itself might be harder to judge. *"We are sure that TV viewers will be impressed with the beauty of the venue,"* said Simon Israel. *"With the skyscrapers as a backdrop and the biggest big wheel in the world, it is a unique décor for a Grand Prix."*

The fact the race was taking place at night, a first for F1, was the hook that Singapore was counting on to assure its popularity. With qualifying starting at 22h00 and the race at 20h00, the cars were running in the absolute dead of night, under incredibly powerful lighting, developed by an Italian company. The system comprised 1485 lamps of 2000 watts each, giving a total output of 3 million watts - not including other additional light sources. On Saturday, the hotels near the track asked their guests to leave their curtains open and the lights on in their rooms, so as to create an even more aesthetic effect when seen from outside!

In terms of ensuring the lights worked, nothing had been left to chance, with twelve separate generators feeding the supply. Even if a giant power cut plunged Singapore into darkness, the circuit would still be lit.

On the technical front, just as on the commercial side, the success of this Grand Prix seemed assured, whoever the winner. In any case, in Singapore, the sporting side of the weekend seemed to take something of a back seat.

> Mansour Ojjeh's wife and Ron Dennis' new companion seemed to appreciate the Singapore atmosphere on the starting grid.

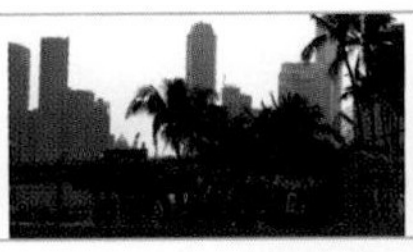

PRACTICE

Date	Weather (AM)	Air temperature	Track temperature	Weather (PM)	Air temperature	Track temperature
Friday September 26, 2008	Stary night, dry	28-31°c	30-34°c	Stary night, dry	28-29°c	28-32°c
Saturday September 27, 2008	Stary night, dry	29-30°c	30-32°c	Stary night, dry	31-30°c	30-29°c

All the time trials

N° Driver	Nat.	N° Chassis- Engine [Nbr. GP]	Pos. Free 1 Friday 16:00-17:30	Laps	Pos. Free 2 Friday 20:00-21:30	Laps	Pos. Free 3 Saturday 17:00-18:00	Laps	Pos. Q1 Saturday 20:00-20:20	Laps	Pos. Q2 Saturday 20:27-20:42	Laps	Pos. Q3 Saturday 20:50-21:00	Laps
1. Kimi Räikkönen	FIN	Ferrari F2008 271 [2]	3. 1:46.961	24	7. 1:46.580	25	17. 1:46.482	10	1. 1:44.282	7	3. 1:44.232	5	3. **1:45.617**	6
2. Felipe Massa	BR	Ferrari F2008 269 [2]	2. 1:45.598	23	3. 1:45.793	31	3. 1:45.246	18	4. 1:44.519	7	1. 1:44.014	3	1. **1:44.801**	6
3. Nick Heidfeld	D	BMW Sauber F1.08-07 [1]	8. 1:46.964	24	16. 1:47.760	36	11. 1:45.689	19	12. 1:45.548	7	8. 1:44.520	6	6. **1:45.964**	6
4. Robert Kubica	PL	BMW Sauber F1.08-05 [2]	5. 1:46.618	23	6. 1:46.384	36	7. 1:45.425	17	5. 1:44.740	6	7. 1:44.519	6	4. **1:45.779**	6
5. Fernando Alonso	E	Renault R28-02 [2]	7. 1:46.725	29	1. 1:45.654	30	1. 1:44.506	19	6. 1:44.971	5	15. **DNS**	1		
6. Nelson Piquet	BR	Renault R28-01 [2]	9. 1:47.175	30	16. 1:47.145	35	4. 1:45.249	18	16. **1:46.037**	6				
7. Nico Rosberg	D	Williams FW30-05 - Toyota [1]	6. 1:46.710	25	5. 1:46.164	34	5. 1:45.386	17	8. 1:45.103	5	5. 1:44.429	6	9. **1:46.611**	6
8. Kazuki Nakajima	J	Williams FW30-04 - Toyota [1]	12. 1:47.662	23	9. 1:47.013	32	12. 1:45.982	18	9. 1:45.127	8	9. 1:44.826	6	10. **1:47.547**	6
9. David Coulthard	GB	Red Bull RB4 4 - Renault [1]	15. 1:48.517	23	15. 1:47.640	31	18. 1:46.794	6	15. 1:46.028	10	14. **1:45.298**	6		
10. Mark Webber	AUS	Red Bull RB4 5 - Renault [2]	20. 1:53.703	4	11. 1:47.137	15	8. 1:45.450	21	11. 1:45.493	6	13. **1:45.212**	6		
11. Jarno Trulli	I	Toyota TF108-05 [2]	19. 1:49.064	29	19. 1:48.059	28	16. 1:46.221	19	13. 1:45.642	6	11. **1:45.038**	6		
12. Timo Glock	D	Toyota TF108-07 [1]	13. 1:47.706	27	10. 1:47.046	22	15. 1:46.180	23	8. 1:45.184	9	6. 1:44.441	6	8. **1:46.328**	6
14. Sébastien Bourdais	F	Toro Rosso STR3-04 - Ferrari [2]	14. 1:48.097	16	14. 1:47.487	24	10. 1:45.599	13	17. **1:46.389**	6				
15. Sebastian Vettel	D	Toro Rosso STR3-03 - Ferrari [2]	11. 1:47.570	28	13. 1:47.300	33	9. 1:45.477	19	7. 1:45.042	6	3. 1:44.261	3	7. **1:46.244**	6
16. Jenson Button	GB	Honda RA108-05 [2]	10. 1:47.277	30	8. 1:46.901	32	6. 1:45.409	20	14. 1:45.660	8	12. **1:45.133**	6		
17. Rubens Barrichello	BR	Honda RA108-03 [2]	16. 1:48.725	19	18. 1:48.009	25	14. 1:46.073	2˙	18. **1:46.583**	7				
20. Adrian Sutil	D	Force India VJM01/06 - Ferrari [1]	17. 1:48.839	24	20. 1:48.311	36	20. 1:47.727	19	19. **1:47.940**	10				
21. Giancarlo Fisichella	I	Force India VJM01/05 - Ferrari [2]	18. 1:48.906	25	17. 1:47.965	12	19. 1:47.166	14	20. **DNF**	2				
22. Lewis Hamilton	GB	McLaren MP4-23 07 - Mercedes [1]	1. 1:45.518	20	2. 1:45.752	28	2. 1:45.119	13	3. 1:44.501	3	10. 1:44.932	5	2. **1:45.465**	6
23. Heikki Kovalainen	FIN	McLaren MP4-23 04 - Mercedes [2] -> [1]	4. 1:46.463	20	4. 1:45.797	31	13. 1:45.985	13	2. 1:44.311	7	2. 1:44.207	6	5. **1:45.873**	3

Fastest lap overall

F. Massa 1:44.014 (175,372 km/h)

Maximum speed

N° Driver	S1 Qualifs	Pos.	S1 Race	Pos.	S2 Qualifs	Pos.	S2 Race	Pos.	Finish Qualifs	Pos.	Finish Race	Pos.	Radar Qualifs	Pos.	Radar Race	Pos.
1. K. Räikkönen	291,1	13	291,0	16	268,3	10	270,2	5	249,4	13	247,5	7	285,7	14	286,5	11
2. F. Massa	290,9	14	291,1	14	268,2	12	268,7	10	253,1	3	249,3	2	287,5	9	287,1	8
3. N. Heidfeld	292,4	10	295,0	5	270,3	4	269,6	8	249,7	10	246,9	10	287,1	11	286,7	10
4. R. Kubica	291,5	12	292,4	11	269,1	7	248,6	6	252,6	4	248,6	6	288,1	6	285,4	13
5. F. Alonso	293,4	6	293,3	9	268,7	9	269,8	7	251,5	7	248,7	5	289,8	3	288,2	2
6. N. Piquet	294,8	5	294,1	7	269,1	6	266,0	16	249,4	12	243,0	16	287,8	8	285,4	12
7. N. Rosberg	292,4	9	293,0	10	267,2	14	268,0	11	251,7	6	247,4	8	287,2	10	288,0	3
8. K. Nakajima	293,1	7	293,3	8	268,7	8	271,0	2	250,9	8	247,0	9	286,8	13	287,0	9
9. D. Coulthard	293,0	8	292,2	12	268,1	13	267,7	12	249,7	11	245,9	13	288,1	7	287,3	7
10. M. Webber	291,5	11	291,9	13	268,3	11	265,1	18	249,2	14	242,3	18	287,1	12	284,2	16
11. J. Trulli	286,3	19	285,1	20	265,5	18	261,6	20	246,8	18	242,3	19	281,7	19	276,4	20
12. T. Glock	288,9	17	289,3	19	266,8	17	266,0	17	250,5	9	246,4	11	283,0	18	280,5	19
14. S. Bourdais	295,8	2	297,9	3	270,3	3	270,6	4	248,9	15	245,7	14	289,1	4	287.6	5
15. S. Vettel	295,3	3	297,7	4	270,2	5	270,0	6	253,4	2	249,1	3	288,4	5	287,6	6
16. J. Button	289,5	15	289,6	17	267,2	15	267,3	13	248,2	16	246,2	12	284,8	15	284,4	14
17. R. Barrichello	289,4	16	289,3	18	266,6	16	264,0	19	247,1	17	242,5	17	284,0	17	281,8	18
20. A. Sutil	288,3	18	294,2	6	265,1	19	266,4	15	244,5	19	241,8	20	284,2	16	284,2	15
21. G. Fisichella	257,8	20	291,0	15	264,2	20	266,6	14	243,2	20	243,1	15	281,1	20	282,0	17
22. L. Hamilton	297,5	1	298,0	2	271,5	2	270,7	3	252,5	5	248,8	4	291,1	1	287,9	4
23. H. Kovalainen	295,0	4	298,5	1	273,1	1	272,3	1	253,6	1	250,4	1	290,0	2	289,6	1

Best sector times

Qualifs	**S1** F. Massa	27.977	**S2** N. Heidfeld	40.315	**S3** F. Massa	35.512	= 1:43.804
Race	**S1** F. Massa	28.314	**S2** L .Hamilton	40.840	**S3** F. Alonso	36.101	= 1:45.075

RACE

Date	Weather	Air temperature	Track temperature	Humidity	Wind speed
Sunday September 28, 2008 (20:00)	Stary night, dry	28°c	32-31°c	78-66%	1.9 m/s

Classification & retirements

Pos.	Driver	Constructor	Tyres	Laps	Time	Km/h
1.	F. Alonso	Renault	USS	61	1:57:16.304	158,068
2.	N. Rosberg	Williams Toyota	USSU	61	+ 2.957	158,002
3.	L. Hamilton	McLaren Mercedes	SSU	61	+ 5.917	157,935
4.	T. Glock	Toyota	SSU	61	+ 8.155	157,885
5.	S. Vettel	STR Ferrari	SSU	61	+ 10.268	157,838
6.	N. Heidfeld	BMW	SSU	61	+ 11.101	157,819
7.	D. Coulthard	Red Bull Renault	SSU	61	+ 16.387	157,701
8.	K. Nakajima	Williams Toyota	SSU	61	+ 18.489	157,654
9.	J. Button	Honda	SSU	61	+ 19.885	157,623
10.	H. Kovalainen	McLaren Mercedes	SSU	61	+ 26.902	157,466
11.	R. Kubica	BMW	SSU	61	+ 27.975	157,442
12.	S. Bourdais	STR Ferrari	SUS	61	+ 29.432	157,410
13.	F. Massa	Ferrari	SSSU	61	+ 35.170	157,282
14.	G. Fisichella	Force India	SU	61	+ 43.571	157,095
15.	K. Räikkönen	Ferrari	SSU	57	4 laps	157,177

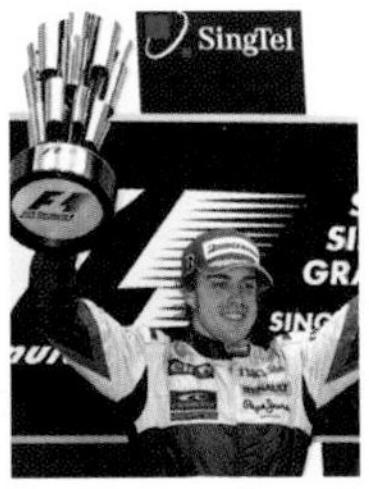

Percute le mur, train AVD arraché

Driver	Constructor	Tyres	Laps	Reason
J. Trulli	Toyota	SU	50	Hydraulik pressure failure
A. Sutil	Force India	SSU	49	Spin... car goes straight on and hits guardrails
M. Webber	Red Bull Renault	SS	29	Gearbox failure
R. Barrichello	Honda	SS	14	Engine
N. Piquet	Renault	S	13	Spin and hits concrete wall

Tyres S: Soft & U: Super soft

Fastest laps

	Driver	Time	Lap	Km/h
1.	K. Räikkönen	1:45.599	14	172,740
2.	F. Massa	1:45.757	13	172,482
3.	F. Alonso	1:45.768	55	172,464
4.	L. Hamilton	1:46.072	14	171,969
5.	N. Rosberg	1:46.454	39	171,352
6.	R. Kubica	1:46.899	14	170,639
7.	J. Trulli	1:46.972	32	170,523
8.	T. Glock	1:47.044	50	170,408
9.	S. Vettel	1:47.271	13	170,047
10.	K. Nakajima	1:47.287	13	170,022
11.	N. Heidfeld	1:47.306	14	169,992
12.	H. Kovalainen	1:47.337	14	169,943
13.	D. Coulthard	1:47.562	41	169,587
14.	S. Bourdais	1:47.820	29	169,181
15.	J. Button	1:48.128	61	168,700
16.	G. Fisichella	1:49.101	28	167,195
17.	M. Webber	1:49.183	13	167,069
18.	A. Sutil	1:49.270	38	166,936
19.	R. Barrichello	1:50.320	13	165,348
20.	N. Piquet	1:50.449	13	165,154

Pit stops

	Driver	Lap	Duration	Stop	Total
1.	F. Alonso	12	28.146	1	28.146
2.	M. Webber	14	31.518	1	31.518
3.	D. Coulthard	14	41.286	1	41.286
4.	R. Barrichello	14	28.532	1	28.532
5.	N. Rosberg	15	27.216	1	27.216
6.	R. Kubica	16	29.399	1	29.399
7.	F. Massa	17	2:03.359	1	2:03.359
8.	L. Hamilton	17	32.638	1	32.638
9.	K. Räikkönen	17	49.568	1	49.568
10.	S. Vettel	17	30.488	1	30.488
11.	T. Glock	17	30.519	1	30.519
12.	H. Kovalainen	17	34.363	1	34.363
13.	N. Heidfeld	17	27.874	1	27.874
14.	K. Nakajima	17	28.094	1	28.094
15.	J. Button	17	26.999	1	26.999
16.	A. Sutil	17	30.550	1	30.550
17.	S. Bourdais	18	25.681	1	25.681
18.	F. Massa	•24•	15.786	2	2:19.145
19.	R. Kubica	•27•	28.782	2	58.181
20.	N. Rosberg	•28•	28.951	2	56.167
21.	G. Fisichella	29	31.375	1	31.375
22.	F. Massa	31	25.866	3	2:45.011
23.	J. Trulli	33	28.346	1	28.346
24.	S. Bourdais	33	27.991	2	53.672
25.	R. Kubica	33	26.591	3	1:24.772
26.	H. Kovalainen	34	26.696	2	1:01.059
27.	J. Button	35	26.839	2	53.838
28.	A. Sutil	39	27.725	2	58.275
29.	N. Rosberg	40	27.090	3	1:23.257
30.	F. Alonso	41	26.160	2	54.306
31.	L. Hamilton	42	25.945	2	58.583
32.	D. Coulthard	42	28.336	2	1:09.622
33.	K. Nakajima	42	26.820	2	54.914
34.	S. Vettel	43	25.779	2	56.267
35.	N. Heidfeld	43	25.125	2	52.999
36.	T. Glock	46	24.648	2	55.167
37.	K. Räikkönen	50	24.974	2	1:14.542

•• Drive-through penalty: Massa.
Unsafe release from pit stop.

Stop-go penalty (10 sec.): Rosberg & Kubica.
•• Refuelling while pit lane closed.

Race leader

Driver	Laps in the lead	Nbr of laps
F. Massa	1 > 17	17
N. Rosberg	18 > 28	11
J. Trulli	29 > 33	5
F. Alonso	34 > 61	28

Driver	Nbr of laps	Kilometers
F. Alonso	28	141,876 km
F. Massa	17	86,002 km
N. Rosberg	11	55,737 km
J. Trulli	5	25,335 km

Gaps on the lead board

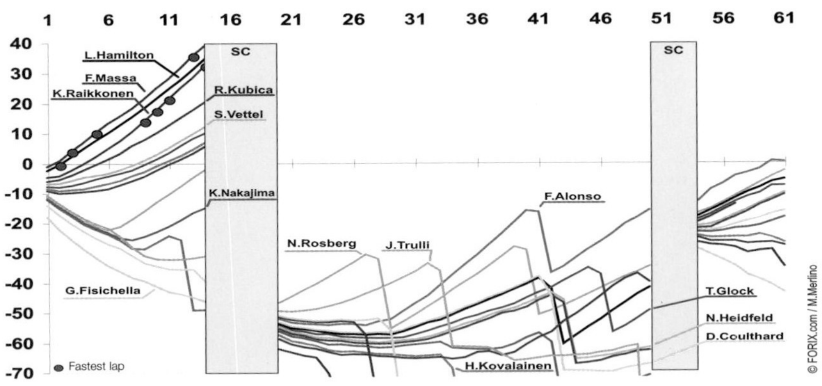

Lap chart

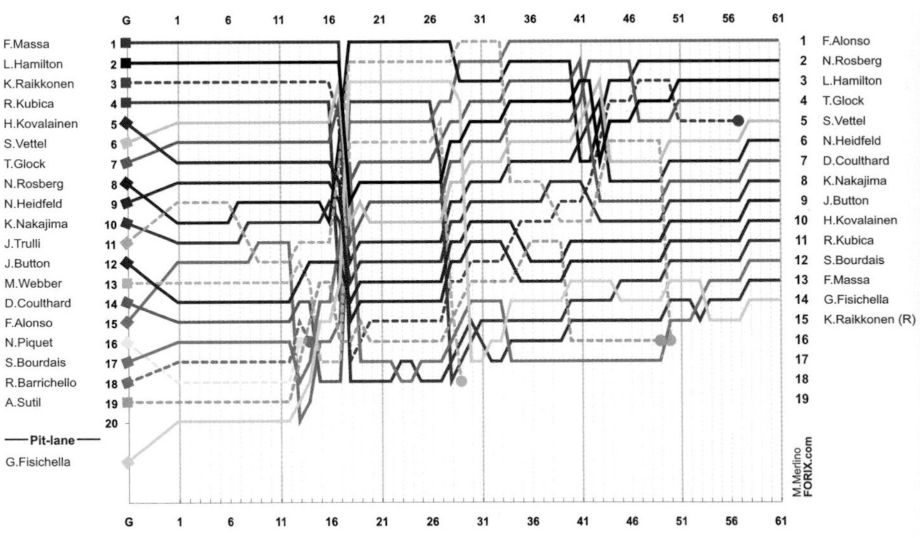

CHAMPIONSHIPS 15/18

Drivers

1.	L. Hamilton	McLaren Mercedes	4🏆	84
2.	F. Massa	Ferrari	5🏆	77
3.	R. Kubica	BMW	1🏆	64
4.	K. Räikkönen	Ferrari	2🏆	57
5.	N. Heidfeld	BMW		56
6.	H. Kovalainen	McLaren Mercedes	1🏆	51
7.	F. Alonso	Renault	1🏆	38
8.	S. Vettel	STR Ferrari	1🏆	27
9.	J. Trulli	Toyota		26
10.	T. Glock	Toyota		20
11.	M. Webber	Red Bull Renault		20
12.	N. Rosberg	Williams Toyota		17
13.	N. Piquet	Renault		13
14.	R. Barrichello	Honda		11
15.	K. Nakajima	Williams Toyota		9
16.	D. Coulthard	Red Bull Renault		8
17.	S. Bourdais	STR Ferrari		4
18.	J. Button	Honda		3
19.	G. Fisichella	Force India		0
20.	A. Sutil	Force India		0
21.	T. Sato	Super Aguri Honda		0
22.	A. Davidson	Super Aguri Honda		0

Constructors

1.	Vodafone McLaren Mercedes	4🏆	135
2.	Scuderia Ferrari Marlboro	7🏆	134
3.	BMW Sauber F1 Team	2🏆	120
4.	ING Renault F1 Team	1🏆	51
5.	Panasonic Toyota Racing		46
6.	Scuderia Torro Rosso	1🏆	31
7.	Red Bull Racing		28
7.	AT&T Williams		26
9.	Honda Racing F1 Team		14
10.	Force India F1 Team		0
11.	Super Aguri F1 Team		0

THE CIRCUIT

Name Marina Bay Street Circuit; Singapore
Lenght 5067 m
Distance 61 laps, 309,087 km
Latitude 1°17'29.05"N
Longitude 103°51'50.93"E

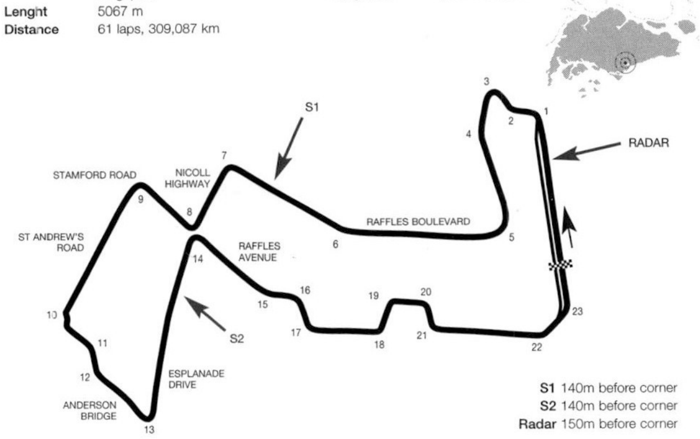

S1 140m before corner
S2 140m before corner
Radar 150m before corner

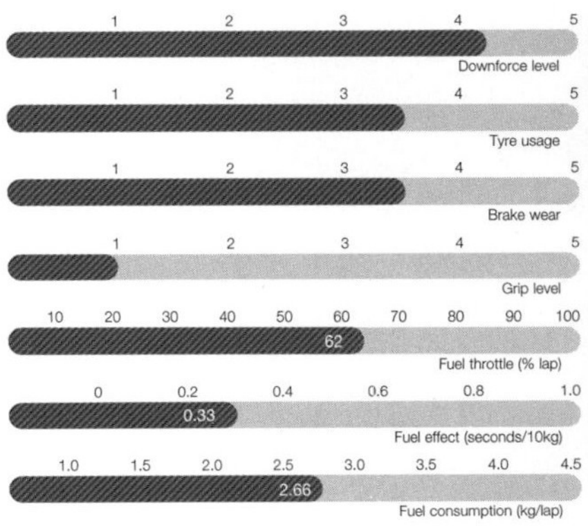

ALO
P1
PIQ
P4

AND THAT MAKES TWO
FOR FERNANDO ALONSO

Fernando Alonso scored a very lucky win in Singapore, nevertheless, he did it again at Mount Fuji. This time, he made the most of the confusion at the first corner, but from then on, he ran his race at a hellish pace, to such an extent that no one was able to challenge him. As for the two title contenders, they both missed out on a good chance to pull out a gap on their rival; Felipe Massa limited the damage by scoring two points, while Lewis Hamilton finished comfortably outside the top eight.

LAST-GASP LEWIS!

Unbelievable. Wild. Fantastic. Crazy. Unthinkable. Words failed when it came to summing up the way the 2008 Formula 1 World Championship finished.

Between laps 69 and 71 the title changed hands twice, passing from Lewis Hamilton to Felipe Massa then back to the British driver in the last corner of the season. After 18 Grands Prix, 1117 laps and 5481 kilometres the title was decided in the final 400 metres when Hamilton passed Timo Glock at Mergulho, the very last corner of a wonderful season.

Never before had a Formula 1 finale given us such tension - a tension that was unbearable by race start, when the heavens opened just before the lights went out. The drivers all started on rain tyres before changing back to dries as the race went on.

Massa took control from the start as Hamilton struggled, but held on to a fourth place that would be good enough for the world title. With seven laps to go, the Sao Paulo rain began again. Once again the drivers stopped for wets, and Hamilton was in trouble. He fluffed his acceleration onto the main straight, and Sebastian Vettel pounced, overtaking him at the start of the antipenultimate lap. One little passing manoeuvre, such huge consequences- the title race had just swung in Massa's favour. When he crossed the line the Brazilian was World Champion. And he would still have been World Champion if Timo Glock hadn't messed up his last braking-point. Struggling with dry-weather tyres on a rain-soaked surface, the German allowed Hamilton ro dive through on the inside and regain the fifth place that made the title his.

So, in the kind of breathtaking script no writer would have dared dream up, the 2008 title came down to the final corner. And Lewis Hamilton took his first crown -- only just, one point ahead of Felipe Massa after a race that summed up an amazing season.

> Felipe Massa fought manfully to hold back the tears on the podium, but one or two escaped. Winning the Grand Prix, he had certainly kept his part of the bargain.

Massa takes the title… and loses it

As the start approaches, a huge crowd has turned up to pack the Interlagos stands. You can feel the tension all around the circuit as they chant Felipe Massa's name and boo Leiws Hamilton.

The plot thickens with just four minutes to go when a storm breaks over the circuit. Virtually all of the drivers go for wet weather tyres.

Massa had only one strategy in mind: winning. The Brazilian led from the start and drove the perfect race. Switching to 'dries' by lap 10, the Ferrari driver made certain of the race win.

Behind him, though, Hamilton was struggling. Between laps 12 and 17 he was out of the top five, where he had to finish if he wanted to take the title. Once back in fourth, he was having to work hard to stay there.

With eight laps remaining, though, the Interlagos rain returned. Hamilton wasn't among the first to come in and found himself in fifth place, just in front of Sebastian Vettel - who passed him on the straight as they finished lap 69. McLaren were stunned: if the Briton finished sixth, he would miss out on the world title.

Hamilton tried everything, risking an off, but just couldn't get past Vettel, which was his only hope (see opposite). On the very last lap the British driver tried an impossible move on the German but it didn't work. But that brought the two men to the final corner of the race, the tight left-hander called 'Mergulho', taken in second.

Up ahead, Timo Glock's Toyota fluffed its braking and slowed - he was on dry-weather tyres in the pouring rain. The German's last lap was a 1:44.7 - 16 seconds slower than the one before. Vettel and Hamilton pounced, passing him on the climb up toward the finishing straight.

Just 400 metres more and the McLaren driver crossed the line in fifth place - the title was his by a single point.

The stunned silence of the previous two laps gave way to an explosion of joy at McLaren; over at Ferrari, joy turned to despair. Sheer happenstance had seen Glock hand the title to Hamilton on a plate.

Massa won for his home crowd, but missed out by one little point. Taking the season as a whole, Hamilton probably deserved the crown, but Massa didn't deserve to lose it in such a cruel way.

> No doubt who was the happiest man on the podium: it was Fernando Alonso, whose second place for Renault was a magnificent way for the French team to finish off their season.

He tried to remain philosophical as he left the podium after a victory in vain. "*Those were the most unbelieveable few minutes of my life. When I crossed the line, I was World Champion. I was waiting for my engineer to tell me that on the radio.*

I was at Turn 3 already when he told me Lewis had overtaken Glock. I couldn't take it in, it was quite surreal. But there you are, the title is Lewis's, congratulations to him - he scored more points than me and he's a great champion. I won the race today, I did what I had to do, and I think I can leave here with my head held high.

It was a perfect day. These things happen, that's racing… God knows his plan. If things turned out this way, it's because they were supposed to."

Lewis: "a terribly difficult race"

Lewis Hamilton's Brazilian Grand Prix was like a nightmare. Fourth, then fifth, then sixth, he reclaimed that crucial fifth place only in the very last few metres of the race: "*God was with me again, as he has been all through my career,*" he said. "*But it was tough! I think it was the hardest race of my career. In the rain everything was fine, I felt quite comfortable. But then when Vettel went past me there were only two laps to go. I did everything I could to get past him again. I was all over the place, I thought my heart was going to burst - I still feel sick, it was that intense. I don't know how I managed to stay calm. I had no idea where Massa was, I presumed he was in front. On the last lap I just told myself I had to get that place back. I didn't have time to lose focus and start feeling sorry for myself - I HAD to get it back. I was trying to work out where I could get back at Vettel, trying* to get the maximum out of the car in every corner. I had no rear tyres left, I could hardly keep up with him. Then the team came on the radio and said, "Glock is ahead of you. He's on slicks. It would be good if you could get past him." There were two corners left. I saw him about to turn in for the last one, and I went for it. I relaxed a bit, thinking it was OK, but then I started panicking: I thought my engineer would be saying, 'Wohoo, you're champion', but there was nothing coming through. But when I crossed the line, they told me. It was such a feeling to see everyone, my family, my friends. It was crazy, but I did exactly what I had to do. And now it's all over. But it hasn't sunk in yet that I'm World Champion. It's fantastic. Never in a million years would I have imagined I could end up here. I've dreamt about it so much, it still seems like a dream.*"

Lewis Hamilton: a perfect champion

Lewis Hamilton won the world title on the slippery slopes of Interlagois in just his 35th Grand Prix.

As soon as the young British driver came into Formula 1 in 2007 it was obvious he had the talent to go all the way. In less than two years, Hamilton has gone from being an unknown to a global star.

His story reads like a modern fairytale. From humble origins in Trinidad and Tobago - his grandfather migrated to the UK and became a taxi-driver - Hamilton began karting at the age of 8.

Two years later, at a motor sport awards evening in 1995, he went up to McLaren boss Ron Dennis to ask for his autograph.

Cheekily he asked if he could drive for McLaren one day. An amused Denis added, beside his signature, "Come and see me in 10 years."

Hamilton didn't wait that long. By 13 he had won every kart title he had entered for. Dennis was convinced he had a future star on his hands and signed a 10-year deal with young Lewis.

Never had McLaren entered a contract with such a young driver.

But they have had no cause to regret it. Karting, Formula Renault, F3, GP2: the super-talented Hamilton won every championship he took part in, prompting Dennis to bring him into Formula 1, though never thinking his young protégé would enjoy such spectacular success.

Hamilton is from the same mould as the great champions of the sport.

Steely resolve and sheer speed, hard work and soft hands in a slide: he has it all, with hardly a weak spot.

A calm demeanour, endless patience with his fans, always thinking of his family and team, he is a thoroughly grounded young man.

Runner-up in his first season, the taking the title in Brazil for the first time, Hamlton has only just started.

If his talent is anything to go by, he may well end up one day among the brightest stars in the motor racing galaxy, alongside such names as Juan Manuel Fangio, Aytron Senna, Alain Prost and Michael Schumacher.

<
Hamilton has his helmet off - and realises he is the 2008 World Champion. One of the mechanics has come up with a suitably inscribed Union Jack for the young Briton to wrap himself in. Time to celebrate…

> For his final Grand Prix David Coulthard had an all-white car in the livery of Austrian charity 'Wings for Life'. Sadly, he was out at the first corner: "I'm really ticked off, that's not the way I wanted to finish," said the Scotsman. "I took it very carefully going into the first corner, leaving plenty of room, but I think it was Rosberg who hit me from behind. I would have been OK but for Nakajima taking my front wing off. I wanted to make it to the finish, then do some doughnuts for the fans, even if you do get fined for doing it."

> The race start: mindful of what happened in 2007, Hamilton doesn't push his luck, going through the first corner in fourth place behind Massa, Trulli and Räikkönen.

David Coulthard calls a halt after 245 Grands Prix

The figures are impressive: 245 races, 13 victories, 353 points, 61 podiums, 12 poles. Since debuting with Williams in 1994, when he took over from Ayrton Senna, David Coulthard has left his own mark on Formula 1 with his laid-back style, his British sense of humour and the build of a Hollywood star.

Most of his racing has been with leading teams, where he always played second fiddle to teammates such as Damon Hil at Williams, Miki Hakkinen and Kimi Raikkonen at McLaren, and Mark Webber at Red Bull.

Any other driver in a similar situation would have expected to see his F1 career cut short, but ever the perfect gentleman, Coulthard, with his gift for setting up a car, his charm and his willingness to go along with all the PR work, has managed to prolong his career.

But now that career has taken a new turn.

"*I suppose I should be really emotional this weekend,*" said the Scot in Sao Paulo, "*but I think that will happen on Sunday when I get out of the car. That will be the end of this part of my life. I'm not stopping because I don't like racing any more, it's because my F1 journey has reached its natural conclusion. When I leave the paddock on Sunday that will be it.*"

His Red Bull race car was repainted for the weekend in the colours of 'Wings for Life', which sponsors research into spinal injuries.

"*I want to thank all the teams for agreeing to the change of livery,*" said Coulthard. "*I think it's a first in modern Formula 1.*"

Rumour had it that the Scot would be taking up a career in television sports commentary with the BBC, the British network that will take over Grand Prix coverage again next year.

He was also said to be staying with Red Bull in a consultancy role, rather like Michael Schumacher's at Ferrari.

SNAPSHOTS OF THE WEEKEND

+ The man at the centre of the last-corner kerfuffle, Timo Glock, said there was nothing he could do to stop Sebastian Vettel and Lewis Hamilton passing him.
"Late in the race I gambled on staying out on dry-weather tyres, and it was so raining so hard I could hardly keep the car on the track," he explained. "But sixth is a pretty good result."

+ "Being on the podium here confirms that we are right back among the front-runners," said a happy Fernando Aloonso after coming home second.
Renault announced their 2009 driver line-up the following week, with both Alonso and Nelsinho Piquet being retained.

+ The two BMW Saubers trailed home 10th and 11th. Robert Kubica was still in the title hunt when they went to Japan, but eventually finished 4th overall, 23 points behind Hamilton. "An end-of-season to forget," acknowledged technical director Willy Rampf. "At the start we gambled on wets, but we got it wrong, it was just too wet."

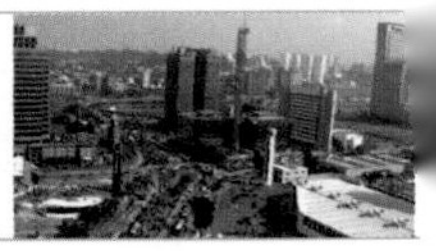

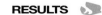

PRACTICE

Date	Weather (AM)	Air temperature	Track temperature	Weather (PM)	Air temperature	Track temperature
Friday October 3, 2008	Cloudy	20-18°c	22-20°c	Cloudy	17-19°c	22-20°c
Saturday November 1st, 2008	Sunny	21-23°c	25-31°c	Sunny	22-24°c	37-40°c

All the time trials

N° Driver	Nat.	N° Chassis- Engine [Nbr. GP]	Pos. Free 1 Friday 10:00-11:30	Laps	Pos. Free 2 Friday 14:00-15:30	Laps	Pos. Free 3 Saturday 11:00-12:00	Laps	Pos. Q1 Saturday 14:00-14:20	Laps	Pos. Q2 Saturday 14:27-14:42	Laps	Pos. Q3 Saturday 14:50-15:00	Laps
1. Kimi Räikkönen	FIN	Ferrari F2008 271 [1]	3. 1:12.507	18	4. 1:12.600	32	12. 1:12.698	10	2. 1:12.083	7	6. 1:11.950	6	3. **1:12.825**	6
2. Felipe Massa	BR	Ferrari F2008 269 [1]	1. 1:12.305	24	2. 1:12.353	41	4. 1:12.312	17	1. 1:11.830	8	4. 1:11.875	3	1. **1:12.368**	6
3. Nick Heidfeld	D	BMW Sauber F1.08-07 [2]	9. 1:13.426	28	13. 1:13.038	49	6. 1:12.402	19	9. 1:1:12.371	7	7. 1:12.026	5	8. **1:13.297**	6
4. Robert Kubica	PL	BMW Sauber F1.08-05 [1]	4. 1:12.874	24	12. 1:12.971	48	14. 1:12.971	22	10. 1:12.381	7	13. **1:12.300**	6		
5. Fernando Alonso	E	Renault R28-02 [1]	6. 1:13.061	26	1. 1:12.296	43	1. 1:12.141	19	4. 1:12.214	6	9. 1:12.090	6	6. **1:12.967**	6
6. Nelson Piquet	BR	Renault R28-01 [1]	8. 1:13.378	39	7. 1:12.703	44	9. 1:12.457	24	7. 1:12.348	7	11. **1:12.137**	6		
7. Nico Rosberg	D	Williams FW30-05 - Toyota [2]	12. 1:13.621	23	8. 1:12.761	42	11. 1:12.625	16	18. **1:13.002**	8				
8. Kazuki Nakajima	J	Williams FW30-04 - Toyota [2]	16. 1:13.806	24	10. 1:12.886	42	15. 1:13.054	19	16. **1:12.800**	9				
9. David Coulthard	GB	Red Bull RB4 3 - Renault [2]	18. 1:13.861	19	11. 1:12.896	38	16. 1:13.058	22	15. **1:12.690**	10				
10. Mark Webber	AUS	Red Bull RB4 4 - Renault [2]	7. 1:13.298	24	5. 1:12.650	45	8. 1:12.453	18	12. 1:12.409	7	12. **1:12.289**	6		
11. Jarno Trulli	I	Toyota TF108-05 [1]	11. 1:13.600	24	3. 1:12.435	44	10. 1:12.457	19	6. 1:12.226	3	10. 1:12.107	6	2. **1:12.737**	6
12. Timo Glock	D	Toyota TF108-07 [1]	10. 1:13.466	33	14. 1:13.041	39	13. 1:12.712	22	5. 1:12.223	9	5. 1:11.909	9	10. **1:14.230**	6
14. Sébastien Bourdais	F	Toro Rosso STR3-04 - Ferrari [1]	13. 1:13.649	30	17. 1:13.273	41	7. 1:12.426	18	13. 1:12.498	7	8. 1:12.075	6	9. **1:14.105**	3
15. Sebastian Vettel	D	Toro Rosso STR3-03 - Ferrari [1]	17. 1:13.836	30	6. 1:12.687	47	5. 1:12.389	19	11. 1:12.390	7	2. 1:11.845	6	7. **1:13.082**	7
16. Jenson Button	GB	Honda RA108-05 [1]	15. 1:13.766	13	18. 1:13.341	49	18. 1:13.278	23	17. **1:12.810**	9				
17. Rubens Barrichello	BR	Honda RA108-03 [1]	14. 1:13.676	28	16. 1:13.221	39	17. 1:13.135	24	14. 1:12.548	8	15. **1:13.139**	6		
20. Adrian Sutil	D	Force India VJM01/06 - Ferrari [2]	19. 1:14.704	21	19. 1:13.428	32	20. 1:13.680	22	20. **1:13.508**	9				
21. Giancarlo Fisichella	I	Force India VJM01/05 - Ferrari [1]	20. 1:14.821	21	20. 1:13.691	33	19. 1:13.460	22	19. **1:13.426**	9				
22. Lewis Hamilton	GB	McLaren MP4-23 05 - Mercedes [2]	2. 1:12.495	23	9. 1:12.827	33	2. 1:12.212	18	3. 1:12.213	3	3. 1:11.856	5	4. **1:12.830**	6
23. Heikki Kovalainen	FIN	McLaren MP4-23 07 - Mercedes [1]	5. 1:12.925	20	15. 1:13.231	37	3. 1:12.225	18	8. 1:12.366	5	1. 1:11.768	6	5. **1:12.917**	6

Fastest lap overall

H. Kovalainen 1:11.768 (216,146 km/h)

Maximum speed

N° Driver	S1 Qualifs	Pos.	S1 Race	Pos.	S2 Qualifs	Pos.	S2 Race	Pos.	Finish Qualifs	Pos.	Finish Race	Pos.	Radar Qualifs	Pos.	Radar Race	Pos.
1. K. Räikkönen	309,1	3	307,6	3	263,2	3	259,1	1	306,7	3	311,8	4	309,0	2	310,8	7
2. F. Massa	307,1	6	307,0	5	261,9	5	257,5	6	304,4	5	311,7	5	306,5	5	311,7	5
3. N. Heidfeld	304,5	11	303,8	13	260,5	12	257,0	10	302,6	9	310,2	8	304,7	10	310,1	8
4. R. Kubica	303,2	17	305,7	9	260,6	11	257,4	8	299,9	18	307,2	12	302,1	17	306,9	14
5. F. Alonso	305,8	7	304,0	12	261,6	6	257,6	4	303,7	6	305,6	17	305,2	7	305,6	17
6. N. Piquet	304,3	12			261,4	7			301,9	10			304,0	11	185,5	19
7. N. Rosberg	303,8	16	303,5	15	259,3	19	255,8	14	300,1	17	307,6	11	302,6	15	308,3	10
8. K. Nakajima	302,6	19	306,0	8	259,5	17	254,8	15	300,5	14	308,8	9	302,6	16	310,9	6
9. D. Coulthard	305,6	9			260,3	13			302,9	8			304,7	9	166,2	20
10. M. Webber	307,6	4	306,1	7	261,2	8	257,6	5	306,2	4	310,6	6	307,6	4	310,0	9
11. J. Trulli	304,0	15	304,2	11	260,0	15	256,1	13	299,5	20	307,2	13	302,0	19	307,5	12
12. T. Glock	304,3	13	303,7	14	261,0	9	256,7	11	299,7	19	307,9	10	302,1	18	307,6	11
14. S. Bourdais	305,7	8	306,8	6	262,0	4	256,4	12	301,5	12	313,4	3	303,2	12	313,5	4
15. S. Vettel	307,1	5	310,3	2	260,8	10	258,2	3	303,1	7	310,3	7	305,6	6	313,5	3
16. J. Button	302,6	20	304,3	10	260,2	14	257,3	9	300,3	15	306,7	14	301,7	20	306,2	15
17. R. Barrichello	304,0	14	301,3	18	259,9	16	252,4	18	300,6	13	306,6	15	302,7	14	305,6	16
20. A. Sutil	303,2	18	301,8	17	258,0	20	254,1	16	300,2	16	305,7	16	303,2	13	305,2	18
21. G. Fisichella	305,4	10	301,8	16	259,4	18	253,5	17	301,5	11	304,5	18	304,9	8	307,4	13
22. L. Hamilton	309,9	2	307,4	4	264,3	2	258,6	2	306,5	3	319,3	1	309,0	3	315,7	1
23. H. Kovalainen	311,5	1	312,4	1	264,5	1	257,5	7	310,7	1	319,2	2	313,4	1	315,0	2

Best sector times

Qualifs	**S1** H. Kovalainen	18.061	**S2** T. Glock	36.311	**S3** H. Kovalainen	17.147	= 1:11.519
Race	**S1** F. Massa	18.756	**S2** T. Glcok	37.473	**S3** H. Kovalainen	17.172	= 1:13.401

RACE

Date	Weather	Air temperature	Track temperature	Humidity	Wind speed
Sunday November 2, 2008 (15:00)	Rain, cloudy	36-38°c	60-61°c	27%	2.1 m/s

Classification & retirements

Pos.	Driver	Constructor	Tyres	Laps	Time	Km/h
1.	F. Massa	Ferrari	WMMW	71	1:34:11.435	194,865
2.	F. Alonso	Renault	WMMW	71	+ 13.298	194,408
3.	K. Räikkönen	Ferrari	WMMW	71	+ 16.235	194,307
4.	S. Vettel	STR Ferrari	WMMMW	71	+ 38.011	193,564
5.	L. Hamilton	McLaren Mercedes	WMMW	71	+ 38.907	193,533
6.	T. Glock	Toyota	WMM	71	+ 44.368	193,348
7.	H. Kovalainen	McLaren Mercedes	WMMW	71	+ 55.074	192,985
8.	J. Trulli	Toyota	WMM	71	+ 68.463	192,533
9.	M. Webber	Red Bull Renault	WMMW	71	+ 79.666	192,157
10.	N. Heidfeld	BMW	WMMW	70	1 lap	191,736
11.	R. Kubica	BMW	WMMW	70	1 lap	190,867
12.	N. Rosberg	Williams Toyota	WMMW	70	1 lap	190,774
13.	J. Button	Honda	WMMME	70	1 lap	190,423
14.	S. Bourdais	STR Ferrari	WMME	70	1 lap	190,305
15.	R. Barrichello	Honda	WMMEW	70	1 lap	189,798
16.	A. Sutil	Force India	WSSEW	69	2 laps	188,714
17.	K. Nakajima	Williams Toyota	WMMMW	69	2 laps	188,329
18.	G. Fisichella	Force India	WSSE	69	2 laps	187,453

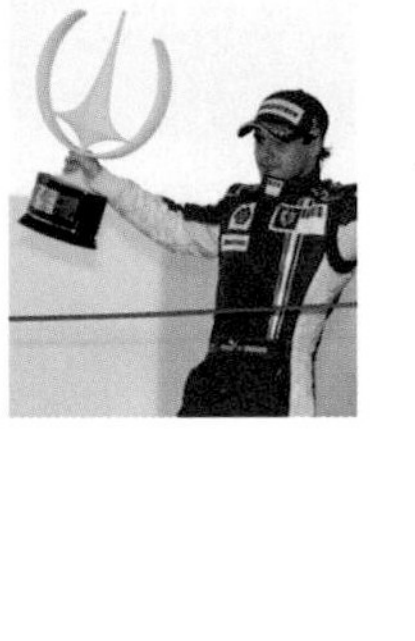

Driver	Constructor	Tyres	Laps	Reason
N. Piquet	Renault	W	0	Went off
D. Coulthard	Red Bull Renault	W	0	Pushed by Rosberg, spin and hits Nakajima

Tyres M: Medium & S: Soft // W: Wet & E: Extreme Wet

Fastest laps

	Driver	Time	Lap	Km/h
1.	F. Massa	1:13.736	36	210,377
2.	T. Glock	1:14.057	32	209,465
3.	K. Räikkönen	1:14.117	59	209,296
4.	L. Hamilton	1:14.159	31	209,177
5.	J. Trulli	1:14.167	40	209,155
6.	H. Kovalainen	1:14.207	36	209,042
7.	S. Vettel	1:14.214	25	209,022
8.	F. Alonso	1:14.229	39	208,980
9.	R. Kubica	1:14.375	61	208,570
10.	N. Heidfeld	1:14.652	41	207,796
11.	J. Button	1:14.759	59	207,498
12.	N. Rosberg	1:14.934	35	207,014
13.	S. Bourdais	1:14.951	57	206,967
14.	M. Webber	1:15.033	40	206,741
15.	G. Fisichella	1:15.212	36	206,249
16.	R. Barrichello	1:15.414	35	205,696
17.	A. Sutil	1:15.773	60	204,721
18.	K. Nakajima	1:15.865	50	204,473

Pit stops

	Driver	Lap	Duration	Stop	Total
1.	G. Fisichella	2	29.588	1	29.588
2.	N. Rosberg	7	28.550	1	28.550
3.	J. Button	7	27.862	1	27.862
4.	S. Bourdais	8	26.686	1	26.686
5.	T. Glock	8	26.160	1	26.160
6.	A. Sutil	8	29.524	1	29.524
7.	K. Nakajima	8	28.506	1	28.506
8.	S. Vettel	9	26.102	1	26.102
9.	F. Alonso	9	27.658	1	27.658
10.	M. Webber	9	28.788	1	28.788
11.	R. Barrichello	9	28.097	1	28.097
12.	F. Massa	10	27.656	1	27.658
13.	H. Kovalainen	10	32.527	1	32.527
14.	N. Heidfeld	10	27.881	1	27.881
15.	R. Kubica	10	27.758	1	27.758
16.	J. Trulli	11	31.122	1	31.122
17.	K. Räikkönen	11	28.870	1	28.870
18.	L. Hamilton	11	28.319	1	28.319
19.	S. Vettel	27	27.515	2	53.617
20.	J. Button	33	26.923	2	54.785
21.	T. Glock	36	35.238	2	1:01.398
22.	F. Massa	38	30.501	2	58.157
23.	G. Fisichella	38	54.619	2	1:24.207
24.	S. Bourdais	38	29.832	2	56.518
25.	F. Alonso	40	29.889	2	57.547
26.	L. Hamilton	40	29.242	2	57.561
27.	R. Barrichello	40	28.881	2	56.978
28.	N. Rosberg	41	29.423	2	57.973
29.	H. Kovalainen	42	29.264	2	1:01.791
30.	N. Heidfeld	42	28.848	2	56.729
31.	K. Räikkönen	43	29.436	2	58.306
32.	J. Trulli	43	29.829	2	1:00.951
33.	A. Sutil	44	30.623	2	1:00.147
34.	R. Kubica	46	27.007	2	54.765
35.	M. Webber	48	27.655	2	56.443
36.	S. Vettel	51	26.626	3	1:20.243
37.	K. Nakajima	51	26.843	2	55.349
38.	J. Button	56	27.450	3	1:22.235
39.	K. Nakajima	62	26.618	3	1:21.967
40.	G. Fisichella	63	46.539	3	2:10.746
41.	N. Heidfeld	64	27.306	3	1:24.035
42.	R. Barrichello	64	28.097	3	1:25.075
43.	N. Rosberg	64	26.862	3	1:24.835
44.	S. Bourdais	64	28.249	3	1:24.767
45.	R. Kubica	64	26.379	3	1:21.144
46.	H. Kovalainen	65	27.229	3	1:29.020
47.	A. Sutil	64	27.733	3	1:27.880
48.	M. Webber	65	28.771	3	1:25.214
49.	F. Alonso	66	26.672	3	1:24.219
50.	K. Räikkönen	66	26.498	3	1:24.804
51.	J. Button	65	27.056	4	1:49.291
52.	L. Hamilton	66	26.483	3	1:24.044
53.	S. Vettel	66	26.810	4	1:47.053
54.	F. Massa	67	27.234	3	1:25.391
55.	R. Barrichello	67	28.370	4	1:53.445

Race leader

Driver	Laps in the lead	Nbr of laps
F. Massa	1 > 9	9
J. Trulli	10 > 11	2
F. Massa	12 > 38	27
F. Alonso	39 > 40	2
K. Räikkönen	41 > 43	3
F. Massa	44 > 71	28

Driver	Nbr of laps	Kilometers
F. Massa	64	275,746 km
K. Räikkönen	3	12,927 km
J. Trulli	2	8,618 km
F. Alonso	2	8,618 km

Gaps on the lead board

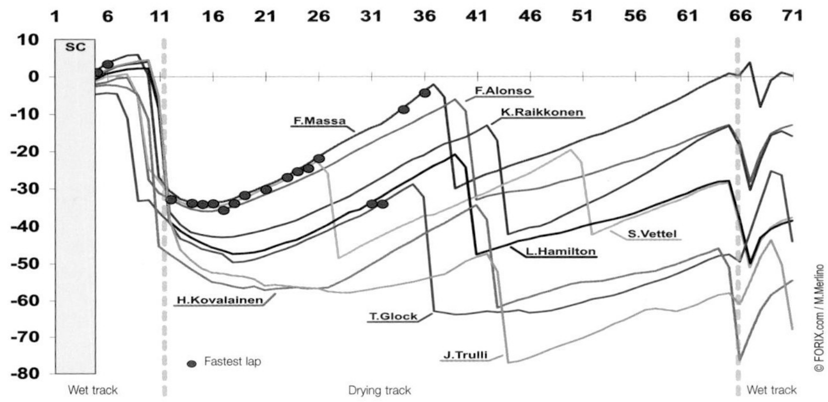
1 6 11 16 21 26 31 36 41 46 51 56 61 66 71
10 0 -10 -20 -30 -40 -50 -60 -70 -80
SC
F.Alonso
K.Raikkonen
F.Massa
S.Vettel
L.Hamilton
H.Kovalainen
T.Glock
J.Trulli
Fastest lap
Wet track
Drying track
Wet track
© FORIX.com / M.Merlino

Lap chart

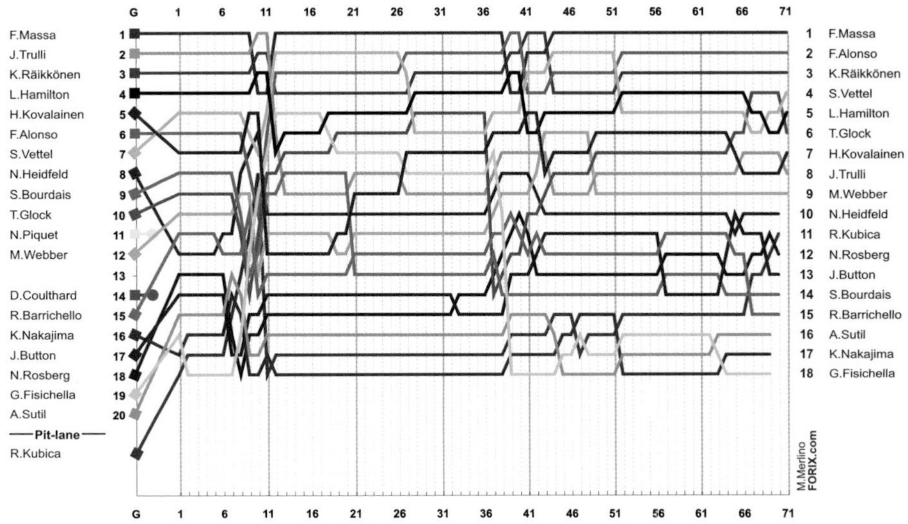
G 1 6 11 16 21 26 31 36 41 46 51 56 61 66 71
F.Massa 1
J.Trulli 2
K.Räikkönen 3
L.Hamilton 4
H.Kovalainen 5
F.Alonso 6
S.Vettel 7
N.Heidfeld 8
S.Bourdais 9
T.Glock 10
N.Piquet 11
M.Webber 12
13
D.Coulthard 14
R.Barrichello 15
K.Nakajima 16
J.Button 17
N.Rosberg 18
G.Fisichella 19
A.Sutil 20
Pit-lane
R.Kubica
1 F.Massa
2 F.Alonso
3 K.Räikkönen
4 S.Vettel
5 L.Hamilton
6 T.Glock
7 H.Kovalainen
8 J.Trulli
9 M.Webber
10 N.Heidfeld
11 R.Kubica
12 N.Rosberg
13 J.Button
14 S.Bourdais
15 R.Barrichello
16 A.Sutil
17 K.Nakajima
18 G.Fisichella
M.Merlino FORIX.com

CHAMPIONSHIPS 18/18

Drivers

	Driver	Constructor	Wins	Points
1.	**L. Hamilton**	**McLaren Mercedes**	5	98
2.	F. Massa	Ferrari	6	97
3.	K. Räikkönen	Ferrari	2	75
4.	R. Kubica	BMW	1	75
5.	F. Alonso	Renault	2	61
6.	N. Heidfeld	BMW		60
7.	H. Kovalainen	McLaren Mercedes	1	53
8.	S. Vettel	STR Ferrari	1	35
9.	J. Trulli	Toyota		31
10.	T. Glock	Toyota		25
11.	M. Webber	Red Bull Renault		21
12.	N. Piquet	Renault		19
13.	N. Rosberg	Williams Toyota		17
14.	R. Barrichello	Honda		11
15.	K. Nakajima	Williams Toyota		9
16.	D. Coulthard	Red Bull Renault		8
17.	S. Bourdais	STR Ferrari		4
18.	J. Button	Honda		3
19.	G. Fisichella	Force India		0
20.	A. Sutil	Force India		0
21.	T. Sato	Super Aguri Honda		0
22.	A. Davidson	Super Aguri Honda		0

Constructors

	Constructor	Wins	Points
1.	**Scuderia Ferrari Marlboro**	8	**172**
2.	Vodafone McLaren Mercedes	5	151
3.	BMW Sauber F1 Team	2	135
4.	ING Renault F1 Team	2	80
5.	Panasonic Toyota Racing		56
6.	Scuderia Torro Rosso	1	39
7.	Red Bull Racing		29
7.	AT&T Williams		26
9.	Honda Racing F1 Team		14
10.	Force India F1 Team		0
11.	Super Aguri F1 Team		0

THE CIRCUIT

Name Autódromo José Carlos Pace; Interlagos, São Paulo
Lenght 4309 m
Distance 71 laps, 305,909 km
Latitude 23°42'13.20"S
Longitude 46°42'00.30"O

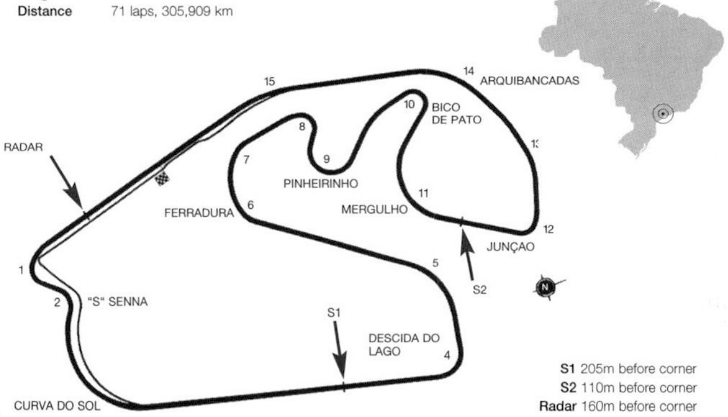
RADAR
1
2
"S" SENNA
CURVA DO SOL
S1
DESCIDA DO LAGO
4
5
6
FERRADURA
7
8
9
PINHEIRINHO
10
BICO DE PATO
11
MERGULHO
12
JUNÇAO
S2
14
ARQUIBANCADAS
15

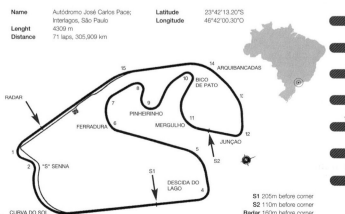

S1 205m before corner
S2 110m before corner
Radar 160m before corner

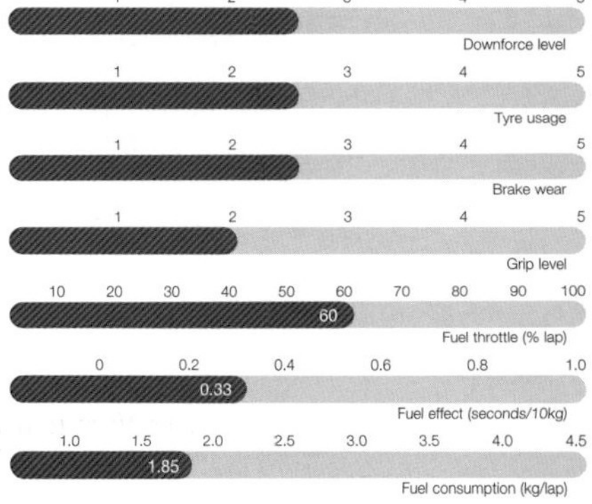
1 2 3 4 5
Downforce level
1 2 3 4 5
Tyre usage
1 2 3 4 5
Brake wear
1 2 3 4 5
Grip level
10 20 30 40 50 60 70 80 90 100
60
Fuel throttle (% lap)
0 0.2 0.4 0.6 0.8 1.0
0.33
Fuel effect (seconds/10kg)
1.0 1.5 2.0 2.5 3.0 3.5 4.0 4.5
1.85
Fuel consumption (kg/lap)

> In Barcelona, during a November test session, the cars ran with "2009 type" wings: huge snow shovels at the front, small wings at the back. What has been lost in the way of aerodynamics has not been gained in aesthetic terms.

Modified aerodynamics, KERS, slick tyres: it's all change in 2009

After the end of the season, all the Formula 1 teams, except Toyota, were back in action again at the Barcelona circuit, from 17 to 19 November, for an intensive three day test session, in early preparation for the 2009 season.

What used to be the traditional testing ban in November, to give team personnel some down time after the season is now a thing of the past. Most of the teams used this session to try out some components they planned to use in 2009.

In order to reduce corner speeds and to encourage more overtaking, the FIA had set

new aerodynamic regulations for 2009, the most visible effect of which is smaller rear wings and new bigger front wings.
BMW was the only team to test the entire package along with the KERS (Kinetic Energy Recovery System) which recovers the energy from braking. It's not compulsory and some teams have already said they will not be using it, at least in the early part of the season.
Other teams opted for running an aero package that approximated to the estimated downforce levels to be found in 2009.
The cars are now definitely faster down the straights, because of reduced drag and are no slower in the corners, because of the return to slick tyres, even at this very first test.
It was Sebastian Vettel who set the best time of the week in Barcelona in 1.19.295, which is around 1.3 seconds faster than the best lap in qualifying for the Spanish Grand Prix, when Felipe Massa lapped in 1.20.584.
At first glance, it looked as though 2009 would beat all records when it came to lap times.
As for making overtaking easier, we will have to wait and see.

> The Doctor puts it off for now: on 20 and 21 November, Valentino Rossi once again tested a Ferrari Formula 1 car at the Mugello circuit. On the second day, rain and an off-track excursion brought the test to a premature end, but the Italian had proved to be relatively competitive, just 3 seconds off a time set by Ferrari's official test driver, Luca Badoer.

Sebastien Loeb in Formula 1!

In the Honda camp, Bruno Lalli (or "Senna") drove a Formula 1 car for the first time. He is rumoured to be replacing Rubens Barrichello in the Japanese team in 2009.

It was a gift from his sponsor, Red Bull, for having won the world rally championship for the fifth time. Sebastien Loeb was given a full day of testing at the wheel of an F1 car, at the first day of the Barcelona test, out on track along with all the other drivers.
The previous week, the Frenchman had been for a seat fitting at the Red Bull Racing factory and then had a shake-down at Silverstone. The real test came in Barcelona, with sixteen other cars out on track.
So, Sebastien Loeb was one of the boys, as he strung together a total of 82 laps, which is more than a grand prix distance! Having spent the morning finding the right balance on his car, the Frenchman began pushing a bit harder in the afternoon, at the wheel of a car fitted with 2009 slick tyres, as next year, the grooved tyres

which have been used since 1998, are being done away with.
Demonstrating his natural talent, Loeb had no problem switching from his Citroen rally car to the Red Bull Racing F1 machine. "I don't think I'd like to have this much horsepower in the forests!" he joked. *"It was a fantastic experience,*

although these cars are definitely more demanding physically than my rally car. The level of grip in the high speed corners is really impressive."
After his fun day, he handed over to Sebastian Vettel, Red Bull Racing's new driver.
Dreams don't last forever...

Sebastien Buemi, a new talent

Sebastien Buemi, reserve and test driver for Red Bull Racing in 2008, drove on all three days of the Barcelona test, having already taken part in a few other F1 tests during the year.

At the time of writing, Toro Rosso had not yet defined its three-driver-line up, after running three drivers at this test: Sebastien Buemi, Takuma Sato and Sebastien Bourdais. Buemi is a graduate of the Red Bull Junior Driver programme and was the only one to drive on all three days.

After a full season in GP2, the young Swiss driver was now ready to take the final step, by the far the most difficult one, into Formula 1.

Extremely talented, Sebastien Buemi has been involved in motor sport since a tender age. His grandfather, Georges Gachnang, was also a driver in his day, taking part in several international endurance races at the beginning of the Sixties. At the same time as his cousin, Natacha Gachnang, who is aiming to be in GP2 in 2009, little Sebastien began trying his hand at karting. He became the Swiss champion in the mini category at the age of nine, before finishing as runner-up in Formula BMW, then Formula 3 and GP2.

His family could not have financed this rise through the ranks, but Buemi had the good fortune to be talent spotted by Red Bull, when he was fifteen. Looking for a future world champion, the drinks company signed him up for five years. In motor sport, one must always take into account the quality of a driver's car when assessing his talent. One can really only compare a driver to his team-mate, the only rival who theoretically has exactly the same equipment.

It's a foolproof method and, during his career, Buemi has always demolished his team-mates. In Formula 3 in Macau, he beat Bruno Senna, the late Ayrton's nephew, by almost two seconds in qualifying, which is a real chasm. This season, he crushed Luca Filippi in GP2, even though the Italian was considered one of the favourites for the title.

Very talented, Buemi is also a driver who knows how to bring his car home: at the wheel of the Arden, considered to be one of the worst cars on the GP2 grid, the Swiss managed to score a total of 50 points this season, finishing almost every weekend in the points in at least one of the two races.

But above all, he pulled off some impressive passing moves and has a real feel for a sliding car. In Magny-Cours, in the GP2 race held as a curtain raiser to the French Grand Prix, he started from 21st on the grid, going on to produce an incredible performance, winning the race by starting on dry weather tyres in the rain. It was a breathtaking climb through the field, during which he displayed true brio, pulling off passing moves that are simply not found in any race driving manual. Just staying on the track in the tricky conditions was in itself an achievement, something which many of his rivals failed to do.

Of the young drivers under contract to Red Bull,

Buemi is the best placed and so he should be in line for one of the two Toro Rosso seats for next season. Sebastian Vettel has been moved to Red Bull Racing and Sebastien Bourdais is not a certainty for the other drive, after some disappointing race performances. So Buemi could well be driving a Toro Rosso in 2009.

As reserve and test driver for Red Bull Racing this year, he has already tested several times for both these teams. He lives in a little flat in Milton Keynes, not far from the Red Bull Racing factory and often pops in to soak up as much information as he can.

Having celebrated his twentieth birthday on 31 October, Sebastien Buemi has the talent and has benefited from an ideal training programme to make it to Formula 1. He is a prototype for the current batch of young drivers and points the way to the future of motor sport: young drivers who are very well prepared, extremely talented, hard working and ready to deal with all the modern demands of marketing and press work.

∧
Sebastien Buemi in the early morning at the Barcelona circuit. Over the three days, the Swiss driver completed 331 laps, or the equivalent of over five Grands Prix.

<
Sebastien Buemi and Sebastien Bourdais share their impressions on setting up the Toro Rosso car.

A recap of the 2008 season

#	Driver	Nat.	Team	Pts	AUS 16/03	MAL 23/03	BAH 06/04	SPA 27/04	TUR 11/05	MON 25/05	CAN 08/06	FRA 22/06	GBR 06/07	GER 20/07	HUN 03/08	EUR 24/08	BEL 07/09	ITA 14/09	SIN 28/09	JAP 12/10	CHI 17/10	BRA 02/11	Poles	Vict.	Fast. laps	Podiums	Scored GP	GP in lead	Laps in lead	Km in lead
1	Lewis HAMILTON	GB	McLaren Mercedes	98	10[1]	4[5]	13	6[3]	8[2]	10[1]	NC	10	10[1]	10[1]	4[5]	8[2]	6[3]	2[7]	6[3]	12	10[1]	4[5]	7	5	1	10	14	11	294	1,419.390
2	Felipe MASSA	BR	Ferrari	97	NC	NC	10[1]	8[2]	10[1]	6[3]	4[5]	10[1]	13	6[3]	17	10[1]	10[1]	3[6]	13	2[7]	8[2]	10[1]	6	6	3	10	13	11	363	1,749.283
3	Kimi RÄIKKÖNEN	FIN	Ferrari	75	1[8]	10[1]	8[2]	10[1]	6[3]	9	NC	8[2]	5[4]	3[6]	6[3]	NC	18	9	15	6[3]	6[3]	6[3]	2	2	10	9	12	7	178	936.926
4	Robert KUBICA	PL	BMW	75	NC	8[2]	6[3]	5[4]	5[4]	8[2]	10[1]	4[5]	NC	2[7]	1[8]	6[3]	3[6]	6[3]	11	8[2]	3[6]	11	1	1	-	7	14	6	67	296.742
5	Fernando ALONSO	E	Renault	61	5[2]	1[8]	10	NC	3[6]	NC	NC	1[8]	3[6]	11	5[4]	NC	5[4]	5[4]	10[1]	10[1]	5[4]	8[2]	-	2	-	3	12	3	62	296.510
6	Nick HEIDFELD	D	BMW	60	8[2]	3[6]	5[4]	9	4[5]	14	8[2]	13	8[2]	5[4]	10	9	8[2]	4[5]	3[6]	9	4[5]	10	-	-	2	4	11	5	22	103.498
7	Heikki KOVALAINEN	FIN	McLaren Mercedes	53	4[5]	6[3]	4[5]	NC	1[8]	9	5[4]	4[5]	4[5]	10[1]	5[4]	10	8[2]	10	NC	NC	2[7]		1	1	2	3	11	7	31	157.249
8	Sebastian VETTEL	D	STR Ferrari	35	NC	NC	NC	17	4[5]	1[8]	NC	NC	NC	3[6]	4[5]	10[1]	4[5]	3[6]	9	5[4]			1	1	-	1	9	1	49	283.548
9	Jarno TRULLI	I	Toyota	31	NC	5[4]	3[6]	1[8]	10	NC	3[6]	6[3]	2[7]	NC	2[7]	4[5]	NC	13	NC	4[5]	NC	1[8]	-	-	-	1	10	4	13	60.927
10	Timo GLOCK	D	Toyota	25	NC	NC	9	11	13	NC	12	NC	NC	8[2]	2[7]	9	11	5[4]	NC	2[7]	3[6]		-	-	-	1	6	1	3	13.033
11	Mark WEBBER	AUS	Red Bull Renault	21	NC	2[7]	2[7]	4[5]	2[7]	5[4]	12	3[6]	10	NC	9	1[8]	1[8]	NC	1[8]	14	9		-	-	-	1	9	-	-	-
12	Nelsinho PIQUET	BR	Renault	19	NC	11	NC	12	NC	NC	2[7]	NC	8[2]	3[6]	NC	NC	10	5[4]	1[8]	NC			-	-	-	1	5	2	13	59.385
13	Nico ROSBERG	D	Williams Toyota	17	6[3]	14	1[8]	NC	1[8]	NC	10	16	NC	14	12	NC	8[2]	15	15	15			-	-	-	2	5	1	11	55.737
14	Rubens BARRICHELLO	BR	Honda	11	DQ	13	11	NC	14	3[6]	2[7]	14	6[3]	NC	16	NC	16	15	NC	15			-	-	-	1	3	1	7	30.527
15	Kazuki NAKAJIMA	J	Williams Toyota	9	3[6]	17	14	2[7]	NC	2[7]	NC	15	1[8]	13	14	12	1[8]	15	12	17			-	-	-	1	5	-	-	-
16	David COULTHARD	GB	Red Bull Renault	8	NC	9	18	12	9	6[3]	9	NC	13	11	17	11	16	2[7]	NC	10			-	-	-	1	2	1	1	4.361
17	Sébastien BOURDAIS	F	STR Ferrari	4	2[7]	NC	15	NC	16	13	17	11	18	10	2[7]	12	10	12	9				-	-	-	2	2	1	3	13.689
18	Jenson BUTTON	GB	Honda	3	NC	10	NC	3[6]	11	11	11	NC	17	12	13	15	9	14	16				-	-	-	1				
19	Giancarlo FISICHELLA	I	Force India Ferrari	0	NC	12	12	10	NC	NC	NC	18	NC	16	15	14	17	NC	14	NC	17	18	-	-	-	-	-	-	-	-
20	Adrian SUTIL	D	Force India Ferrari	0	NC	NC	19	16	NC	NC	19	NC	15	NC	NC	13	19	NC	NC	NC	18		-	-	-	-	-	-	-	-
21	Takuma SATO	J	Super Aguri Honda	0	NC	16	17	13															-	-	-	-	-	-	-	-
22	Anthony DAVIDSON	GB	Super Aguri Honda	0	NC	15	16	NC															-	-	-	-	-	-	-	-

#	Team	Nat.	Pts	AUS	MAL	BAH	SPA	TUR	MON	CAN	FRA	GBR	GER	HUN	EUR	BEL	ITA	SIN	JAP	CHI	BRA	Poles	Vict.	Fast. laps	Podiums	Scored GP	GP in lead	Laps in lead	Km in lead
1	Ferrari	I	172	1	10	18	18	16	6	4	18	5	9	6	10	10	3		8	14	16	8	8	13	19	17	13	541	2,686.209
2	McLaren-Mercedes	GB	151	14	10	4	6	8	11		5	14	14	14	13	6	10	6		10	6	8	6	3	13	16	12	325	1,576.639
3	BMW Sauber	D	135	8	11	11	5	9	8	18	4	8	7	1	6	11	10	3	8	7		1	1	2	11	17	9	89	400.240
4	Renault	F	80	5	1			3			3	3	8	8		5	5	10	15	6	8	-	2	-	4	13	4	75	355.895
5	Toyota	J	36		5	3	1			8	6	2		10	6		5	4	2	4		-	-	-	2	12	4	16	74.010
6	STR-Ferrari	I	39	2				4	1			1		3	6	10	4	3		5		1	1	-	1	10	2	52	297.237
7	Red Bul-Renault	A	29		2	2	4	2	5	6	3				1	1	2	1				-	-	-	1	11	1	1	4.361
8	Williams-Toyota	GB	26	9		1	2	1	2			1			1		9					-	-	-	2	8	1	11	55.737
9	Honda	J	14			3		3	2	6												-	-	-	1	4	1	7	30.527
10	Force India-Ferrari	IND	0																			-	-	-	-	-	-	-	-
11	Super Aguri-Honda	J	0																			-	-	-	-	-	-	-	-

Family picture of the 2008 World Championship.
From left to right, standing: Sébastien Bourdais, Sebastian Vettel, Takuma Sato, Anthony Davidson, Giancarlo Fisichella, Adrian Sutil, Nico Rosberg & Kazuki Nakajima.
In the middle: Jarno Trulli, Timo Glock, Mark Webber, David Coulthard, Jenson Button, Rubens Barrichello.
Sitting: Nick Heidfeld, Robert Kubica, Felipe Massa, Kimi Räikkönen, Lewis Hamilton, Heikki Kovalainen, Fernando Alonso & Nelsinho Piquet.

Number of kms and laps raced in 2008

		Maximum 5,480.855 km	Maximum 1,117 laps	GP finished	GP classified	GP raced
1.	N. Heidfeld	5,463.186	1,112	18	18	18
2.	R. Kubica	5,310.252	1,084	16	16	18
3.	N. Rosberg	5,271.460	1,068	6	16	18
4.	L. Hamilton	5,253.032	1,065	17	17	18
5.	F. Massa	5,159.525	1,057	15	16	18
6.	K. Räikkönen	5,127.484	1,042	13	16	18
7.	K. Nakajima	5,010.587	1,024	16	16	18
8.	H. Kovalainen	4,983.027	1,011	14	15	18
9.	J. Trulli	4,908.462	1,010	15	16	18
10.	F. Alonso	4,901.145	1,000	15	15	18
11.	M. Webber	4,877.079	998	15	15	18
12.	R. Barrichello	4,791.447	986	14	13	18
13.	T. Glock	4,653.260	950	14	14	18
14.	J. Button	4,571.950	936	14	14	18
15.	S. Bourdais	4,425.371	887	13	14	18
16.	D. Coulthard	4,127.433	812	13	13	18
17.	G. Fisichella	3,968.534	810	11	11	18
18.	S. Vettel	3,939.727	810	12	12	18
19.	N. Piquet	3,828.904	776	9	9	18
20.	A. Sutil	3,356.274	687	7	7	18
21.	T. Sato	1,074.293	207	3	3	4
22.	A. Davidson	644.805	119	2	2	4

		Maximum 10,961.710	Max. 2,234			
1.	BMW	10,773.438	2,196	34	34	36
2.	Ferrari	10,287.009	2,099	28	32	36
3.	Williams Toyota	10,282.047	2,092	32	32	36
4.	McLaren Mercedes	10,146.059	2,076	31	32	36
5.	Toyota	9,561.722	1,960	29	29	36
6.	Honda	9,363.397	1,922	28	27	36
7.	Red Bull Renault	9,004.512	1,810	28	28	36
8.	Renault	8,730.049	1,776	24	24	36
9.	STR Ferrari	8,365.098	1,697	25	26	36
10.	Force India-Ferrari	7,324.808	1,497	18	18	36
11.	Super Aguri Honda	1,719.098	326	5	5	8

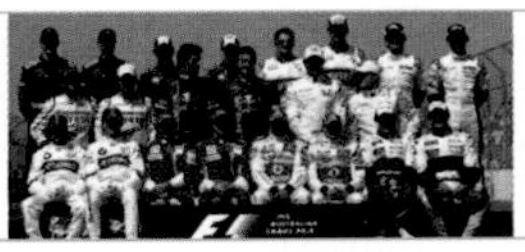

Drivers: GP raced

BARRICHELLO Rubens	268	STUCK Hans Joachim	74	ASCARI Alberto	32
PATRESE Riccardo	256	BRAMBILLA Vittorio	74	COLLINS Peter	32
SCHUMACHER Michael	249	NAKAJIMA Satoru	74	LAMY Pedro	32
COULTHARD David	246	GUGELMIN Mauricio	74	TAKAGI Tora	32
FISICHELLA Giancarlo	212	CLARK Jim	72	VILLORESI Luigi	31
BERGER Gerhard	210	PACE Carlos	72	NILSSON Gunnar	31
De CESARIS Andrea	208	De La ROSA Pedro	72	De ADAMICH Andrea	30
PIQUET Nelson	204	PIRONI Didier	70	REVSON Peter	30
ALESI Jean	201	MODENA Stefano	70	GETHIN Peter	30
PROST Alain	199	GIACOMELLI Bruno	69	MANZON Robert	28
TRULLI Jarno	199	WURZ Alexander	69	BEUTTLER Mike	28
ALBORETO Michele	194	VILLENEUVE Gilles	67	BERNOLDI Enrique	28
MANSELL Nigel	187	MORBIDELLI Gianni	67	Da MATTA Cristiano	28
SCHUMACHER Ralf	180	MOSS Stirling	66	SPEED Scott	28
LAFFITE Jacques	176	FABI Teo	64	TAYLOR Trevor	27
HILL Graham	175	SUZUKI Aguri	64	COURAGE Piers	27
LAUDA Niki	171	LEHTO JJ	62	ROSSET Ricardo	27
BOUTSEN Thierry	163	BLUNDELL Mark	61	GONZALEZ Jose-Froilan	26
VILLENEUVE Jacques	163	RINDT Jochen	60	Von TRIPS Wolfgang	26
SENNA Ayrton	161	COMAS Erik	59	GODIN de BEAUFORT Carel	26
HERBERT Johnny	161	MERZARIO Arturo	57	PEREZ-SALA Luis	26
HAKKINEN Mika	161	PESCAROLO Henri	56	VETTEL Sebastian	26
BRUNDLE Martin	158	CAFFI Alex	56	MAGGS Tony	25
PANIS Olivier	158	SCHELL Harry	55	ANDERSON Bob	25
FRENTZEN Heinz-Harald	156	RODRIGUEZ Pedro	54	KEEGAN Rupert	25
BUTTON Jenson	153	BEHRA Jean	53	ROTHENGATTER Huub	25
WATSON John	152	STOMMELEN Rolf	53	MAGNUSSEN Jan	25
HEIDFELD Nick	150	STREIFF Philippe	53	SALAZAR Eliseo	24
ARNOUX René	149	ROSBERG Nico	53	BRABHAM David	24
REUTEMANN Carlos	146	GINTHER Richie	52	MARQUES Tarso	24
WARWICK Derek	146	FANGIO Juan-Manuel	51	DAVIDSON Anthony	24
IRVINE Eddie	146	IRELAND Innes	50	CLAES Johnny	23
FITTIPALDI Emerson	144	HAILWOOD Mike	50	MUSSO Luigi	23
RAIKKONEN Kimi	139	OLIVER Jackie	49	BOESEL Raul	23
JARIER Jean-Pierre	134	JABOUILLE Jean-Pierre	49	LAMMERS Jan	23
REGAZZONI Clay	132	DALY Derek	49	DALMAS Yannick	23
CHEEVER Eddie	132	LARINI Nicola	49	De GRAFFENRIED Emmanuel	22
ANDRETTI Mario	128	BADOER Luca	49	WISELL Reine	22
BRABHAM Jack	123	HILL Phil	47	GLOCK Timo	22
PETERSON Ronnie	123	WINKELHOCK Manfred	47	BAGHETTI Giancarlo	21
ALONSO Fernando	122	GACHOT Bertrand	47	GUERRERO Roberto	21
WEBBER Mark	121	SALVADORI Roy	46	MAZZACANE Gaston	21
MARTINI Pierluigi	118	CEVERT François	46	BELLOF Stefan	20
JONES Alan	116	KLIEN Christian	46	MONTERMINI Andrea	20
HILL Damon	115	ALBERS Christijan	46	BAUMGARTNER Zsolt	20
ICKX Jacky	114	HAWTHORN Mike	45	PIZZONIA Antonio	20
ROSBERG Keke	114	BERNARD Eric	45	BIRA Prince	19
TAMBAY Patrick	114	BANDINI Lorenzo	42	ERTL Harald	19
HULME Denny	112	PRYCE Tom	42	HENTON Brian	19
SCHECKTER Jody	112	MORENO Roberto	42	HESNAULT François	19
SURTEES John	111	REBAQUE Hector	41	KARTHIKEYAN Narain	19
SALO Mika	110	GROUILLARD Olivier	41	NAKAJIMA Kazuki	19
ALLIOT Philippe	109	WENDLINGER Karl	41	TARUFFI Piero	18
De ANGELIS Elio	108	ZANARDI Alessandro	41	SCHECKTER Ian	18
VERSTAPPEN Jos	107	FITTIPALDI Christian	40	SERRA Chico	18
MASS Jochen	105	KUBICA Robert	40	CECOTTO Johnny	18
MASSA Felipe	105	LIUZZI Vitantonio	39	INOUE Taki	18
BONNIER Jo	103	ROSIER Louis	38	BRUNI Gimmi	18
STEWART Jackie	99	BROOKS Tony	38	BOURDAIS Sébastien	18
McLAREN Bruce	98	GREGORY Masten	38	PIQUET Nelsinho	18
DINIZ Pedro	98	TARQUINI Gabriele	38	MIERES Roberto	17
SIFFERT Jo	96	PIRRO Emanuele	37	HERRMANN Hans	17
AMON Chris	96	ZONTA Ricardo	37	BIANCHI Lucien	17
DEPAILLER Patrick	95	MONTEIRO Tiago	37	GALLI Nanni	17
KATAYAMA Ukyo	95	SPENCE Mike	36	CAMPOS Adrian	17
MONTOYA Juan-Pablo	94	BALDI Mauro	36	ALLISON Cliff	16
CAPELLI Ivan	93	DANNER Christian	36	ATTWOOD Dick	16
HUNT James	92	GENE Marc	36	TUERO Esteban	16
SATO Takuma	90	GANLEY Howden	35	McNISH Allan	16
GURNEY Dan	86	FITTIPALDI Wilson	35	WILSON Justin	16
BELTOISE Jean-Pierre	85	HAMILTON Lewis	35	BONETTO Felice	15
PALMER Jonathan	83	KOVALAINEN Heikki	35	CHIRON Louis	15
SURER Marc	82	SUTIL Adrian	35	WHARTON Ken	15
TRINTIGNANT Maurice	81	SCHENKEN Tim	34	BURGESS Ian	15
JOHANSSON Stefan	79	LUNGER Brett	34	SULLIVAN Danny	15
GHINZANI Piercarlo	76	FARINA Giuseppe	33	DUMFRIES Johnny	15
NANNINI Alessandro	76	NAKANO Shinji	33	BURTI Luciano…	15

Drivers: GP in the lead

SCHUMACHER Michael	141	ALBORETO Michele	10	IRELAND Innes	2
SENNA Ayrton	86	KOVALAINEN Heikki	10	REVSON Peter	2
PROST Alain	84	GONZALEZ Jose-Froilan	9	MASS Jochen	2
COULTHARD David	62	TAMBAY Patrick	9	De CESARIS Andrea	2
PIQUET Nelson	58	GINTHER Richie	8	JOHANSSON Stefan	2
MANSELL Nigel	55	IRVINE Eddie	8	WARWICK Derek	2
STEWART Jackie	51	HEIDFELD Nick	8	CAPELLI Ivan	2
RAIKKONEN Kimi	51	KUBICA Robert	8	SALO Mika	2
ALONSO Fernando	51	COLLINS Peter	7	VETTEL Sebastian	2
HAKKINEN Mika	48	BEHRA Jean	7	PIQUET Nelsinho	2
HILL Damon	45	BANDINI Lorenzo	7	HOLLAND Bill	1
BARRICHELLO Rubens	45	RODRIGUEZ Pedro	7	ROSE Mauri	1
CLARK Jim	43	AMON Chris	7	SOMMER Raymond	1
LAUDA Niki	41	PACE Carlos	7	DAVIES Jimmy	1
FANGIO Juan-Manuel	38	JABOUILLE Jean-Pierre	7	GREEN Cecil	1
BERGER Gerhard	33	BROOKS Tony	6	WALLARD Lee	1
HILL Graham	32	DEPAILLER Patrick	6	VILLORESI Luigi	1
MONTOYA Juan-Pablo	32	RATHMANN Jim	5	BONETTO Felice	1
MOSS Stirling	31	McLAREN Bruce	5	TARUFFI Piero	1
PATRESE Riccardo	29	SIFFERT Jo	5	AGABASHIAN Fred	1
BRABHAM Jack	28	CEVERT François	5	DAYWALT Jimmy	1
PETERSON Ronnie	28	BOUTSEN Thierry	5	MIERES Roberto	1
ARNOUX René	25	VUKOVICH Bill	4	SWEIKERT Bob	1
MASSA Felipe	25	McGRATH Jack	4	MENDITEGUY Carlos	1
HUNT James	24	BONNIER Jo	4	LEWIS-EVANS Stuart	1
JONES Alan	24	Von TRIPS Wolfgang	4	BETTENHAUSEN Tony	1
SCHECKTER Jody	23	BELTOISE Jean-Pierre	4	AMICK George	1
HAMILTON Lewis	23	BRAMBILLA Vittorio	4	BOYD Johnny	1
ANDRETTI Mario	22	De ANGELIS Elio	4	GENDEBIEN Olivier	1
ASCARI Alberto	21	HERBERT Johnny	4	BAGHETTI Giancarlo	1
SCHUMACHER Ralf	21	WEBBER Mark	4	TAYLOR Trevor	1
REGAZZONI Clay	20	FAGIOLI Luigi	3	MAIRESSE Willy	1
ROSBERG Keke	20	KLING Karl	3	SCARFIOTTI Ludovico	1
VILLENEUVE Jacques	20	SCHELL Harry	3	PARKES Mike	1
ICKX Jacky	19	CASTELLOTTI Eugenio	3	LOVE John	1
REUTEMANN Carlos	19	HANKS Sam	3	SERVOZ-GAVIN Johnny	1
ALESI Jean	19	MUSSO Luigi	3	COURAGE Piers	1
FITTIPALDI Emerson	18	TRINTIGNANT Maurice	3	GETHIN Peter	1
VILLENEUVE Gilles	18	BRYAN Jimmy	3	HAILWOOD Mike	1
SURTEES John	17	RUTTMAN Troy	3	STOMMELEN Rolf	1
HULME Denny	17	THOMSON Johnny	3	PRYCE Tom	1
GURNEY Dan	16	OLIVER Jackie	3	NILSSON Gunnar	1
FARINA Giuseppe	14	JARIER Jean-Pierre	3	STUCK Hans Joachim	1
LAFFITE Jacques	14	NANNINI Alessandro	3	GIACOMELLI Bruno	1
FISICHELLA Giancarlo	14	CROSS Art	2	MARTINI Pierluigi	1
TRULLI Jarno	14	FREELAND Don	2	PANIS Olivier	1
FRENTZEN Heinz-Harald	13	PARSONS Johnnie	2	Da MATTA Cristiano	1
BUTTON Jenson	13	O'CONNOR Pat	2	SATO Takuma	1
HAWTHORN Mike	12	RUSSO Paul	2	PIZZONIA Antonio	1
RINDT Jochen	12	FLAHERTY Pat	2	WINKELHOCK Markus	1
HILL Phil	10	GREGORY Masten	2	GLOCK Timo	1
PIRONI Didier	10	SACHS Eddie	2	ROSBERG Nico	1
WATSON John	10	WARD Rodger	2	BOURDAIS Sébastien	1

Drivers: laps in the lead

SCHUMACHER Michael	5,108	AMON Chris	183	NILSSON Gunnar	21
SENNA Ayrton	2,931	JABOUILLE Jean-Pierre	179	NANNINI Alessandro	21
PROST Alain	2,683	HILL Phil	172	DAVIES Jimmy	18
MANSELL Nigel	2,091	WALLARD Lee	165	KLING Karl	18
CLARK Jim	1,940	DEPAILLER Patrick	164	BOYD Johnny	18
STEWART Jackie	1,921	BOUTSEN Thierry	164	AMICK George	18
PIQUET Nelson	1,600	TRULLI Jarno	160	Da MATTA Cristiano	17
LAUDA Niki	1,592	IRVINE Eddie	157	WARWICK Derek	16
HAKKINEN Mika	1,488	Von TRIPS Wolfgang	156	PANIS Olivier	16
HILL Damon	1,358	FRENTZEN Heinz-Harald	150	ROSE Mauri	15
FANGIO Juan-Manuel	1,347	RATHMANN Jim	147	SCHELL Harry	15
ALONSO Fernando	1,221	BANDINI Lorenzo	143	STUCK Hans Joachim	14
MOSS Stirling	1,181	HANKS Sam	140	PIQUET Nelsinho	14
HILL Graham	1,101	BONNIER Jo	139	GREGORY Masten	13
RAIKKONEN Kimi	1,027	FLAHERTY Pat	138	LOVE John	13
ASCARI Alberto	927	BROOKS Tony	133	ROSBERG Nico	11
COULTHARD David	897	PARSONS Johnnie	131	WEBBER Mark	10
BRABHAM Jack	825	CEVERT François	129	HOLLAND Bill	8
MASSA Felipe	819	COLLINS Peter	127	FAGIOLI Luigi	8
ANDRETTI Mario	798	GINTHER Richie	116	DAYWALT Jimmy	8
BERGER Gerhard	748	BEHRA Jean	107	STOMMELEN Rolf	8
BARRICHELLO Rubens	729	BUTTON Jenson	104	FREELAND Don	7
PETERSON Ronnie	707	BELTOISE Jean-Pierre	101	BAGHETTI Giancarlo	7
SCHECKTER Jody	675	SIFFERT Jo	99	PARKES Mike	7
HUNT James	666	SWEIKERT Bob	86	MUSSO Luigi	6
REUTEMANN Carlos	649	RODRIGUEZ Pedro	86	WINKELHOCK Markus	6
VILLENEUVE Jacques	633	JARIER Jean-Pierre	79	SOMMER Raymond	5
HAMILTON Lewis	615	TRINTIGNANT Maurice	78	GREEN Cecil	5
MONTOYA Juan-Pablo	605	KUBICA Robert	74	LEWIS-EVANS Stuart	5
JONES Alan	589	McGRATH Jack	71	HAILWOOD Mike	5
PATRESE Riccardo	565	REVSON Peter	63	MASS Jochen	5
VILLENEUVE Gilles	534	RUTTMAN Troy	59	LARINI Nicola	5
ICKX Jacky	529	THOMSON Johnny	55	MIERES Roberto	4
ROSBERG Keke	512	SCARFIOTTI Ludovico	55	TAYLOR Trevor	4
ARNOUX René	507	VETTEL Sebastian	52	GENDEBIEN Olivier	3
VUKOVICH Bill	485	PACE Carlos	50	MAIRESSE Willy	3
FITTIPALDI Emerson	478	TARUFFI Piero	46	SERVOZ-GAVIN Johnny	3
HULME Denny	435	O'CONNOR Pat	46	GETHIN Peter	3
SCHUMACHER Ralf	401	CAPELLI Ivan	46	JOHANSSON Stefan	3
RINDT Jochen	387	HERBERT Johnny	44	GLOCK Timo	3
REGAZZONI Clay	360	IRELAND Innes	43	BOURDAIS Sébastien	3
FARINA Giuseppe	336	McLAREN Bruce	41	VILLORESI Luigi	2
SURTEES John	308	KOVALAINEN Heikki	40	COURAGE Piers	2
PIRONI Didier	295	MENDITEGUY Carlos	39	PRYCE Tom	2
WATSON John	287	OLIVER Jackie	36	SALO Mika	2
LAFFITE Jacques	283	RUSSO Paul	35	SATO Takuma	2
GONZALEZ Jose-Froilan	272	CROSS Art	32	BONETTO Felice	1
ALESI Jean	265	BRAMBILLA Vittorio	32	AGABASHIAN Fred	1
HAWTHORN Mike	225	De CESARIS Andrea	32	MARTINI Pierluigi	1
ALBORETO Michele	218	GIACOMELLI Bruno	31	PIZZONIA Antonio	1
BRYAN Jimmy	216	De ANGELIS Elio	28		
FISICHELLA Giancarlo	210	HEIDFELD Nick	25		
GURNEY Dan	203	BETTENHAUSEN Tony	24		
AMBAY Patrick	195	SACHS Eddie	22		
WARD Rodger	188	CASTELLOTTI Eugenio	21		

Drivers: points

SCHUMACHER Michael	1,369	SALVADORI Roy	19
PROST Alain	798.5	PRYCE Tom	19
SENNA Ayrton	614	PIQUET Nelsinho	19
ALONSO Fernando	551	ROSIER Louis	18
COULTHARD David	535	BRYAN Jimmy	18
RAIKKONEN Kimi	531	GENDEBIEN Olivier	18
BARRICHELLO Rubens	530	MARTINI Pierluigi	18
PIQUET Nelson	485.5	BONETTO Felice	17.5
MANSELL Nigel	482	KLING Karl	17
LAUDA Niki	420.5	SCARFIOTTI Ludovico	17
HAKKINEN Mika	420	SURER Marc	17
BERGER Gerhard	385	MODENA Stefano	17
STEWART Jackie	360	VERSTAPPEN Jos	17
HILL Damon	360	MANZON Robert	16
SCHUMACHER Ralf	329	LEWIS-EVANS Stuart	16
REUTEMANN Carlos	310	NAKAJIMA Satoru	16
MONTOYA Juan-Pablo	307	BRAMBILLA Vittorio	15.5
MASSA Felipe	298	DALY Derek	15
HILL Graham	289	MORENO Roberto	15
FITTIPALDI Emerson	281	WARD Rodger	14
PATRESE Riccardo	281	PARKES Mike	14
FANGIO Juan-Manuel	277.64	BAGHETTI Giancarlo	14
CLARK Jim	274	STOMMELEN Rolf	14
FISICHELLA Giancarlo	267	PALMER Jonathan	14
BRABHAM Jack	261	GIACOMELLI Bruno	14
SCHECKTER Jody	255	WENDLINGER Karl	14
HULME Denny	248	KLIEN Christian	14
ALESI Jean	241	MIERES Roberto	13
VILLENEUVE Jacques	235	WISELL Reine	13
BUTTON Jenson	232	OLIVER Jackie	13
LAFFITE Jacques	228	REBAQUE Hector	13
TRULLI Jarno	214	Da MATTA Cristiano	13
REGAZZONI Clay	212	PARSONS Johnnie	12
HAMILTON Lewis	207	ARUNDELL Peter	12
PETERSON Ronnie	206	PESCAROLO Henri	12
JONES Alan	206	FITTIPALDI Christian	12
HEIDFELD Nick	200	FRERE Paul	11
McLAREN Bruce	196.5	BETTENHAUSEN Tony	11
IRVINE Eddie	191	ALLISON Cliff	11
MOSS Stirling	186.64	ATTWOOD Dick	11
ALBORETO Michele	186.5	GETHIN Peter	11
ICKX Jacky	181	MERZARIO Arturo	11
ARNOUX René	181	STREIFF Philippe	11
SURTEES John	180	FISCHER Rudi	10
ANDRETTI Mario	180	THOMSON Johnny	10
HUNT James	179	HERRMANN Hans	10
FRENTZEN Heinz-Harald	174	GANLEY Howden	10
WATSON John	169	GUGELMIN Mauricio	10
ROSBERG Keke	159.5	LEHTO JJ	10
DEPAILLER Patrick	141	BERNARD Eric	10
ASCARI Alberto	140.14	DINIZ Pedro	10
GURNEY Dan	133	RUTTMAN Troy	9.5
BOUTSEN Thierry	132	WALLARD Lee	9
HAWTHORN Mike	127.64	PARNELL Reg	9
FARINA Giuseppe	127.33	McGRATH Jack	9
De ANGELIS Elio	122	De GRAFFENRIED Emmanuel	9
KUBICA Robert	120	MENDITEGUY Carlos	9
RINDT Jochen	109	SERVOZ-GAVIN Johnny	9
GINTHER Richie	107	NAKAJIMA Kazuki	9
VILLENEUVE Gilles	107	RUSSO Paul	8.5
TAMBAY Patrick	103	MORBIDELLI Gianni	8.5
PIRONI Didier	101	MARIMON Onofre	8.14
WEBBER Mark	100	NAZARUK Mike	8
HILL Phil	98	CROSS Art	8
BRUNDLE Martin	98	BIRA Prince	8
HERBERT Johnny	98	SWEIKERT Bob	8
CEVERT François	89	FLAHERTY Pat	8
JOHANSSON Stefan	88	ANDERSON Bob	8
AMON Chris	83	TAYLOR Trevor	8
KOVALAINEN Heikki	83	ELFORD Vic	8
GONZALEZ Jose-Froilan	77.64	REDMAN Brian	8
BELTOISE Jean-Pierre	77	DONOHUE Mark	8
PANIS Olivier	76	SUZUKI Aguri	8
BROOKS Tony	75	PIZZONIA Antonio	8
TRINTIGNANT Maurice	72.33	MAIRESSE Willy	7
RODRIGUEZ Pedro	71	SCHENKEN Tim	7
MASS Jochen	71	ANDRETTI Michael	7
WARWICK Derek	71	ALLIOT Philippe	7
CHEEVER Eddie	70	COMAS Erik	7
SIFFERT Jo	68	LARINI Nicola	7
NANNINI Alessandro	65	MONTEIRO Tiago	7
REVSON Peter	61	CARTER Duane	6.5
De CESARIS Andrea	59	HOLLAND Bill	6
BANDINI Lorenzo	58	AMICK George	6
PACE Carlos	58	GODIA-SALES Chico	6
Von TRIPS Wolfgang	56	GOLDSMITH Paul	6
BEHRA Jean	51.14	BIANCHI Lucien	6
VILLORESI Luigi	49	LOVE John	6
COLLINS Peter	47	De ADAMICH Andrea	6
IRELAND Innes	47	CAFFI Alex	6
WURZ Alexander	45	GIRAUD-CABANTOUS Yves	5
MUSSO Luigi	44	PERDISA Cesare	5
SATO Takuma	44	LINDEN Andy	5
TARUFFI Piero	41	FLOCKHART Ron	5
VETTEL Sebastian	41	FAIRMAN Jack	5
ROSBERG Nico	41	FOLLMER George	5
BONNIER Jo	39	BALDI Mauro	5
SALO Mika	33	GACHOT Bertrand	5
FAGIOLI Luigi	32	KATAYAMA Ukyo	5
SCHELL Harry	32	GENE Marc	5
BLUNDELL Mark	32	KARTHIKEYAN Narain	5
JARIER Jean-Pierre	31.5	LIUZZI Vitantonio	5
NILSSON Gunnar	31	ROSE Mauri	4
CAPELLI Ivan	31	WHITEHEAD Peter	4
RATHMANN Jim	29	MANTOVANI Sergio	4
HAILWOOD Mike	29	De PORTAGO Alfonso	4
STUCK Hans Joachim	29	CHIRON Louis	4
De la ROSA Pedro	29	DAVIES Jimmy	4
SPENCE Mike	27	BOYD Johnny	4
GLOCK Timo	27	FREELAND Don	4
MAGGS Tony	26	RODRIGUEZ Ricardo	4
FABI Teo	23	GODIN de BEAUFORT Carel	4
GREGORY Masten	21	BELLOF Stefan	4
JABOUILLE Jean-Pierre	21	DANNER Christian	4
HANKS Sam	20	BOURDAIS Sébastien	4
COURAGE Piers	20	…	
CASTELLOTTI Eugenio	19.5	SUTIL Adrian	1
VUKOVICH Bill	19		

Drivers: podiums

SCHUMACHER Michael	154	REGAZZONI Clay	28	GONZALEZ Jose-Froilan	15	KUBICA Robert	8
PROST Alain	106	McLAREN Bruce	27	BOUTSEN Thierry	15	MUSSO Luigi	7
SENNA Ayrton	80	SCHUMACHER Ralf	27	BUTTON Jenson	15	RODRIGUEZ Pedro	7
BARRICHELLO Rubens	62	MASSA Felipe	27	GINTHER Richie	14	HERBERT Johnny	7
COULTHARD David	62	PETERSON Ronnie	26	RINDT Jochen	13	FAGIOLI Luigi	6
PIQUET Nelson	60	IRVINE Eddie	26	CEVERT François	13	Von TRIPS Wolfgang	6
MANSELL Nigel	59	ICKX Jacky	25	VILLENEUVE Gilles	13	SIFFERT Jo	6
RAIKKONEN Kimi	57	MOSS Stirling	24	PIRONI Didier	13	PACE Carlos	6
LAUDA Niki	54	SURTEES John	24	JOHANSSON Stefan	12	TARUFFI Piero	5
ALONSO Fernando	52	JONES Alan	24	AMON Chris	11	De CESARIS Andrea	5
HAKKINEN Mika	51	HUNT James	23	TAMBAY Patrick	11	PANIS Olivier	5
BERGER Gerhard	48	ALBORETO Michele	23	HEIDFELD Nick	11	HANKS Sam	4
REUTEMANN Carlos	45	VILLENEUVE Jacques	23	TRINTIGNANT Maurice	10	RATHMANN Jim	4
STEWART Jackie	43	ARNOUX René	22	BROOKS Tony	10	IRELAND Innes	4
HILL Damon	42	HAMILTON Lewis	22	BEHRA Jean	9	NILSSON Gunnar	4
PATRESE Riccardo	37	FARINA Giuseppe	20	COLLINS Peter	9	WARWICK Derek	4
HILL Graham	36	WATSON John	20	De ANGELIS Elio	9	KOVALAINEN Heikki	4
FANGIO Juan-Manuel	35	GURNEY Dan	19	CHEEVER Eddie	9	…	
FITTIPALDI Emerson	35	DEPAILLER Patrick	19	NANNINI Alessandro	9	WEBBER Mark	2
HULME Denny	33	ANDRETTI Mario	19	BRUNDLE Martin	9	ROSBERG Nico	2
SCHECKTER Jody	33	HAWTHORN Mike	18	VILLORESI Luigi	8	SATO Takuma	1
CLARK Jim	32	FRENTZEN Heinz-Harald	18	BANDINI Lorenzo	8	PIQUET Nelsinho	1
LAFFITE Jacques	32	FISICHELLA Giancarlo	18	REVSON Peter	8	GLOCK Timo	1
ALESI Jean	32	ASCARI Alberto	17	BELTOISE Jean-Pierre	8	VETTEL Sebastian	1
BRABHAM Jack	31	ROSBERG Keke	17	MASS Jochen	8		
MONTOYA Juan-Pablo	30	HILL Phil	16	TRULLI Jarno	8		

Drivers: pole positions

SCHUMACHER Michael	68	LAFFITE Jacques	7	NALON Duke	1
SENNA Ayrton	65	HILL Phil	6	AGABASHIAN Fred	1
CLARK Jim	33	FITTIPALDI Emerson	6	VUKOVICH Bill	1
PROST Alain	33	JABOUILLE Jean-Pierre	6	McGRATH Jack	1
MANSELL Nigel	32	JONES Alan	6	HOYT Jerry	1
FANGIO Juan-Manuel	29	REUTEMANN Carlos	6	CASTELLOTTI Eugenio	1
HAKKINEN Mika	26	SCHUMACHER Ralf	6	FLAHERTY Pat	1
LAUDA Niki	24	FARINA Giuseppe	5	O'CONNOR Pat	1
PIQUET Nelson	24	AMON Chris	5	RATHMANN Dick	1
HILL Damon	20	REGAZZONI Clay	5	THOMSON Johnny	1
ANDRETTI Mario	18	TAMBAY Patrick	5	BONNIER Jo	1
ARNOUX René	18	ROSBERG Keke	5	SACHS Eddie	1
STEWART Jackie	17	HAWTHORN Mike	4	Von TRIPS Wolfgang	1
ALONSO Fernando	17	PIRONI Didier	4	BANDINI Lorenzo	1
MOSS Stirling	16	GONZALEZ Jose-Froilan	3	PARKES Mike	1
RAIKKONEN Kimi	16	BROOKS Tony	3	REVSON Peter	1
MASSA Felipe	15	GURNEY Dan	3	HULME Denny	1
ASCARI Alberto	14	JARIER Jean-Pierre	3	DEPAILLER Patrick	1
HUNT James	14	CHECKTER Jody	3	PACE Carlos	1
PETERSON Ronnie	14	De ANGELIS Elio	3	BRAMBILLA Vittorio	1
HILL Graham	13	FABI Teo	3	PRYCE Tom	1
BRABHAM Jack	13	TRULLI Jarno	3	GIACOMELLI Bruno	1
ICKX Jacky	13	FISICHELLA Giancarlo	3	De CESARIS Andrea	1
VILLENEUVE Jacques	13	BUTTON Jenson	3	BOUTSEN Thierry	1
BARRICHELLO Rubens	13	LEWIS-EVANS Stuart	2	HEIDFELD Nick	1
MONTOYA Juan-Pablo	13	SIFFERT Jo	2	KUBICA Robert	1
HAMILTON Lewis	13	WATSON John	2	KOVALAINEN Heikki	1
BERGER Gerhard	12	VILLENEUVE Gilles	2	VETTEL Sebastian	1
COULTHARD David	12	ALBORETO Michele	2		
RINDT Jochen	10	ALESI Jean	2		
SURTEES John	8	FRENTZEN Heinz-Harald	2		
PATRESE Riccardo	8	FAULKNER Walt	1		

Drivers: fastest laps

SCHUMACHER Michael	76	GURNEY Dan	6	VILLORESI Luigi	1
PROST Alain	41	FITTIPALDI Emerson	6	McGRATH Jack	1
RAIKKONEN Kimi	35	REUTEMANN Carlos	6	HERRMANN Hans	1
MANSELL Nigel	30	LAFFITE Jacques	6	MARIMON Onofre	1
CLARK Jim	28	FRENTZEN Heinz-Harald	6	BEHRA Jean	1
HAKKINEN Mika	25	FARINA Giuseppe	5	KLING Karl	1
LAUDA Niki	24	PACE Carlos	5	MIERES Roberto	1
FANGIO Juan-Manuel	23	SCHECKTER Jody	5	RUSSO Paul	1
PIQUET Nelson	23	PIRONI Didier	5	MUSSO Luigi	1
BERGER Gerhard	21	WATSON John	5	BETTENHAUSEN Tony	1
MOSS Stirling	19	ALBORETO Michele	5	THOMSON Johnny	1
SENNA Ayrton	19	SIFFERT Jo	4	TRINTIGNANT Maurice	1
HILL Damon	19	BELTOISE Jean-Pierre	4	IRELAND Innes	1
COULTHARD David	18	DEPAILLER Patrick	4	BAGHETTI Giancarlo	1
STEWART Jackie	15	ALESI Jean	4	SCARFIOTTI Ludovico	1
REGAZZONI Clay	15	VUKOVICH Bill	3	ATTWOOD Dick	1
BARRICHELLO Rubens	15	BROOKS Tony	3	RODRIGUEZ Pedro	1
ICKX Jacky	14	McLAREN Bruce	3	OLIVER Jackie	1
JONES Alan	13	GINTHER Richie	3	PESCAROLO Henri	1
PATRESE Riccardo	13	RINDT Jochen	3	HAILWOOD Mike	1
ASCARI Alberto	12	AMON Chris	3	BRAMBILLA Vittorio	1
BRABHAM Jack	12	JARIER Jean-Pierre	3	HASEMI Masahiro	1
ARNOUX René	12	ROSBERG Keke	3	NILSSON Gunnar	1
MONTOYA Juan-Pablo	12	HAMILTON Lewis	3	SURER Marc	1
SURTEES John	11	RATHMANN Jim	2	HENTON Brian	1
ALONSO Fernando	11	BANDINI Lorenzo	2	De CESARIS Andrea	1
MASSA Felipe	11	CEVERT François	2	PALMER Jonathan	1
HILL Graham	10	MASS Jochen	2	GUGELMIN Mauricio	1
ANDRETTI Mario	10	TAMBAY Patrick	2	NAKAJIMA Satoru	1
HULME Denny	9	WARWICK Derek	2	BOUTSEN Thierry	1
PETERSON Ronnie	9	FABI Teo	2	GACHOT Bertrand	1
VILLENEUVE Jacques	9	NANNINI Alessandro	2	MORENO Roberto	1
HUNT James	8	FISICHELLA Giancarlo	2	WURZ Alexander	1
VILLENEUVE Gilles	8	KOVALAINEN Heikki	2	IRVINE Eddie	1
SCHUMACHER Ralf	8	HEIDFELD Nick	2	DE LA ROSA Pedro	1
GONZALEZ Jose-Froilan	6	PARSONS Johnnie	1	ROSBERG Nico	1
HAWTHORN Mike	6	WALLARD Lee	1		
HILL Phil	6	TARUFFI Piero	1		

Number of Constructors'Championships

(since 1958)

<u>16 titles</u>
Ferrari 1961-1964
1975-1976-1977-1979-1982-
1983-1999-2000-2001-2002-
2003-2004-2007-2008

<u>9 titles</u>
Williams 1980-1981-1986-
1987-1992-1993-1994-1996-
1997

<u>8 titles</u>
McLaren 1974
1984-1985-1988-1989
1990-1991-1998

<u>7 titles</u>
Lotus 1963-1965-1968
1970-1972-1973-1978

<u>2 titles</u>
Cooper 1959-1960
Brabham 1966-1967
Renault 2005-2006

<u>1 title</u>
Vanwall 1958
BRM 1962
Matra 1969
Tyrrell 1971
Benetton 1995

Constructors: Grands Prix

Ferrari	776	RAM	28	Trevis	4
McLaren	648	Eagle	25	Emeryson	4
Williams	529	Spirit	23	Martini	4
Lotus	491	Forti	23	Deidt	3
Tyrrell	430	Pacific	22	Pawl	3
Brabham	394	Simtek	21	Moore	3
Minardi	340	Rial	20	Dunn	3
Ligier	326	Fondmetal	19	Gilby	3
Arrows	291	Midland	18	Token	3
Benetton	260	Force India	18	LEC	3
Jordan	250	Connaught	17	RAM March	3
Renault	245	Spyker	17	Marchese	2
Sauber	215	Parnelli	16	Sherman	2
BRM	197	Onyx	16	Aston	2
March	197	Venturi	16	BMW	2
Lola	149	Simca Gordini	14	Nichels	2
Osella	132	HWM	14	Pankratz	2
Cooper	128	Eurobrun	14	Ewing	2
Toyota	122	Talbot Lago	13	Christensen	2
Surtees	118	BRP	13	Scarab	2
B·A·R	117	Coloni	13	Alfa Special	2
Alfa Romeo	110	Mercedes	12	Bellasi	2
Shadow	104	Kurtis Kraft	12	Kojima	2
Ensign	99	Kuzma	10	Olson	1
Footwork	91	De Tomaso	10	Langley	1
ATS	89	Tecno	10	Rae	1
Honda	88	Hill	10	Wetteroth	1
Jaguar	85	Merzario	10	Snowberger	1
Prost	83	Lesovsky	9	Adams	1
Dallara	78	Watson	9	Hall	1
Copersucar	71	Eifelland March	8	Del Roy	1
Red Bull	71	ERA	7	Turner	1
Maserati	70	Phillips	7	EMW	1
Matra	60	Veritas	6	Klenk	1
Toleman	57	Stevens	6	Bugatti	1
Zakspeed	53	A-T-S	6	Elder	1
Toro Rosso	53	Trojan	6	Sutton	1
BMW Sauber	53	Boro	6	Tec Mec	1
Hesketh	52	Lamborghini	6	Meskowski	1
Stewart	49	Alta	5	Ferguson	1
Wolf	47	Epperly	5	ENB	1
AGS	47	Aston Martin	5	Stebro	1
Penske	40	JBW	5	Shannon	1
Super Aguri	39	Scirocco	5	Protos	1
Theodore	34	LDS	5	Politoys	1
Gordini	33	Maserati Milano	4	Connew	1
Fittipaldi	32	Frazer Nash	4	Amon	1
Larrousse	32	OSCA	4	Lyncar	1
Porsche	31	AFM	4	Rebaque	1
Iso-Marlboro	30	Bromme	4	Monteverdi	1
Leyton House	30	Schroeder	4	Andrea Moda	1
Vanwall	28	Lancia	4		

Constructors: victories

Ferrari	209	Mercedes	9	Epperly	2
McLaren	162	Maserati	9	Kuzma	1
Williams	113	Vanwall	9	Porsche	1
Lotus	79	Matra	9	Eagle	1
Brabham	35	Ligier	9	Hesketh	1
Renault	35	Kurtis Kraft	5	Penske	1
Benetton	27	Jordan	4	Shadow	1
Tyrrell	23	Watson	3	Stewart	1
BRM	17	March	3	BMW Sauber	1
Cooper	16	Wolf	3	Toro Rosso	1
Alfa Romeo	10	Honda	3		

Constructors: pole positions

Ferrari	203	Ligier	9	Honda	2
McLaren	141	Mercedes	8	Stevens	1
Williams	125	Vanwall	7	Lesovsky	1
Lotus	107	Kurtis	6	Ewing	1
Renault	50	March	5	Lola	1
Brabham	39	Matra	4	Porsche	1
Benetton	15	Shadow	3	Wolf	1
Tyrrell	14	Lancia	2	Arrows	1
Alfa Romeo	12	Watson	2	Toleman	1
Cooper	11	Jordan	2	Stewart	1
BRM	11	B·A·R	2	BMW Sauber	1
Maserati	10	Toyota	2	Toro Rosso	1

Constructors: fastest laps

Ferrari	218	Matra	12	Toleman	2
McLaren	137	Mercedes	9	Jordan	2
Williams	129	Ligier	9	BMW Sauber	2
Lotus	71	Kurtis Kraft	7	Gordini	1
Brabham	41	March	7	Lancia	1
Benetton	36	Vanwall	6	Lesovsky	1
Renault	27	Surtees	3	Watson	1
Tyrrell	20	Epperly	2	Hesketh	1
Maserati	15	Eagle	2	Parnelli	1
BRM	15	Honda	2	Kojima	1
Cooper	14	Shadow	2	Ensign	1
Alfa Romeo	14	Wolf	2	Toyota	1

Constructors: points

Ferrari	4,023.5	Red Bull	103	Dallara	15
McLaren	3,310.5	Wolf	79	Fittipaldi	12
Williams	2,565.5	Shadow	67.5	BRP	11
Lotus	1,368	Vanwall	57	Leyton House	8
Renault	1,056	Surtees	53	ATS	7
Brabham	864	Alfa Romeo	50	Maserati	6
Benetton	851.5	Jaguar	49	Iso-Marlboro	6
Tyrrell	621	Porsche	48	Parnelli	6
BRM	433	Hesketh	48	Rial	6
Ligier	388	Toro Rosso	48	Onyx	6
Cooper	342	Stewart	47	Osella	5
Jordan	291	Lola	43	Larrousse	5
BMW Sauber	272	Minardi	38	Super Aguri	4
B·A·R	227	Prost	35	Hill	3
Toyota	219	Copersucar	32	Theodore	2
Sauber	195	Toleman	26	Zakspeed	2
March	173.5	Footwork	25	AGS	2
Matra	163	Penske	23	Tecno	1
Arrows	142	Ensign	19	Venturi	1
Honda	154	Eagle	17	Spyker	1

Constructors: one-two

Ferrari	79	Mercedes	5	Renault	2
McLaren	44	BRM	5	Benetton	2
Williams	33	Alfa Romeo	4	Maserati	1
Lotus	8	Kurtis Kraft	2	Ligier	1
Brabham	8	Epperly	2	Jordan	1
Tyrrell	8	Watson	2	BMW Sauber	1
Cooper	6	Matra	2		

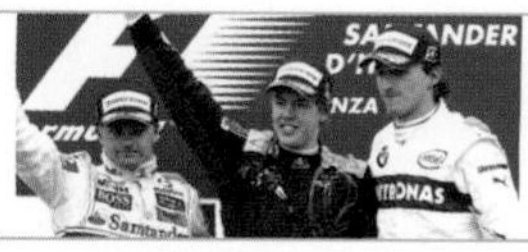

	GB	MC	INDY 500	CH	B	F	I	D	E	NL	RA	PESCARA	P	MA	USA	ZA	MEX
1950	Farina Alfa Romeo	Fangio Alfa Romeo	Parsons Kurtis Kraft Offenhauser	Farina Alfa Romeo	Fangio Alfa Romeo	Fangio Alfa Romeo	Farina Alfa Romeo										
1951	Gonzalez Ferrari		Wallard Kurtis Kraft Offenhauser	Fangio Alfa Romeo	Farina Alfa Romeo	Fagioli/Fangio Alfa Romeo	Ascari Ferrari	Ascari Ferrari	Fangio Alfa Romeo								
1952	Ascari Ferrari		Ruttman Kuzma Offenhauser	Taruffi Ferrari	Ascari Ferrari	Ascari Ferrari	Ascari Ferrari	Ascari Ferrari		Ascari Ferrari							
1953	Ascari Ferrari		Vukovich Kurtis Kraft Offenhauser	Ascari Ferrari	Ascari Ferrari	Hawthorn Ferrari	Fangio Maserati	Farina Ferrari		Ascari Ferrari	Ascari Ferrari						
1954	Gonzalez Ferrari		Vukovich Kurtis Kraft Offenhauser	Fangio Mercedes	Fangio Maserati	Fangio Mercedes	Fangio Mercedes	Fangio Mercedes	Hawthorn Ferrari		Fangio Maserati						
1955	Moss Mercedes	Trintignant Ferrari	Sweikert Kurtis Kraft Offenhauser		Fangio Mercedes		Fangio Mercedes			Fangio Mercedes	Fangio Mercedes						
1956	Fangio Ferrari	Moss Maserati	Flaherty Watson Offenhauser		Collins Ferrari	Collins Ferrari	Moss Maserati	Fangio Ferrari			Musso/Fangio Ferrari						
1957	Brooks / Moss Vanwall	Fangio Maserati	Hanks Epperly Offenhauser			Fangio Maserati	Moss Vanwall	Fangio Maserati			Fangio Maserati	Moss Vanwall					
1958	Collins Ferrari	Trintignant Cooper-Climax	Bryan Epperly Offenhauser		Brooks Vanwall	Hawthorn Ferrari	Brooks Vanwall	Brooks Vanwall		Moss Vanwall	Moss Cooper-Climax		Moss Vanwall	Moss Vanwall			
1959	Brabham Cooper-Climax	Brabham Cooper-Climax	Ward Watson Offenhauser			Brooks Ferrari	Moss Cooper-Climax	Brooks Ferrari		Bonnier BRM			Moss Cooper-Climax		McLaren Cooper-Climax		
1960	Brabham Cooper-Climax	Moss Lotus-Climax	Rathmann Watson Offenhauser		Brabham Cooper-Climax	Brabham Cooper-Climax	P. Hill Ferrari			Brabham Cooper-Climax	McLaren Cooper-Climax		Brabham Cooper-Climax		Moss Lotus-Climax		
1961	Von Trips Ferrari	Moss Lotus-Climax			Hill Ferrari	Baghetti Ferrari	P. Hill Ferrari	Moss Lotus-Climax		Von Trips Ferrari					Ireland Lotus-Climax		
1962	Clark Lotus-Climax	McLaren Cooper-Climax			Clark Lotus-Climax	Gurney Porsche	G. Hill BRM	G. Hill BRM		G. Hill BRM					Clark Lotus-Climax	G. Hill BRM	
1963	Clark Lotus-Climax	G. Hill BRM			Clark Lotus-Climax	Clark Lotus-Climax	Clark Lotus-Climax	Surtees Ferrari		Clark Lotus-Climax					G. Hill BRM	Clark Lotus-Climax	Clark Lotus-Climax
1964	Clark Lotus-Climax	G. Hill BRM			Clark Lotus-Climax	Gurney Brabham-Climax	Surtees Ferrari	Surtees Ferrari		Clark Lotus-Climax					G. Hill BRM		Gurney Brabham-Climax
1965	Clark Lotus-Climax	G. Hill BRM			Clark Lotus-Climax	Clark Lotus-Climax	Stewart BRM	Clark Lotus-Climax		Clark Lotus-Climax					G. Hill BRM	Clark Lotus-Climax	G nther Honda
1966	Brabham Brabham-Repco	Stewart BRM			Surtees Ferrari	Brabham Brabham-Repco	Scarfiotti Ferrari	Brabham Brabham-Repco		Brabham Brabham-Repco					Clark Lotus-BRM		Surtees Cooper-Maserati
1967	Clark Lotus-Ford	Hulme Brabham-Repco			Gurney Eagle-Weslake	Brabham Brabham-Repco	Surtees Honda	Hulme Brabham-Repco		Clark Lotus-Ford					Clark Lotus-Ford	Rodriguez Cooper-Maserati	Clark Lotus-Ford
1968	Siffert Lotus-Ford	G. Hill Lotus-Ford			McLaren McLaren-Ford	Ickx Ferrari	Hulme McLaren-Ford	Stewart Matra-Ford	G. Hill Lotus-Ford	Stewart Matra-Ford					Stewart Matra-Ford	Clark Lotus-Ford	G. Hill Lotus-Ford
1969	Stewart Matra-Ford	G. Hill Lotus-Ford				Stewart Matra-Ford	Stewart Matra-Ford	Ickx Brabham-Ford	Stewart Matra-Ford	Stewart Matra-Ford					Rindt Lotus-Ford	Stewart Matra-Ford	Hulme McLaren-Ford
1970	Rindt Lotus-Ford	Rindt Lotus-Ford			Rodriguez BRM	Rindt Lotus-Ford	Regazzoni Ferrari	Rindt Lotus-Ford	Stewart March-Ford	Rindt Lotus-Ford					E. Fittipaldi Lotus-Ford	Brabham Brabham-Ford	Ickx Ferrari
1971	Stewart Tyrrell-Ford	Stewart Tyrrell-Ford				Stewart Tyrrell-Ford	Gethin BRM	Stewart Tyrrell-Ford	Stewart Tyrrell-Ford	Ickx Ferrari					Cevert Tyrrell-Ford	Andretti Ferrari	
1972	E. Fittipaldi Lotus-Ford	Beltoise BRM			E. Fittipaldi Lotus-Ford	Stewart Tyrrell-Ford	E. Fittipaldi Lotus-Ford	Ickx Ferrari	E. Fittipaldi Lotus-Ford		Stewart Tyrrell-Ford				Stewart Tyrrell-Ford	Hulme McLaren-Ford	
1973	Revson McLaren-Ford	Stewart Tyrrell-Ford			Stewart Tyrrell-Ford	Peterson Lotus-Ford	Peterson Lotus-Ford	Stewart Tyrrell-Ford	E. Fittipaldi Lotus-Ford	Stewart Tyrrell-Ford	E. Fittipaldi Lotus-Ford				Peterson Lotus-Ford	Stewart Tyrrell-Ford	
1974	Scheckter Tyrrell-Ford	Peterson Lotus-Ford			E. Fittipaldi McLaren-Ford	Peterson Lotus-Ford	Peterson Lotus-Ford	Regazzoni Ferrari	Lauda Ferrari	Lauda Ferrari	Hulme McLaren-Ford				Reutemann Brabham-Ford	Reutemann Brabham-Ford	
1975	E. Fittipaldi McLaren-Ford	Lauda Ferrari			Lauda Ferrari	Lauda Ferrari	Regazzoni Ferrari	Reutemann Brabham-Ford	Mass McLaren-Ford	Hunt Hesketh-Ford	E. Fittipaldi McLaren-Ford				Lauda Ferrari	Scheckter Tyrrell-Ford	
1976	Lauda Ferrari	Lauda Ferrari			Lauda Ferrari	Hunt McLaren-Ford	Peterson March-Ford	Hunt McLaren-Honda	Hunt McLaren-Ford	Hunt McLaren-Ford						Lauda Ferrari	
1977	Hunt McLaren-Ford	Scheckter Wolf-Ford			Nilsson Lotus-Ford	M. Andretti Lotus-Ford	M. Andretti Lotus-Ford	Lauda Ferrari	M. Andretti Lotus-Ford	Lauda Ferrari	Scheckter Wolf-Ford					Lauda Ferrari	
1978	Reutemann Ferrari	Depailler Tyrrell-Ford			M. Andretti Lotus-Ford	M. Andretti Lotus-Ford	Lauda Brabham- Alfa Romeo	M. Andretti Lotus-Ford	M. Andretti Lotus-Ford	M. Andretti Lotus-Ford	M. Andretti Lotus-Ford					Peterson Lotus-Ford	
1979	Regazzoni Williams-Ford	Scheckter Ferrari			Scheckter Ferrari	Jabouille Renault	Scheckter Ferrari	Jones Williams-Ford	Depailler Ligier-Ford	Jones Williams-Ford	Laffite Ligier-Ford					G. Villeneuve Ferrari	
1980	Jones Williams-Ford	Reutemann Williams-Ford			Pironi Ligier-Ford	Jones Williams-Ford	Piquet Brabham-Ford	Laffite Ligier-Ford		Piquet Brabham-Ford	Jones Williams-Ford					Arnoux Renault	
1981	Watson McLaren-Ford	G. Villeneuve Ferrari			Reutemann Williams-Ford	Prost Renault	Prost Renault	Piquet Brabham-Ford	G. Villeneuve Ferrari	Prost Renault	Piquet Brabham-Ford						
1982	Lauda McLaren-Ford	Patrese Brabham-Ford		K. Rosberg Williams-Ford	Watson McLaren-Ford	Arnoux Renault	Arnoux Renault	Tambay Ferrari		Pironi Ferrari						Prost Renault	
1983	Prost Renault	K. Rosberg Williams-Ford			Prost Renault	Prost Renault	Piquet Brabham-BMW	Arnoux Ferrari		Arnoux Ferrari						Patrese Brabham-BMW	
1984	Lauda McLaren- TAG Porsche	Prost McLaren- TAG Porsche			Alboreto Ferrari	Lauda McLaren- TAG Porsche	Lauda McLaren- TAG Porsche	Prost McLaren- TAG Porsche		Prost McLaren- TAG Porsche			Prost McLaren- TAG Porsche		K. Rosberg Williams-Honda	Lauda McLaren- TAG Porsche	
1985	Prost McLaren- TAG Porsche	Prost McLaren- TAG Porsche			Senna Lotus-Renault	Piquet Brabham-BMW	Prost McLaren- TAG Porsche	Alboreto Ferrari		Lauda McLaren- TAG Porsche			Senna Lotus-Renault		K. Rosberg Williams-Honda	Mansell Williams-Honda	
1986	Mansell Williams-Honda	Prost McLaren- TAG Porsche			Mansell Williams-Honda	Mansell Williams-Honda	Piquet Williams-Honda	Piquet Williams-Honda	Senna Lotus-Renault				Mansell Williams-Honda		Senna Lotus-Renault		Berger Benetton-BMW
1987	Mansell Williams-Honda	Senna Lotus-Honda			Prost McLaren- TAG Porsche	Mansell Williams-Honda	Piquet Williams-Honda	Piquet Williams-Honda	Mansell Williams-Honda				Prost McLaren- TAG Porsche		Senna Lotus-Honda		Mansell Williams-Honda
1988	Senna McLaren-Honda	Prost McLaren-Honda			Senna McLaren-Honda	Prost McLaren-Honda	Berger Ferrari	Senna McLaren-Honda	Prost McLaren-Honda				Prost McLaren-Honda		Senna McLaren-Honda		Prost McLaren-Honda
1989	Prost McLaren-Honda	Senna McLaren-Honda			Senna McLaren-Honda	Prost McLaren-Honda	Prost McLaren-Honda	Senna McLaren-Honda	Senna McLaren-Honda				Berger Ferrari		Prost Ferrari		Senna McLaren-Honda
1990	Prost Ferrari	Senna McLaren-Honda			Senna McLaren-Honda	Prost Ferrari	Senna McLaren-Honda	Senna McLaren-Honda	Prost Ferrari				Mansell Ferrari		Senna McLaren-Honda		Prost Ferrari
1991	Mansell Williams-Renault	Senna McLaren-Honda			Senna McLaren-Honda	Mansell Williams-Renault	Mansell Williams-Renault	Mansell Williams-Renault	Mansell Williams-Renault				Patrese Williams-Renault		Senna McLaren-Honda		Patrese Williams-Renault
1992	Mansell Williams-Renault	Senna McLaren-Honda			M. Schumacher Benetton-Ford	Mansell Williams-Renault	Senna McLaren-Honda	Mansell Williams-Renault	Mansell Williams-Renault				Mansell Williams-Renault			Mansell Williams-Renault	Mansell Williams-Renault
1993	Prost Williams-Renault	Senna McLaren-Ford			D. Hill Williams-Renault	Prost Williams-Renault	D. Hill Williams-Renault	Prost Williams-Renault	Prost Williams-Renault				M. Schumacher Benetton-Ford			Prost Williams-Renault	
1994	D. Hill Williams-Renault	M. Schumacher Benetton-Ford			D. Hill Williams-Renault	M. Schumacher Benetton-Ford	D. Hill Williams-Renault	Berger Ferrari	D. Hill Williams-Renault				D. Hill Williams-Renault				
1995	Herbert Benetton-Renault	M. Schumacher Benetton-Renault			M. Schumacher Benetton-Renault	M. Schumacher Benetton-Renault	Herbert Benetton-Renault	M. Schumacher Benetton-Renault	M. Schumacher Benetton-Renault		D. Hill Williams-Renault		Coulthard Williams-Renault				
1996	J. Villeneuve Williams-Renault	Panis Ligier- Mugen Honda			M. Schumacher Ferrari	D. Hill Williams-Renault	M. Schumacher Ferrari	D. Hill Williams-Renault	M. Schumacher Ferrari		D. Hill Williams-Renault		J. Villeneuve Williams-Renault				
1997	J. Villeneuve Williams-Renault	M. Schumacher Ferrari			M. Schumacher Ferrari	M. Schumacher Ferrari	Coulthard McLaren-Mercedes	Berger Benetton-Renault	J. Villeneuve Williams-Renault		J. Villeneuve Williams-Renault						
1998	M. Schumacher Ferrari	Häkkinen McLaren-Mercedes			D. Hill Jordan- Mugen Honda	M. Schumacher Ferrari	M. Schumacher Ferrari	Häkkinen McLaren-Mercedes	Häkkinen McLaren-Mercedes		M. Schumacher Ferrari						
1999	Coulthard McLaren-Mercedes	M. Schumacher Ferrari			Coulthard McLaren-Mercedes	Frentzen Jordan Mugen Honda	Frentzen Jordan Mugen Honda	Irvine Ferrari	Häkkinen McLaren-Mercedes								
2000	Coulthard McLaren-Mercedes	Coulthard McLaren-Mercedes			Häkkinen McLaren-Mercedes	Coulthard McLaren-Mercedes	M. Schumacher Ferrari	Barrichello Ferrari	Häkkinen McLaren-Mercedes						M. Schumacher Ferrari		
2001	Häkkinen McLaren-Mercedes	M. Schumacher Ferrari			M. Schumacher Ferrari	M. Schumacher Ferrari	Montoya Williams-BMW	R. Schumacher Williams-BMW	M. Schumacher Ferrari						Häkkinen McLaren-Mercedes		
2002	M. Schumacher Ferrari	Coulthard McLaren-Mercedes			M. Schumacher Ferrari	M. Schumacher Ferrari	Barrichello Ferrari	M. Schumacher Ferrari	M. Schumacher Ferrari						Barrichello Ferrari		
2003	Barrichello Ferrari	Montoya Williams-BMW				R. Schumacher Williams-BMW	M. Schumacher Ferrari	Montoya Williams-BMW	M. Schumacher Ferrari						M. Schumacher Ferrari		
2004	M. Schumacher Ferrari	Trulli Renault			Räikkönen McLaren-Mercedes	M. Schumacher Ferrari	Barrichello Ferrari	M. Schumacher Ferrari	M. Schumacher Ferrari						M. Schumacher Ferrari		
2005	Montoya McLaren-Mercedes	Räikkönen McLaren-Mercedes			Räikkönen McLaren-Mercedes	Alonso Renault	Montoya McLaren-Mercedes	Alonso Renault	Räikkönen McLaren-Mercedes						M. Schumacher Ferrari		
2006	Alonso Renault	Alonso Renault				M. Schumacher Ferrari	M. Schumacher Ferrari	M. Schumacher Ferrari	Alonso Renault						M. Schumacher Ferrari		
2007	Räikkönen Ferrari	Alonso McLaren-Mercedes			Räikkönen Ferrari	Räikkönen Ferrari	Alonso McLaren-Mercedes		Massa Ferrari						Hamilton McLaren-Mercedes		
2008	Hamilton McLaren-Mercedes	Hamilton McLaren-Mercedes			Massa Ferrari	Massa Ferrari	Vettel STR-Ferrari	Hamilton McLaren-Mercedes	Räikkönen Ferrari								

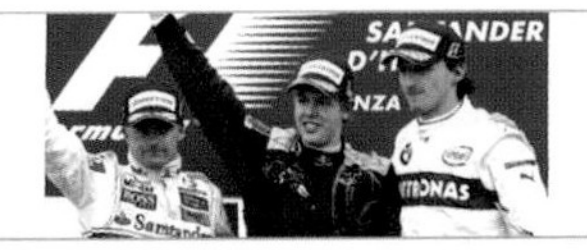

Year	A	CDN	BR	S	USA-W (Long Beach)	USA-E	J	RSM	LAS VEGAS	EUR	AUS	H	PACIFIC	L	MAL	BRN	PRC	TR
1950																		
1951																		
1952																		
1953																		
1954																		
1955																		
1956																		
1957																		
1958																		
1959																		
1960																		
1961																		
1962																		
1963																		
1964	Bandini Ferrari																	
1965																		
1966																		
1967		Brabham Brabham-Repco																
1968		Hulme McLaren-Ford																
1969		Ickx Brabham-Ford																
1970	Ickx Ferrari	Ickx Ferrari																
1971	Siffert BRM	Stewart Tyrrell-Ford																
1972	E. Fittipaldi Lotus-Ford	Stewart Tyrrell-Ford																
1973	Peterson Lotus-Ford	Revson McLaren-Ford	E. Fittipaldi Lotus-Ford	Hulme McLaren-Ford														
1974	Reutemann Brabham-Ford	E. Fittipaldi McLaren-Ford	E. Fittipaldi McLaren-Ford	Scheckter Tyrrell-Ford														
1975	Brambilla March-Ford		Pace Brabham-Ford	Lauda Ferrari														
1976	Watson Penske-Ford	Hunt McLaren-Ford	Lauda Ferrari	Scheckter Tyrrell-Ford	Regazzoni Ferrari	Hunt McLaren-Ford	M. Andretti Lotus-Ford											
1977	Jones Shadow-Ford	Scheckter Wolf-Ford	Reutemann Ferrari	Laffite Ligier-Matra	Andretti Lotus-Ford	Hunt McLaren-Ford	Hunt McLaren-Ford											
1978	Peterson Lotus-Ford	G. Villeneuve Ferrari	Reutemann Ferrari	Lauda Brabham- Alfa Romeo	Reutemann Ferrari	Reutemann Ferrari												
1979	Jones Williams-Ford	Jones Williams-Ford	Laffite Ligier-Ford		G. Villeneuve Ferrari	G. Villeneuve Ferrari												
1980	Jabouille Renault	Jones Williams-Ford	Arnoux Renault		Piquet Brabham-Ford	Jones Williams-Ford												
1981	Laffite Ligier-Matra	Laffite Ligier-Matra	Reutemann Williams-Ford		Jones Williams-Ford			Piquet Brabham-Ford	Jones Williams-Ford									
1982	De Angelis Lotus-Ford	Piquet Brabham-BMW	Prost Renault		Lauda McLaren-Ford	Watson McLaren-Ford		Pironi Ferrari	Alboreto Tyrrell-Ford									
1983	Prost Renault	Arnoux Ferrari	Piquet Brabham-BMW		Watson McLaren-Ford	Alboreto Tyrrell-Ford		Tambay Ferrari		Piquet Brabham-BMW								
1984	Lauda McLaren- TAG Porsche	Piquet Brabham-BMW	Prost McLaren- TAG Porsche			Piquet Brabham-BMW		Prost McLaren- TAG Porsche		Prost McLaren- TAG Porsche								
1985	Prost McLaren- TAG Porsche	Alboreto Ferrari	Prost McLaren- TAG Porsche					De Angelis Lotus-Renault		Mansell Williams-Honda	K. Rosberg Williams-Honda							
1986	Prost McLaren- TAG Porsche	Mansell Williams-Honda	Piquet Williams-Honda					Prost McLaren- TAG Porsche			Prost McLaren- TAG Porsche	Piquet Williams-Honda						
1987	Mansell Williams-Honda		Prost McLaren- TAG Porsche				Berger Ferrari	Mansell Williams-Honda			Berger Ferrari	Piquet Williams-Honda						
1988		Senna McLaren-Honda	Prost McLaren-Honda				Senna McLaren-Honda	Senna McLaren-Honda			Prost McLaren-Honda	Senna McLaren-Honda						
1989		Boutsen Williams-Renault	Mansell Ferrari				Nannini Benetton-Ford	Senna McLaren-Honda			Boutsen Williams-Renault	Mansell Ferrari						
1990		Senna McLaren-Honda	Prost Ferrari				Piquet Benetton-Ford	Patrese Williams-Renault			Piquet Benetton-Ford	Boutsen Williams-Renault						
1991		Piquet Benetton-Ford	Senna McLaren-Honda				Berger McLaren-Honda	Senna McLaren-Honda			Senna McLaren-Honda	Senna McLaren-Honda						
1992		Berger McLaren-Honda	Mansell Williams-Renault				Mansell Williams-Renault	Mansell Williams-Renault			Berger McLaren-Honda	Senna McLaren-Honda						
1993		Prost Williams-Renault	Senna McLaren-Ford				Senna McLaren-Ford	Prost Williams-Renault		Senna McLaren-Ford	Senna McLaren-Ford	D. Hill Williams-Renault						
1994		M. Schumacher Benetton-Ford	M. Schumacher Benetton-Ford				D. Hill Williams-Renault	M. Schumacher Benetton-Ford		M. Schumacher Benetton-Ford	Mansell Williams-Renault	M. Schumacher Benetton-Ford	M. Schumacher Benetton-Ford					
1995		Alesi Ferrari	M. Schumacher Benetton-Renault				M. Schumacher Benetton-Renault	D.Hill Williams-Renault		M. Schumacher Benetton-Renault	D. Hill Williams-Renault	D. Hill Williams-Renault	M. Schumacher Benetton-Renault					
1996		D. Hill Williams-Renault	D. Hill Williams-Renault				D. Hill Williams-Renault	D. Hill Williams-Renault		J. Villeneuve Williams-Renault	D. Hill Williams-Renault	J. Villeneuve Williams-Renault						
1997	J. Villeneuve Williams-Renault	M. Schumacher Ferrari	J. Villeneuve Williams-Renault				M. Schumacher Ferrari	Frentzen Williams-Renault		Häkkinen McLaren-Mercedes	Coulthard McLaren-Mercedes	J. Villeneuve Williams-Renault		J. Villeneuve Williams-Renault				
1998	Häkkinen McLaren-Mercedes	M. Schumacher Ferrari	Häkkinen McLaren-Mercedes				Häkkinen McLaren-Mercedes	Coulthard McLaren-Mercedes			Häkkinen McLaren-Mercedes	M. Schumacher Ferrari		Häkkinen McLaren-Mercedes				
1999	Irvine Ferrari	Häkkinen McLaren-Mercedes	Häkkinen McLaren-Mercedes				Häkkinen McLaren-Mercedes	M. Schumacher Ferrari		Herbert Stewart-Ford	Irvine Ferrari	Häkkinen McLaren-Mercedes			Irvine Ferrari			
2000	Häkkinen McLaren-Mercedes	M. Schumacher Ferrari	M. Schumacher Ferrari				M. Schumacher Ferrari	M. Schumacher Ferrari		M. Schumacher Ferrari	M. Schumacher Ferrari	Häkkinen McLaren-Mercedes			M. Schumacher Ferrari			
2001	Coulthard McLaren-Mercedes	R. Schumacher Williams-BMW	Coulthard McLaren-Mercedes				M. Schumacher Ferrari	R. Schumacher Williams-BMW		M. Schumacher Ferrari	M. Schumacher Ferrari	M. Schumacher Ferrari			M. Schumacher Ferrari			
2002	M. Schumacher Ferrari	M. Schumacher Ferrari	M. Schumacher Ferrari				M. Schumacher Ferrari	M. Schumacher Ferrari		Barrichello Ferrari	M. Schumacher Ferrari	Barrichello Ferrari			M. Schumacher Ferrari			
2003	M. Schumacher Ferrari	M. Schumacher Ferrari	Fisichella Jordan-Ford				Barrichello Ferrari	M. Schumacher Ferrari		R. Schumacher Williams-BMW	Coulthard McLaren-Mercedes	Alonso Renault			Räikkönen McLaren-Mercedes			
2004		M. Schumacher Ferrari	Montoya Williams-BMW				M. Schumacher Ferrari	M. Schumacher Ferrari		M. Schumacher Ferrari	M. Schumacher Ferrari	M. Schumacher Ferrari			M. Schumacher Ferrari	M. Schumacher Ferrari	Barrichello Ferrari	
2005		Räikkönen McLaren-Mercedes	Montoya McLaren-Mercedes				Räikkönen McLaren-Mercedes	Alonso Renault		Alonso Renault	Fisichella Renault	Räikkönen McLaren-Mercedes			Alonso Renault	Alonso Renault	Alonso Renault	Räikkönen McLaren-Mercedes
2006		Alonso Renault	Massa Ferrari				Alonso Renault	M. Schumacher Ferrari		M. Schumacher Ferrari	Alonso Renault	Button Honda			Fisichella Renault	Alonso Renault	M. Schumacher Ferrari	Massa Ferrari
2007		Hamilton McLaren-Mercedes	Räikkönen Ferrari				Hamilton McLaren-Mercedes			Alonso McLaren-Mercedes	Räikkönen Ferrari	Hamilton McLaren-Mercedes	SGP		Alonso McLaren-Mercedes	Massa Ferrari	Räikkönen Ferrari	Massa Ferrari
2008		Kubica BMW	Massa Ferrari				Alonso Renault			Massa Ferrari	Hamilton McLaren-Mercedes	Kovalainen McLaren-Mercedes	Alonso Renault		Räikkönen Ferrari	Massa Ferrari	Hamilton McLaren-Mercedes	Massa Ferrari

Drivers: victories

Driver	Victories	Driver	Victories
SCHUMACHER Michael	91	HILL Phil	3
PROST Alain	51	PIRONI Didier	3
SENNA Ayrton	41	BOUTSEN Thierry	3
MANSELL Nigel	31	FRENTZEN Heinz-Harald	3
STEWART Jackie	27	HERBERT Johnny	3
CLARK Jim	25	FISICHELLA Giancarlo	3
LAUDA Niki	25	VUKOVICH Bill	2
FANGIO Juan-Manuel	24	GONZALEZ Jose-Froilan	2
PIQUET Nelson	23	TRINTIGNANT Maurice	2
HILL Damon	22	Von TRIPS Wolfgang	2
ALONSO Fernando	21	RODRIGUEZ Pedro	2
HAKKINEN Mika	20	SIFFERT Jo	2
RAIKKONEN Kimi	17	REVSON Peter	2
MOSS Stirling	16	DEPAILLER Patrick	2
HILL Graham	14	JABOUILLE Jean-Pierre	2
BRABHAM Jack	14	TAMBAY Patrick	2
FITTIPALDI Emerson	14	De ANGELIS Elio	2
ASCARI Alberto	13	PARSONS Johnnie	1
COULTHARD David	13	WALLARD Lee	1
ANDRETTI Mario	12	FAGIOLI Luigi	1
REUTEMANN Carlos	12	TARUFFI Piero	1
JONES Alan	12	RUTTMAN Troy	1
VILLENEUVE Jacques	11	SWEIKERT Bob	1
MASSA Felipe	11	MUSSO Luigi	1
HUNT James	10	FLAHERTY Pat	1
PETERSON Ronnie	10	HANKS Sam	1
SCHECKTER Jody	10	BRYAN Jimmy	1
BERGER Gerhard	10	WARD Rodger	1
BARRICHELLO Rubens	9	BONNIER Jo	1
HAMILTON Lewis	9	RATHMANN Jim	1
ICKX Jacky	8	BAGHETTI Giancarlo	1
HULME Denny	8	IRELAND Innes	1
ARNOUX René	7	BANDINI Lorenzo	1
MONTOYA Juan-Pablo	7	GINTHER Richie	1
BROOKS Tony	6	SCARFIOTTI Ludovico	1
SURTEES John	6	GETHIN Peter	1
RINDT Jochen	6	CEVERT François	1
VILLENEUVE Gilles	6	BELTOISE Jean-Pierre	1
LAFFITE Jacques	6	PACE Carlos	1
PATRESE Riccardo	6	MASS Jochen	1
SCHUMACHER Ralf	6	BRAMBILLA Vittorio	1
FARINA Giuseppe	5	NILSSON Gunnar	1
REGAZZONI Clay	5	NANNINI Alessandro	1
WATSON John	5	ALESI Jean	1
ALBORETO Michele	5	PANIS Olivier	1
ROSBERG Keke	5	TRULLI Jarno	1
GURNEY Dan	4	BUTTON Jenson	1
McLAREN Bruce	4	KUBICA Robert	1
IRVINE Eddie	4	KOVALAINEN Heikki	1
HAWTHORN Mike	3	VETTEL Sebastian	1
COLLINS Peter	3		

The 59 World Champions

Year	Driver	Nationality	Team	GP	Poles	Victories	Fastests laps
1950	Giuseppe Farina	I	Alfa Romeo	7	2	3	3
1951	Juan Manuel Fangio	RA	Alfa Romeo	8	4	3	5
1952	Alberto Ascari	I	Ferrari	8	5	6	5
1953	Alberto Ascari	I	Ferrari	9	6	5	4
1954	Juan Manuel Fangio	RA	Mercedes/Maserati	9	5	6	3
1955	Juan Manuel Fangio	RA	Mercedes	7	3	4	3
1956	Juan Manuel Fangio	RA	Lancia/Ferrari	8	5	3	3
1957	Juan Manuel Fangio	RA	Maserati	8	4	4	2
1958	Mike Hawthorn	GB	Ferrari	11	4	1	5
1959	Jack Brabham	AUS	Cooper Climax	9	1	2	1
1960	Jack Brabham	AUS	Cooper Climax	10	3	5	3
1961	Phil Hill	USA	Ferrari	8	5	2	2
1962	Graham Hill	GB	BRM	9	1	4	3
1963	Jim Clark	GB	Lotus Climax	10	7	7	6
1964	John Surtees	GB	Ferrari	10	2	2	2
1965	Jim Clark	GB	Lotus Climax	10	6	6	6
1966	Jack Brabham	AUS	Brabham Repco	9	3	4	1
1967	Denny Hulme	NZ	Brabham Repco	11	0	2	2
1968	Graham Hill	GB	Lotus Ford	12	2	3	0
1969	Jackie Stewart	GB	Matra Ford	11	2	6	5
1970	Jochen Rindt	A	Lotus Ford	13	3	5	1
1971	Jackie Stewart	GB	Tyrrell Ford	11	6	6	3
1972	Emerson Fittipaldi	BR	Lotus Ford	12	3	5	0
1973	Jackie Stewart	GB	Tyrrell Ford	15	3	5	1
1974	Emerson Fittipaldi	BR	McLaren Ford	15	2	3	0
1975	Niki Lauda	A	Ferrari	14	9	5	2
1976	James Hunt	GB	McLaren Ford	16	8	6	2
1977	Niki Lauda	A	Ferrari	17	2	3	3
1978	Mario Andretti	USA	Lotus Ford	16	8	6	3
1979	Jody Scheckter	ZA	Ferrari	15	1	3	1
1980	Alan Jones	AUS	Williams Ford	14	3	5	5
1981	Nelson Piquet	BR	Brabham Ford	15	4	3	1
1982	Keke Rosberg	FIN	Williams Ford	16	1	1	0
1983	Nelson Piquet	BR	Brabham BMW Turbo	15	1	3	4
1984	Niki Lauda	A	McLaren TAG Porsche Turbo	16	0	5	5
1985	Alain Prost	F	McLaren TAG Porsche Turbo	16	2	5	5
1986	Alain Prost	F	McLaren TAG Porsche Turbo	16	1	4	2
1987	Nelson Piquet	BR	Williams Honda Turbo	16	4	3	4
1988	Ayrton Senna	BR	McLaren Honda Turbo	16	13	8	3
1989	Alain Prost	F	McLaren Honda	16	2	4	5
1990	Ayrton Senna	BR	McLaren Honda	16	10	6	2
1991	Ayrton Senna	BR	McLaren Honda	16	8	7	2
1992	Nigel Mansell	GB	Williams Renault	16	14	9	8
1993	Alain Prost	F	Williams Renault	16	13	7	6
1994	Michael Schumacher	D	Benetton Ford	14	6	8	9
1995	Michael Schumacher	D	Benetton Renault	17	4	9	7
1996	Damon Hill	GB	Williams Renault	16	9	8	5
1997	Jacques Villeneuve	CDN	Williams Renault	17	10	7	3
1998	Mika Häkkinen	FIN	McLaren Mercedes	16	9	8	6
1999	Mika Häkkinen	FIN	McLaren Mercedes	16	11	5	6
2000	Michael Schumacher	D	Ferrari	17	9	9	2
2001	Michael Schumacher	D	Ferrari	17	11	9	3
2002	Michael Schumacher	D	Ferrari	17	7	11	7
2003	Michael Schumacher	D	Ferrari	16	5	6	5
2004	Michael Schumacher	D	Ferrari	18	8	13	10
2005	Fernando Alonso	E	Renault	19	6	7	2
2006	Fernando Alonso	E	Renault	18	6	7	5
2007	Kimi Räikkönen	FIN	Ferrari	17	3	6	6
2008	Lewis Hamilton	GB	McLaren Mercedes	18	7	5	1